Money Adviser 2000

Lisa Ellis
and the Editors of Money

MONEY BOOKS

Time Inc. Home Entertainment / 1271 Avenue of the Americas / New York, NY 10020

Manufactured in the United States of America
First Printing 2000

MONEY MAGAZINE

MANAGING EDITOR Robert Safian **EXECUTIVE EDITOR** Denise B. Martin **ASSISTANT MANAGING EDITORS** Glenn Coleman, Loren Feldman, Eric Gelman, Craig Matters, Sheryl Hilliard Tucker **EDITORS-AT-LARGE** Jean Sherman Chatzky, Michael Sivy **SENIOR EDITORS** Marion Asnes, Jim Frederick, Jon Gertner, William Green, Ellen Stark, Teresa Tritch, Walter Updegrave, Nelson Wang **SENIOR WRITER/COLUMNIST** Jason Zweig **ASSOCIATE EDITOR** Scott Medintz **SENIOR WRITERS** Peter Carbonara, Jerry Edgerton, John Helyar, Peter J. Keating, Penelope Wang, Suzanne Woolley **STAFF WRITERS** Lisa Reilly Cullen, Amy Feldman, David Futrelle, Pablo Galarza, Jeanne Lee, Lani Luciano, Mari McQueen, Pat Regnier, James E. Reynolds, Sarah A. Rose, Rob Turner **WRITER-REPORTERS** Joan Caplin, Brian L. Clark, Michael Powe, Laura Washington **CONTRIBUTING WRITERS** Paul Lukas, Bethany McLean, Joseph Nocera, Andrew Serwer **ART DIRECTOR** Syndi C. Becker **DEPUTY ART DIRECTOR** Scott A. Davis **SENIOR ASSOCIATE ART DIRECTOR** MaryAnn Salvato **ASSOCIATE ART DIRECTORS** John Dixon, Andrea Dunham **DESIGNER** Semi Kang **INFORMATION GRAPHICS DESIGNER** Myra Klockenbrink **ART PRODUCTION COORDINATOR** Tommy McCall **PHOTOGRAPHY PICTURE EDITOR** Jane Clark **DEPUTY PICTURE EDITORS FEATURES** Cathy Mather, Betsy Keating **ASSISTANT PICTURE EDITOR** Shawn Vale **REPORTERS CHIEF** Katharine B. Drake **SENIOR STAFF** Judy Feldman, Roberta Kirwan **STAFF** Adrienne Carter, Erica Garcia, Patrice D. Johnson, D. Mosher (mail), Brian P. Murphy, Natasha Rafi **EDITORIAL PRODUCTION MANAGER** Allegra-Jo Lagani **COPY CHIEF** Patricia A. Feimster **OPERATIONS CHIEF** Lionel P. Vargas **STAFF** Sukey Rosenbaum (senior coordinator), Sally Boggan, Martha E. Bula Torres, John D'Antonio, Judith Ferbel, Emily Harrow, Eve Sennett, Libby Stephens **PUBLIC RELATIONS ASSISTANT DIRECTOR** Dianne Milton **ASSISTANT TO THE MANAGING EDITOR** Tanya Shaw **ADMINISTRATIVE COORDINATOR DESIGN** Nikki Robinson **STAFF** Merrily Brooks, Llubia Reyes **CORRESPONDENTS** Linda Berlin, Barbara Hordern, Ann S. Knol, Stephen Marsh, Melanie J. Mavrides, Laura Mecoy, Marcia R. Pledger, Elizabeth S. Roberts, Carol F. Shepley, Nancy Stesin, Jeff Wuorio **CONTRIBUTING TAX EDITOR** Mary L. Sprouse **DIRECTOR OF IMAGING** Richard J. Sheridan **IMAGING STAFF** Janet Miller (manager), Michael D. Brennan, Edward G. Carnesi, Vanessa R. Etherington, Kyle Hislip, Marco Lau, Angel A. Mass, Stanley E. Moyse, Claudio M. Muller, Richard K. Prue, Lorri O. Stenton, Paul Tupay **DIRECTOR OF TECHNOLOGY** Jeffrey W. Fulton **TECHNOLOGY STAFF** Al Criscuolo, Kevin Kersey (technology managers), Lawrence J. Shine (database administrator), Thomas J. Miller (systems administrator), Frank B. Cuffe, Joe Z. Peng, Andrew M. Ross **MONEY NEW MEDIA EDITOR** William D. McGuire **DESIGN DIRECTOR** Caldwell Toll **PRODUCTION DIRECTOR** Mark Thomas **PRODUCTION MANAGER** Tim Ungs **PRODUCER** Waits May **PROGRAMMER** German Todorov **ASSOCIATE PRODUCER** Borzou Daragahi **PRODUCTION ASSISTANT** Eric Mortensen **ADMINISTRATIVE ASSISTANT** Savy Mangru

TIME INC. HOME ENTERTAINMENT

PRESIDENT Stuart Hotchkiss **EXECUTIVE DIRECTOR, BRANDED BUSINESSES** David Arfine **EXECUTIVE DIRECTOR, NON-BRANDED BUSINESSES** Alicia Longobardo **EXECUTIVE DIRECTOR, TIME INC. BRAND LICENSING** Risa Turken **DIRECTOR, MARKETING SERVICES** Michael Barrett **DIRECTOR, RETAIL & SPECIAL SALES** Tom Mifsud **ASSOCIATE DIRECTORS** Roberta Harris, Kenneth Maehlum **PRODUCT MANAGERS** Andre Okolowitz, Niki Viswanathan, Daria Raehse **ASSOCIATE PRODUCT MANAGERS** Dennis Sheehan, Meredith Shelley, Bill Totten, Lauren Zaslansky **ASSISTANT PRODUCT MANAGERS** Victoria Alfonso, Jennifer Dowell, Ann Gillespie **LICENSING MANAGER** JoAnna West **ASSOCIATE LICENSING MANAGER** Regina Feiler **ASSOCIATE MANAGER, RETAIL & NEW MARKETS** Bozena Szwagulinski **EDITORIAL OPERATIONS DIRECTOR** John Calvano **BOOK PRODUCTION MANAGER** Jessica McGrath **ASSISTANT BOOK PRODUCTION MANAGER** Jonathan Polsky **BOOK PRODUCTION COORDINATOR** Kristen Lizzi **FULFILLMENT MANAGER** Richard Perez **ASSISTANT FULFILLMENT MANAGER** Tara Schimming **FINANCIAL DIRECTOR** Tricia Griffin **FINANCIAL MANAGER** Robert Dente **ASSOCIATE FINANCIAL MANAGER** Steven Sandonato **EXECUTIVE ASSISTANT** Mary Jane Rigoroso **SPECIAL THANKS TO** Emily Rabin, Jennifer Bomhoff, Alison Ehrmann

MONEY BOOK SERIES

DESIGNER Laura Ierardi, LCI Design

ISSN: 1522-7618   ISBN: 1-883013-89-5

We welcome your comments and suggestions about MONEY Books. Please write to us at:

MONEY Books
Attention: Book Editors
PO Box 11016
Des Moines, IA 50336-1016

If you would like to order any of our Hard Cover Collector Edition books, please call us at 1-800-327-6388
(Monday through Friday, 7 a.m. to 8 p.m. or Saturday, 7 a.m. to 6 p.m. Central Time).

❧ Contents

Chapter 1

Prospering In the New Century

*M*any Americans began the new millennium better off than they ever imagined. In the most phenomenal bull market in U.S. history, any investor who owned a Standard & Poor's 500-stock index fund has seen his or her account more than triple in size over the past five years. Of course, lots of us did not own such a fund. And as the market rises, it seems possible that the end of the fun could mar 2000. If you haven't already bought in, you may be wondering if it's too late now. If you have been in the game, you can't help but ponder if it's time to get out while the getting is still so good. Still, the economy is booming and consumer confidence is strong. Where do you fit into this picture of financial nirvana? Are you taking full advantage of these good times? Could you be doing a better job of building wealth? Are you on track to realize your American Dream? This book strives to answer these questions as well as provide benchmarks and worksheets that will help you figure out where you stand.

The past decade of unprecedented prosperity ended on a high note for Americans like Dan and Cathy Keefe. Thanks to a healthy economy and solid financial planning, the Keefes and their infant son Sam enjoy an enviable lifestyle. They have an executive-level income, a swelling investment portfolio and status toys such as the new Ford Expedition in the driveway of their Minnetonka, Minn. home. But for Dan Keefe, living well means living anxiously. "We're on track with our plan to retire early," says the 36-year-old chief operating officer of an information management firm. "Still, I'm nervous about how long this expansion will last. I want to be prepared for the downside."

Keefe's combination of satisfaction and trepidation reflects the tone of our latest *Americans and Their Money* survey. The poll was mailed to more than 4,500 households, covered a vast array of financial topics and had a margin of error of plus or minus 3%. To flesh out our statistical findings, we interviewed 15 typical investors about their personal finances. As we analyzed the results of this poll, one sentiment came through clearly. Americans strongly associate how much control we have over our lives with how well we manage our finances. Lately, however, the volatility of the stock market is leaving us a little uncertain. So read on to find out how we are dealing with our fears and what we expect in the new century.

Why We're Confident in the Future

The good news from our survey is that two thirds of us are satisfied with our financial situation. That's the highest level since our 1991 poll. Not surprisingly, people with household incomes of less than $50,000 are less enthusiastic. Some 48% feel they've missed the party. These economic good times have changed the lifestyle of the average American family, our survey takers agree. But they do not all perceive the same changes. Those with household incomes of $100,000 or more observe that the strong economy has helped families invest more money. Those in the $50,000 to $99,999 income bracket are concerned that prosperous times have made us more interested in obtaining material things. And the least affluent believe that average folks are now more anxious about how they're doing financially.

We have realistic financial expectations. Looking ahead, four out of five Americans expect their standard of living to rise in the future. Indeed, the Conference Board's Consumer Confidence Index reflects how self-assured we've become since the market took off. The confidence index has been at historically high levels of 130 to 140 for the past three years, after sliding to around 47 in February 1992 in the midst of a wave of downsizing. Lately, however, the Conference Board reports that confidence is waning—a finding that our survey echoes. According to our poll, almost 30% of us think the economy will cool off within the next six months to a year. Some 54% anticipate that inflation will rise. And a hefty 67% of us believe there will be a pick-up in mortgage interest rates.

Skepticism also pervades our expectations for the stock market. One third of the surveyed group say stocks will go down over the next year, the largest percentage with such a view since our survey was launched in 1983. Another third think that the market will go up. The remaining third is convinced that the market will continue on its current course. That could be good or bad, depending on how you think the market is valued right now. But common sense tells us that we've been skating on thin ice for a while.

We aren't worried about employment. What's fueling optimism about our personal well-being? Well, for one thing, we don't seem to be worried about job security. Even with the unemployment rate close to its lowest point in three decades, 63% of us expect it to stay about the same in 2000. Only 11% were apprehensive about losing their jobs. "Most consumers pay far more attention to the unemployment rate than the stock market," says Conference Board economist Ken Goldstein. "Low unemployment numbers, plus the fact that they may be getting a bit more in their paycheck, are enough to keep most people happy." But simply having a job may not keep us financially content for long if our paychecks don't continue to grow. In fact, the prospect of low raises tops the list of our most pressing job concerns. That fear may be real. A new survey from Hewitt Associates, a benefits consulting firm, projects average increases of about 4% for 2000.

We're not obsessed with the stock market. Here's a snapshot of how individual investors with incomes over $50,000 are doing. Nearly 30% claim their portfolios of stocks or stock funds outperformed the S&P 500 index in the past year. When asked to detail their investment gains, however, only about 15% actually report returns that exceeded the S&P's. That may be why a mere 4% point to buying a great stock or mutual fund as their smartest money move. (For most Americans, buying a house is still No. 1 in this category.) It also may be the reason why "investing in real estate" and "starting a business" edged out "investing in stocks" as the best way to get rich in America.

The 22% of our $50,000-plus group who believe that they can whip the S&P over time expect to do so in one of four ways—by diversifying their portfolios, by investing in cutting-edge tech firms, by making high-risk investments or by investing in new business ventures. But investing in new businesses can be hazardous. For instance, Franz Huber, the 54-year-old chief scientist for a technology company in Denver, recalls the "dark moment" when he lost $10,000 in one weekend after he was asked to cover payroll expenses at the small start-up where he was a principal. "The then president said a second round of financing was all lined up but that he needed $10,000 to pay the staff," says Huber. "Then the financing fell through, and the company eventually went bankrupt."

Investing in technology is always tricky, even for stock pick-ers with a solid track record. Last year the financial media were loaded with stories about investors making big scores on the net. But there were a lot of misfires we don't hear about.

Dr. Steven Paul, a 43-year-old veterinarian in Coral Springs, Fla. knows what it feels like to both win and lose on net bets. After making a nice gain in an internet auction stock, Paul thought he saw a trend and jumped on another internet auction play. Wrong move. "It almost went bust," he says. "I bought it at its high and now it's at its low." Lesson learned? "I'd probably investigate a net stock a little bit more the next time," says Paul. In our survey, 12% of those with incomes of $100,000-plus regret buying investments without doing research. Paul, who also owns an internet mutual fund, is one of just 9% of Americans who invested in net-related stocks or mutual funds last year. Investing in the internet tends to be tightly correlated with income. Folks in the $100,000-plus set are three times more likely to invest in net stocks than are less affluent investors.

We're focused on retirement goals. The big news in retirement savings is that participation in employee plans such as 401(k)s spiked from 45% in 1997 to 60% last year (78% for the $50,000-plus bunch). In fact, when asked what money move they're most proud of, these higher-income folks point to getting an early start on retirement saving. Still, one in five Americans saved nothing last year. As you would expect, the annual savings story gets brighter as the income level goes up. Some 28% of households with $50,000-plus incomes expect to put away between $10,000 and $19,999, while 12% plan to save between $20,000 and $29,999.

Our poster couple for retirement savings is Sharon and James Leshikar of Sugarland, Texas, 32 and 38, respectively. When they married 10 years ago, they set an annual savings goal of $20,000, which is why they now have about $300,000 in IRAs. "It was tough when we first got married because we didn't have much money," recalls Sharon. "And then I quit work two years ago to stay home with our two girls. Nevertheless, we're still committed to meeting our goal, which is easier now that James is earning more money."

While 31% of respondents want to retire by 55, only 9% expect to do so. That's because early retirees often forgo full pension packages, resulting in reduced income and health benefits. "We're living 31 years longer than we did at the beginning of the last century," notes Steven Camp, a Fort Lauderdale financial planner. "I see people who won't be able to keep up with the cost of living unless they triple their income in retirement." Some 29% of women surveyed won't have saved anything this year. Thus it's not surprising that more women than men (14% to 9%) say they won't really have enough to meet living expenses later on in life. One out of four respondents, male and female, say they'll have just enough to cover their needs. As you would expect, upper income folks are not as worried. About 83% of the $50,000-plus crowd expect to be comfortable in their golden years.

We're high on real estate, especially our own. We may be a bit worried about this year's raises and more than a bit skeptical about the life expectancy of the bull market. But we are remarkably upbeat about the value of real estate. More than half of us expect our homes to appreciate, with those between the ages of 35 and 49 the most bullish, at 56%. The higher our income, the greater the confidence. And many believe that residential and commercial real estate have an important place in a diversified portfolio. But our faith that our homes will continue to appreciate isn't always realistic, says Lou Stanasolovich, president of Legend Financial Advisors in Pittsburgh. "I always chuckle when people think their homes will go up in value," he says. His affluent clients, a number of whom lost jobs to corporate merger mania, have houses whose values range from $250,000 to $400,000. Many are selling their homes at a loss rather than waiting up to two years to get the price they want.

We're still hooked on easy credit. What do we think are our "dumbest" financial moves? Going into debt, followed by getting a late start on saving for retirement. While 86% of us say we try to pay cash whenever possible, we don't seem to be succeeding. In fact, the percentage of people paying with cash rather than plastic has dropped significantly across all age groups since 1997. We talk a lot about reducing our debt load. But the latest figures from the Federal Reserve show that the amount of outstanding consumer credit grew at a 9.5% annual rate. Compared with our last survey in 1997, twice as many households report having an outstanding credit-card balance of $2,000 (35% vs. 17% in 1997).

We're more comfortable going online. The interest in investing in technology goes hand in hand with increased computer use. These days, more than three fourths of households with incomes of more than $50,000 use their PCs to manage or invest their money. The percentage was 60% in 1997. Of those who venture online today, 71% use the web for financial news or data, compared with 43% two years ago.

It's no surprise then that two thirds of the computer users in our survey who earn more than $50,000 track their portfolios online. Two years ago, only a third of respondents did. In 1999, about 31% bought or sold stocks and funds online. A few more, 33%, say they plan to trade online within this year. Other projected internet activities include buying items with a credit card (40%), booking a vacation or buying airline tickets (40%) and banking by computer (39%). Younger folks are the most likely to integrate net use into their everyday lives. For instance, 62% of those under 35 shop online; 34% use the net to research a mortgage. Only 9% of our survey takers say they chat online with other investors or experts.

✍ *Where You Stand in Year 2000*

A rising economic tide may lift virtually all boats. But it doesn't lift them equally. Despite the surging popularity of stocks, mutual funds and 401(k) plans, an estimated 57% of U.S. households still don't own stocks in any form. So for the majority of us, following the Dow is a spectator sport. Even if you're among those who do own stock, directly or through funds or retirement accounts, your fortunes can vary dramatically depending on exactly what you hold.

To find out how you're doing now, complete the worksheet "Put Your Family's Wealth to the Test" at right. The results will let you compare your success at nurturing a nest egg with that of people in your age and income brackets. What you won't find on these pages are the Top 10 Secrets that magically will transform you into a millionaire. We know that there is no secret path to wealth. So do you. For most Americans, achieving a comfortable lifestyle is a long-term process of saving as much as our circumstances allow and then investing wisely. Why should you bother with such a time-consuming exercise? Measuring the way your income and assets interact can give you a better understanding of the internal dynamics of your finances. The idea isn't so much to dictate where you should invest but to make you aware of what you're doing. Such understanding can help you make more informed decisions.

Then go to the heart of your finances by filling out the worksheet "What Your Family Is Worth" on page 10. Net worth is the value of your assets minus your liabilities. It's the measure that provides a bottom-line snapshot of the financial reserves you can tap for goals such as paying for retirement. By taking that snapshot at least once a year, you can track how quickly your wealth is growing. Determining how much you plan to save each year and the projected return on your assets can help you gauge how long it will take to meet your retirement goals.

Put Your Family's Wealth to the Test

This worksheet will tell you how your wealth building compares against that of others in your age and income brackets. The test is based on surveys of about 11,000 individuals with high incomes and net worths. The survey was conducted by Thomas Stanley and William Danko, authors of the best-selling *Millionaire Next Door*. Fill out the questionnaire to see how you rank in the scoring section below. The higher your score, the more your investing and saving habits resemble those of wealthy Americans.

	EXAMPLE	YOUR FIGURES
1. Your household income from all sources excluding inheritance	$75,000	**1.**
2. Your age (If both spouses work, average your ages.)	40	**2.**
3. Multiply your income by your age.	$3,000,000	**3.**
4. Divide line 3 by 10. The figure you get is the expected average net worth for someone of your age and income.	$300,000	**4.**
5. Total the value of your assets (worksheet on page 10, line 5) excluding inheritance.	$450,000	**5.**
6. Total your debt (worksheet on page 10, line 6).	$50,000	**6.**
7. Subtract line 6 from line 5 to arrive at your net worth.	$400,000	**7.**
8. Divide line 7 by line 4. **This is your final score.**	1.33	**8.**

SCORING:

Above 2.0: Congratulations! You rank in the top 25% of American wealth builders, according to our experts. **1 to 2.00:** You rank in the top half of the population in terms of wealth creation but need to improve some. **0.51 to 0.99:** You're a below-average generator of wealth. Better get back to our worksheets and look for places to improve. **0.50 or lower:** Uh oh. Unless you plan on working until you drop, you had better start saving and investing more than you do now.

As you would expect after years of economic expansion, the wealth of Americans overall has been growing. Our median net worth recently climbed to an estimated $79,600, roughly a 7% increase after inflation since 1994. Net worth tends to increase with age and income. So check the charts entitled "How Your Finances Compare" on page 11 to see how you stack up with people who are close to you in age and income.

Income is the benchmark of financial achievement most of us think of first. Here too most Americans appear to be doing better than ever before. After dipping somewhat during and after

What Your Family Is Worth

Jot down the value of your assets and liabilities in the spaces provided below. Then subtract your liabilities from your assets to arrive at your net worth now.

	AMOUNT
ASSETS	
Cash and Savings (savings accounts, money-market funds, Treasury bills)	**1.**
Taxable investments (excluding retirement accounts)	
Stocks and stock mutual funds	
Bonds and bond mutual funds	
Stock options (if exercised today)	
Value of privately owned business	
Investment real estate	
Cash value of life insurance policies	
Other investments	
Total taxable investments	**2.**
Retirement Accounts	
IRAs	
Employer savings plans, 401(k), 403(b)	
Self-employed plans, Keogh, SEP, etc.	
Annuities	
Estimated value of company pension	
Total retirement accounts	**3.**
Home and Personal Property	
Home	
Vacation home	
Cars, recreational vehicles	
Art, collectibles, jewelry and furnishings	
Other personal assets	
Total home and personal property	**4.**
TOTAL ASSETS (Add lines 1, 2, 3 and 4.)	**5.**
LIABILITIES	
Mortgage debt (balance of mortgages and home-equity borrowings)	
Car loans and leases	
Student loans	
Credit-card balances	
Other loans (401(k), installment, personal lines of credit, etc.)	
Other debt	
TOTAL LIABILITIES	**6.**
NET WORTH (Subtract line 6 from line 5.)	**7.**

How Your Finances Compare

From the top two pyramids below, you can tell how your earning power and wealth compare with that of U.S. households overall. Note that net worth generally rises with income. So review the bottom left-hand chart to see how your wealth stacks up against that of Americans whose income is similar to yours. Since net worth and income tend to increase as you age, use the bottom right-hand chart to compare your wealth and income with that of your peers. In addition to earnings from your job, the income figure you use here should include interest and dividends but not capital gains.

HOUSEHOLD INCOME

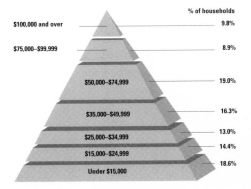

% of households

$100,000 and over	9.8%
$75,000–$99,999	8.9%
$50,000–$74,999	19.0%
$35,000–$49,999	16.3%
$25,000–$34,999	13.0%
$15,000–$24,999	14.4%
Under $15,000	18.6%

MEDIAN HOUSEHOLD INCOME: $38,300

HOUSEHOLD NET WORTH

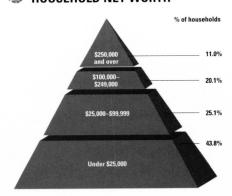

% of households

$250,000 and over	11.0%
$100,000–$249,000	20.1%
$25,000–$99,999	25.1%
Under $25,000	43.8%

MEDIAN HOUSEHOLD NET WORTH: $79,600

NET WORTH BY INCOME

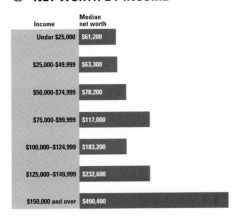

Income	Median net worth
Under $25,000	$61,200
$25,000–$49,999	$63,300
$50,000–$74,999	$78,200
$75,000–$99,999	$117,000
$100,000–$124,999	$183,200
$125,000–$149,999	$232,600
$150,000 and over	$490,400

Source: Claritas

NET WORTH AND INCOME BY AGE

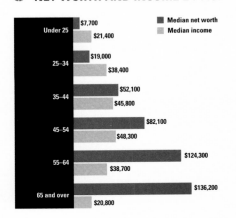

■ Median net worth
■ Median income

Age	Median net worth	Median income
Under 25	$7,700	$21,400
25–34	$19,000	$38,400
35–44	$52,100	$45,800
45–54	$82,100	$48,300
55–64	$124,300	$38,700
65 and over	$136,200	$20,800

the recession of 1990-1991, the median income for U.S. households in constant dollars rose steadily to hit a record of $38,300 recently. Another sign of Americans' more robust earning power can be seen in the increasing number of people climbing into the upper ranges of the income ladder each year. For example, Census Bureau statistics show that the percentage of families earning $100,000 or more nearly doubled to 9% since 1980. Private forecasters estimate that around 10% of households hit the $100,000 or better mark last year.

Many are doing a lot better than even these figures suggest. That's because these stats don't include forms of compensation such as stock awards and stock options, which an increasing number of companies are offering to employees. At salary levels below $100,000, incentives such as stock options can boost base pay by just under 20%. People in higher salary ranges can see increases of 100% to 300%. To see where you rank in terms of raw earning power, refer to the charts on page 11.

Despite rising incomes, middle- and upper-income Americans often complain of having to work harder and harder just to maintain a relatively decent standard of living. In *The Overspent American*, author Juliet Schor points to one survey in which 33% of people earning between $75,000 and $100,000 and 19% of those pulling down more than $100,000 claim that they must spend nearly all their money on the basic necessities of life. Small wonder then that many people pine for a kinder, gentler Leave It to Beaver era when the money we took home bought more and made us happier.

The single largest asset for most Americans remains their home, with an average value of roughly $130,300. In fact, only at a household income above $200,000 does the value of securities exceed that of the old homestead. That said, the portion of assets most of us devote to securities and other financial assets rose steadily throughout the 1990s. The latest Federal Reserve statistics show that financial assets have increased from 28% to 34% of total assets owned by U.S. households. Financial assets are likely to occupy an even larger place on our personal balance sheets given the seemingly insatiable interest in the stock market and the fact that baby boomers are focusing on the need to invest for their retirement.

How High Can Stocks Rise?

It's easy to find reassurance about the longevity of the bull market at the beginning of this new century. Indeed, proclaiming the good news of stock market gains has become something of a cottage industry for a handful of super bulls.

At the relatively cautious end of the spectrum is Wharton professor Jeremy Siegel, whose 1994 book *Stocks for the Long Run* has become a new bible for long-term investors. The book is now in its second edition, and Siegel has developed a lucrative career as a public speaker in the hire of a mutual fund company that pays him more than $10,000 a speech. On the radical side, journalist James Glassman and former Federal Reserve economist Kevin Hassett have been making headlines with a new book, *Dow 36,000*, that says the market is poised to more than triple in value. And then there's Harry Dent, author of the business bestseller *The Roaring 2000s* and its new sequel *The Roaring 2000s Investor*. Dent, who charges $40,000 a speech and even has a new mutual fund named after him, has turned himself into a virtual brand by predicting that the market will rise for another decade until the Dow peaks at 41,000.

The messages of these optimists are certainly appealing. And they have a better record than the bearish pundits who have complained for years that by traditional measures the stock market is overpriced. But do Siegel, Glassman and Hassett, and Dent really have the tools to predict what's going to happen over the next year, the next decade or even further?

The Bull Market's Academic Adviser

The late 1990s rally has been a more democratic affair than those of the 1960s and the 1980s. About half of American adults are invested in the stock market today, up from a fifth a decade ago. There are lots of reasons, including the rise of 401(k) plans, the glamour of internet stocks and the boom in mutual funds and discount brokerages. But perhaps most important is that investors now take it as an article of faith, contrary to the conventional

How Stocks Have Outperformed Bonds

Siegel found that stocks return more than bonds over time.

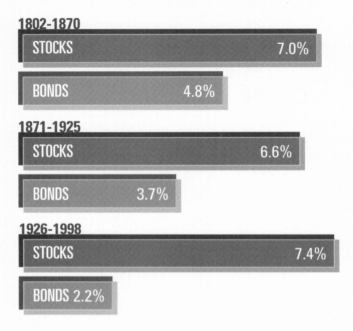

1802-1870

STOCKS	7.0%
BONDS	4.8%

1871-1925

STOCKS	6.6%
BONDS	3.7%

1926-1998

STOCKS	7.4%
BONDS	2.2%

Note: Average annual returns after inflation. **Source:** *Stocks for the Long Run* by Jeremy Siegel.

wisdom of just 20 years ago, that stocks are a safe investment for the long term. Directly or indirectly, they learned that lesson from Jeremy Siegel and his seminal 300-page book. So you might call the Wharton professor the academic adviser to the bull market.

He showed in *Stocks for the Long Run* that over most long periods of time, stocks have offered higher returns than have bonds, as depicted in the chart "How Stocks Have Outperformed Bonds" above. This argument wasn't completely new. Roger Ibbotson at Yale had already convinced institutional investors that stocks had been a consistently good investment since 1926. Even the great crash of '29 doesn't look so bad when it's buried within a 30-year average. But with a little creative archival work, Siegel was able to stretch the numbers back to 1802.

More important, Siegel wasn't afraid to use his numbers to draw dramatic conclusions and give simple advice. Take the notorious Nifty Fifty, a group of well-known big-cap stocks like Coca-Cola and McDonald's that got crushed by the '70s bear market. He showed they were good investments if you hung on to them long enough. He suggested that bonds, if you accounted for inflation, were actually riskier than stocks in the long pull. And he recommended that even conservative investors stash about 70% of their long-term money in the stock market and that aggressive types should borrow to get 130% exposure.

The book soon found an eager audience among financial planners, who were able to use Siegel's numbers to talk nervous clients into stocks. Planners sometimes mail Siegel boxes full of copies of *Stocks for the Long Run* for him to autograph. He says he always obliges. Siegel also became a staple source for financial journalists who wanted to make the same point.

Some of Siegel's biggest fans, however, are executives at financial services firms. Not long after his book came out, he was invited to speak at a Dean Witter conference. He guesses he's done more than 200 such speeches since, all the while maintaining a full teaching load. Recently, he became "senior adviser for investor strategies" for the Chicago-based fund company Nuveen, which means he's on retainer to speak to their shareholders and the brokers who sell their funds. He makes more from speaking these days than he does from teaching.

Siegel's speeches, like his book, focus on the importance of staying in stocks. "Having a Wharton professor say this works better for our clients," says John Waterman, managing director of investments at Rittenhouse, the subsidiary of Nuveen that runs stock funds. This message has helped make a lot of ordinary investors quite rich over the past five years. But is it still the right message today?

Broadly speaking, the answer is probably yes. Still, Siegel's data don't add up to an ironclad rule that stocks are always a great buy. The data on stocks in the early 19th century are sketchy. The indexes Siegel uses track mostly banks and, later, transportation companies. Siegel argues that these companies make up the best possible proxy for corporate America in those days. But there were countless other companies, ranging from turnpikes to land developers to taverns, that were sporadically selling stock to investors. And there are no good data to account for their performance. So Siegel may be overstating the success of 19th-century stocks by tracking only the best companies.

Tracking stocks back in history, of course, doesn't prove a thing about what they will do in the future. There simply are no guarantees, especially now that everyone knows, thanks in part to Siegel, that stocks beat bonds. As a result, stocks are a lot more popular than they used to be, which means they are also much more expensive as measured by their PE (price/earnings) ratio. Thus there may be less room for them to rise.

In fact, that's essentially the argument Siegel himself makes in a new paper published last fall. "The divergence between increased historical returns and lower future returns could set the stage for some significant investor disappointment," he notes dryly. In other words, the party may be over.

This message is certainly less optimistic than the ones Siegel delivers in his book and speeches. "People have said to me, 'In professional circles you seem more cautious than you do when you're addressing investors,'" Siegel admits. "The major reason for that is I don't want to give investors the idea that I'm saying stocks are a bad buy now." What is he saying, then? Siegel hastens to point out that he is not predicting a crash. He's just suggesting that the market may be relatively flat in the long term. He also thinks that stocks still look better than bonds, which he says are not likely to return more than 4% after inflation in the coming years.

To Siegel's credit, he has long urged investors to have reasonable expectations for stock returns. He has been telling audiences to expect stocks to produce 5% to 8% average real returns (that is, adjusted for inflation) in the long run. That's a far cry from the double-digit gains we've gotten used to. And it's almost bearish compared with the predictions others have made using Siegel's data.

❧ Would You Believe Dow 36,000 in 2004?

No one could have predicted that Jim Glassman would come to be viewed by many as a member of the market's lunatic fringe.

How to Solve the Stock Premium Puzzle

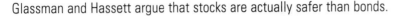

Glassman and Hassett argue that stocks are actually safer than bonds.

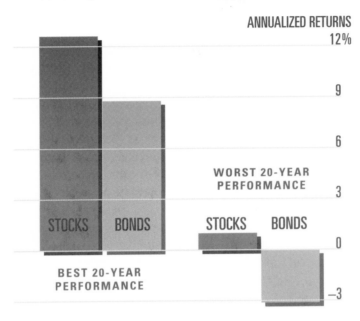

ANNUALIZED RETURNS

12%

9

6

WORST 20-YEAR
PERFORMANCE

3

STOCKS   BONDS

0

STOCKS   BONDS

−3

BEST 20-YEAR
PERFORMANCE

Note: Based on rolling 20-year periods since 1802. **Source:** *Stocks for the Long Run* by Jermey Siegel.

He is far more business-savvy than your average journalist. He's had to meet payrolls as a publisher of the *New Republic* and co-owner of *Roll Call*, a newspaper that covers Capitol Hill. Until recently, he was a columnist at the *Washington Post*. He's now a fellow at the American Enterprise Institute, an influential conservative think tank in Washington. Nevertheless, he and his colleague Kevin Hassett have taken Siegel's work and pushed it to its theoretical extreme. They are utterly convinced that the great bull market ride has only just begun.

Glassman and Hassett believe that we need to rethink the traditional measure of whether a stock is fairly priced. While Siegel frets that the bellwether S&P 500 index may be expensive at a recent 28 times earnings (14 is the historic average PE for stocks), Glassman and Hassett have used his data to argue that stocks are really worth as much as 100 times earnings. Siegel has said publicly that his research does not support this theory. But Glassman and Hassett are undaunted. "Sometimes the people who come up with new data are most resistant to its implications," says Glassman.

Glassman and Hassett began plotting their theory during chats at the American Enterprise Institute. The conversation eventually turned to what academicians call the stock premium puzzle. If stocks are safer than bonds over long periods, as Siegel's numbers show, then why don't they cost at least as much as bonds? Reference "How to Solve the Stock Premium Puzzle" on page 17. In other words, investors should have to pay a comparable price to get comparable peace of mind. Glassman and Hassett believe investors will wake up to this fact over the next five years or so. In response, stocks will finally become fairly priced, pushing the Dow toward 36,000, at least a triple from recent levels.

There are problems with the Dow 36,000 theory, however. For one thing, the premium puzzle isn't so puzzling if you think about your own behavior as an investor. Even if you plan to hold, say, an S&P 500 index fund for 30 years, you would probably get upset if the fund lost 25% over the next two years. That kind of loss can be terrifying even with Siegel's assurances that things will be okay if you just ride it out. And that helps explain why, in the history of stock markets, investors have never been willing to pay as much for stocks as they do for bonds. People just hate to lose money, and they're not good at looking out 30 years. The University of Chicago's Richard Thaler, a pioneer in the field of behavioral finance, calls this overreaction to short-term volatility "myopic loss aversion." He says it's a basic psychological trait of most investors.

What might the world look like if investors had so much confidence in stocks that they would routinely pay 100 times earnings? The capital markets could become a free money machine for businesses, as some critics have pointed out, meaning your local dry cleaner and favorite corner pub might start issuing stock. Because they are much more likely to go out of business than, say, Philip Morris, these companies would make the stock market a much more volatile, speculative investment than it's been the past 200 years. It's arguably happening right now, as internet companies with no earnings command stratospheric stock prices.

Doesn't this make the market riskier? "The notion that the risk characteristics of the market might change is a neat and interesting thought," concedes Hassett. But neither he nor Glassman think that such a dramatic rush to go public, if it happened, would torpedo either the market or their theory. "The value of stocks owned by U.S. households has grown from $2 trillion 10 years ago, to $11 trillion today, without untoward consequences," Glassman says. "But this is a worthwhile point. As the Dow rises, investors must become more choosy." In fact, Glassman and Hassett devote the second half of their book to outlining a particularly choosy, even conservative, investment strategy. Among their favorite stocks is Tootsie Roll Industries, which trades at a relatively modest 18 times its expected 2000 earnings.

Glassman and Hassett have found defenders, if not exactly true believers, within the financial services industry. Recently retired Vanguard Funds chairman Jack Bogle devotes an appendix in his latest book to questioning Glassman and Hassett's calculations. Yet he also gave a carefully worded endorsement for the back of their book: "*Dow 36,000* offers superb advice." Another blurber, David Malpass, chief international strategist for the brokerage firm Bear Stearns, says: "I don't particularly want to defend the 36,000 [projection]. I want to defend the idea that new thinking on valuation is important and timely." Perhaps when none of the old rules seem to apply, even fringe ideas begin to sound respectable.

☙ The Trouble With Harry's Forecast

The amazing thing about Harry Dent is that the idea on which his success is based is so tiny. He believes that the economy, and therefore the stock market, can be predicted based solely on demographics. If there are a lot of people in the high-spending stage of their lives, such as today's baby boomers, the economy and the stock market go up. If not, they go down. And that's it.

From that idea has grown a one-man empire that Dent runs from his home office high in the Oakland Hills, where he enjoys

Getting in Sync With the Spending Wave

Dent uses this chart to assert that birth rates drive the market.

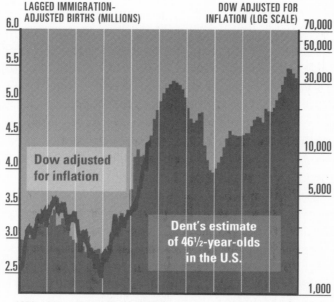

LAGGED IMMIGRATION-ADJUSTED BIRTHS (MILLIONS)

DOW ADJUSTED FOR INFLATION (LOG SCALE)

Dow adjusted for inflation

Dent's estimate of 46½-year-olds in the U.S.

1953 1963 1973 1983 1993 2003 2013 2023 2033 2043 2053

Source: H.S. Dent Foundation.

a stunning view of the San Francisco Bay. His speaking schedule makes Siegel's look like a mere hobby. One day last summer, he says, he gave five talks to groups of individual investors and brokers. Houston's AIM Funds recently launched the Dent Demographic Trends. Dent doesn't actually run the fund; he simply sends faxes with broad sector picks to lead manager Lanny Sachnowitz. But Dent pockets a portion of the fund's management fees (he won't say how much).

Dent claims to prove his theory using the "Spending Wave," shown in the chart "Getting in Sync With the Spending Wave" above. It illustrates how the Dow, after being adjusted for inflation, seems to move in step with the number of 46.5-year-olds in

America. Age 46, Dent asserts, is the age when people spend the most, and the ranks of 46-year-olds are still swelling. He believes this model proves that the market will keep going up and also shows when it will turn down. He thinks all this talk from Siegel, Glassman and Hassett about stocks being a safe investment over the long run is just nuts. He starts most of his speeches by showing how dangerous it can be to be in stocks at the wrong time. "What if you had been in the stock market from 1929 to 1942?" he asks. "That's 13 years of a bear market. Or '68 to '82? A 14-year bear market." According to Dent, stocks will be great until 2008, when the number of 46-year-olds peaks. After that, he says, you'll want to own real estate and bonds: "You have to fit your investment strategy and portfolio to the season."

Dent's reputation as a seer was established by his 1993 book, *The Great Boom Ahead*. In it, he predicted that the end of the biting recession was at hand and that the '90s would be a decade of economic prosperity. One good macroeconomic call like that can be all it takes to make a guru's career. "I didn't think of it this way," says Dent. "But that's what you have to do in economics. You have to make some bold predictions."

The problem with Dent as a market sage is that he may be confusing description and prediction. Spending by many baby boomers is vital to the economy, and it sure does seem likely that they'll spend more over the next decade. But we already know this. It's part of the reason we've been willing to pay such high PEs for companies like Starbucks, Microsoft, Citigroup and Dell. Just as investors drive up prices as soon as it becomes clear that stocks are historically "safe," so too do they drive up prices when it's clear that the economy is prosperous. Many market experts believe that this good news is already reflected in stock prices. On the flip side, the news that people will spend less after 2008 may also find its way into stock prices as that date gets nearer. So you could be in trouble if you wait until then to move into bonds.

Dent doesn't ignore the valuation issue completely. "The last two years, it's been…the biggest issue," says Dent. "And how I finally addressed it, and the best way I can see it for now, was to put the stock market in a channel." Dent relies on a simple but unorthodox market-timing tool called the Dow Channel. In essence, he takes the average performance of the Dow since the early '80s, when the population of 46-year-olds began its rise, and projects it out to the year 2008. That's how he gets his bold Dow 41,000 projection.

The Dow Channel also helps Dent explain the seemingly paradoxical fact that he has grown more bullish as stocks have gotten more expensive. When Dent first predicted the Great Boom in 1993, he used his Spending Wave model to predict that the Dow would rise to about 8,500 by 2007. When the Dow passed that number almost a decade ahead of schedule, Dent didn't simply declare the market fully valued. "As the market started surprising us," he explains, "I had to go back and look at my assumptions. I don't think the market is stupid." So in his 1998 book, *The Roaring 2000s*, he adjusted his population data to account for immigration and added a Dow Channel projection to predict that the Dow would peak between 21,500 and 35,000 in 2008. Dent's latest book pushes his projection to 41,000.

Asked if he might not be too flexible with his numbers, Dent is unapologetic. All that really matters, he insists, is that his Spending Wave indicates the general direction of the market. "The real truth," he says, "is that over time, as long as the economy is growing, the market is going to go up an average of 16% a year with 20% volatility on either side." Why? Because, Dent says, that's what it's been doing.

🌱 *When Stocks Are Priced for Perfection*

Although the ideas of Siegel, Dent, Glassman and Hassett all have their inconsistencies, it's not hard to paint a rosy picture for stock investors. Inflation is still low, while economic productivity is high. The economy is going global, and tech-savvy U.S. corporations are leading the way. Innovative new business models have made the economy more efficient and business cycles less volatile. Few warning lights are going off. What better vehicle could an investor choose right now than stocks?

On the other hand, our sense of safety, our confidence that things are going well, just makes disappointment more likely. Dent and Siegel don't really agree on much. But they both joked in interviews that as soon as everyone understood what they were saying in their books, the market would become overvalued and eventually topple. You could argue, of course, that everyone already knows stocks have been safe historically and that baby boomers are a powerful economic force. These observations may have been fresh once. But now they seem obvious. And they may already be priced into the market. Or is it possible that Glassman and Hassett are right, and there are still investors who have yet to learn what a great deal stocks are?

The only thing that's certain is that after five years of almost uninterrupted prosperity, we're in uncharted territory now. The future isn't bullish, and it isn't bearish. The future is a secret. Perhaps the best advice—don't be too sure of anything.

✒ *Generals in the War for Your Wallet*

Transformed by technology and looser regulations, the biggest names in financial services are gunning for your money as never before. Over the next year, they'll spend upwards of $4 billion talking to you about their latest innovations. Full-service brokers like Merrill Lynch are offering point-and-click online trading. Internet outfits like E Trade are moving into banking and insurance. The people at Vanguard are building an internal army of financial planners. Tellers at Citibank are pushing mutual funds. The line between brokers, bankers and insurers is blurring beyond distinction. Even the high-end world of private banking is losing its edge. Formerly snooty J.P. Morgan, where you were once shown the door if you had less than a million bucks to invest, is now targeting folks with as little as $250,000.

Longtime players and upstarts are at one another's throats, fighting to pull Americans' savings and investment dollars into their coffers. Financial services is a lucrative business; the more of your resources any firm can capture, the more it will earn. The typical American now uses 15 banking and investment products—checking, credit cards, mortgage, mutual funds, life insurance and so on—from five companies. The industry's best minds believe conditions are ripe for consolidating that scattered business into a single brand-name shop.

The evolving industry will provide more convenience for some people, more choice for others. Analysts estimate that up to 20% of Americans will become highly practiced do-it-yourself investors who use only digital providers. An equal number will depend solely on an adviser. In between is the great middle (about 65 million households) with allegiances in both camps.

Those who understand the transition that's under way will have the best opportunity to take advantage of it, both as consumers and as investors. To help you in this process, we interviewed five key leaders and innovators in the financial services industry. All have helped shape today's money business and will be masterminding the ways you buy financial advice for years to come.

Wells Fargo's Richard Kovacevich. Back in the 1970s, when Kovacevich was a Citibank executive in New York City, he helped introduce something called an automated teller machine as a new consumer convenience. Now we can't imagine how anyone ever managed without ATMs. After Citibank, Kovacevich moved on to head Norwest Bank in Minneapolis. There, he gave customers what they wanted—a personal Midwest style of service. And he handed out stock options to lowly tellers, so they were better motivated. Kovacevich transformed his branches (he insists on calling them "stores") into the most envied cross-sellers in the industry. Veteran customers have an average 4.6 financial products from Norwest, easily twice the industry rate. "Most banks," says the lanky Kovacevich, "have not done a very good job of focusing on the customer."

These days the 56-year-old is the San Francisco-based chief executive of Wells Fargo, which merged with Norwest in 1998. His plan is to combine his two great strengths, deploying cutting-edge technology and sales techniques, to create a full-service financial superstore on a scale never seen. His arsenal recently included $207 billion in assets, 15 million customers, about 5,900 branches (No. 1 in North America), 1,200 supermarket sites (tops again) and 6,500 ATMs (the third largest U.S. network, with some machines even dispensing ski-lift tickets). And Wells Fargo is the No. 1 internet bank, with nearly 1.5 million online accounts.

Kovacevich wants to take advantage of all these channels, to use the industry's latest jargon, to spike Wells Fargo's average product count per customer to eight. That's almost twice as many as even Norwest could muster. Although skeptics abound, Kovacevich is adamant. "Five years from now, we will be perceived as much more than a bank," he says, noting that his company already helps sell cars and houses through its website, in addition to financing their purchase.

Then there's the coming introduction of bill-presentment technology, in which bills go directly to your bank or cash manager so that you can automatically pay them online. The service could turn a place like Wells Fargo into a powerful middleman between consumers and merchants. Kovacevich paints the picture: "We'll electronically present the bill to the customer, who can look at it and click, 'Yes, pay it.' Think of all the cost and time that is saved. Is it financial services? Is it processing? Is it the post office?" Kovacevich clearly relishes the idea of creating something new. And there's one thing he's certain of: "At least half the population want multiple products. In some cases it's more like 75%. We will be one of the few financial services companies that will give customers every channel and product they want."

Intuit's Scott Cook. His wife no longer spends hours slogging through her checkbook. That's because, 16 years ago, Cook got fed up and created Intuit's Quicken, now the best name in do-it-yourself finance. Eleven million people use the software, an 80% share in a market where Microsoft is a rare second. About 6 million visit Quicken.com each month via Intuit's websites and online partnerships with AOL and Excite.

Unlike Kovacevich at Wells Fargo, Cook isn't focused on selling more of his own products to his customers. Indeed, the chairman of Intuit's executive committee is downright dismissive of that idea. "We're not a factory," he sniffs from company headquarters in Mountain View, Calif. Rather, Cook expects Intuit to be a virtual adviser, providing tools that consumers can use to direct them to the ideal financial instrument for their needs at the most reasonable price. If each product happens to be sold by a completely different institution, what does it matter?

Cook, who founded the company after stints as a management consultant and a Procter & Gamble marketing exec, is slim and bespectacled and speaks in a thoughtful half-whisper reminiscent of a National Public Radio host. But the 47-year-old doesn't pull many of his punches. Financial planning as it is practiced elsewhere, he says, "is another word for selling." Not at Quicken.com, where users can create their own plan, pick among recommended funds, finance a house, buy insurance, download stock research and obtain just about any financial product one gets from more traditional sources. And the range of available services is only going to expand.

Intuit and other would-be internet portals want to create a new kind of one-stop shop by acting as "infomediaries" between buyer and seller, making money from both sides of the transaction. Their image of objectivity is their key advantage. The ideal infomediary has no interest in the sale of a particular brand or product. And Cook says it certainly won't be peddling your juiciest personal information to third parties without your permission. "We'll be your data custodian," he says.

Technology that's coming in the near future could make it easier to replace an adviser with an electronic infomediary. Email alerts tied to changes in the size or composition of your portfolio would tell you when it's time to rebalance your holdings or walk through a series of estate-planning steps or consider this type of insurance and that type of tax shelter. Artificial intelligence would work its own sales magic. You'll sit down at your PC, and up pops a message that says: "We've shopped your mortgage and found you could save $200 a month."

In Cook's world of the future, however, the only voice most consumers would have to listen to would be their own.

Charles Schwab's David Pottruck. Two years ago Pottruck persuaded founder Chuck Schwab to bet the company's future on a risky strategy. They eliminated Schwab's two-tiered trading system, which offered cheap transactions to online customers and the pricier traditional version to the rest, and instead offered everyone web trades at $30 a pop. The gambit would halve Schwab's average commission and, some feared, trim revenues by $125 million. But better to lead now than follow later, Schwab decided. The price cut attracted new customers and ignited trading volume. The company used the money it saved by doing more of its brokerage business online to expand investor services and draw even more clients. Total accounts at San Francisco-based Schwab recently totaled 6.6 million, up from 4.8 million in 1997, as customer assets swelled to $621 billion from $354 billion. Many still consider Schwab an online discounter. But Pottruck, president and now co-CEO, argues: "We've repositioned as the new model of full-service brokerage."

No competitor has the company's most potent weapon—an outside network of 5,600 financial advisers who work for themselves and use Schwab as their back office. The independent advisers' link to Schwab adds greatly to the company's image as distant from the hard-sell culture of Wall Street. That degree of separation also helps Schwab as it builds an inhouse corps of 7,000 investment specialists to help customers handle their money. Despite all the cyberinvesting hype, the fact is that 70% of new assets last year walked into one of Schwab's 319 branches. And half of its new customers have no brokerage experience. So the internal advice effort will likely grow. "I could imagine," Pottruck says, "Schwab being in the more simplified version of financial planning and leaving the more involved level to the adviser network. We're just beginning to understand how you take your people channels and technology channels and blend them."

Pottruck, 51, a college wrestler, knows the value of a well-timed move and the potential of the other side to grapple. He can't push too far into the independent advisers' planning turf because their accounts represent a third of the company's assets and 15% of its revenues. And their business is growing 30% a year. Nor can Pottruck underestimate the threat from full-service firms and their legions of brokers. Merrill Lynch, for example, is a superpower that serves 8.7 million U.S. households and manages $1.5 trillion of their assets through more brokers (14,000) than any other financial services company. "The full-service guys like Merrill and Morgan Stanley are moving downstream," says Hambrecht & Quist analyst Gregory Smith. "And the deep discounters are moving upstream." For now, Schwab is the model in the middle, the place where everyone else wants to be.

E Trade's Christos Cotsakos. As usual, the online broker's high-profile chief wastes no time making his point. "Who wants an insurance guy sitting in your house for three hours?"

he asks from company headquarters in Menlo Park, Calif. Then again, the hyperkinetic Cotsakos might wear you down himself as he hurls words like "revolution" and "fundamental philosophical movement" throughout a conversation. Fortunately, Cotsakos has a good product to pitch. E Trade's 14% market share ranks second in a five-year-young field that has exploded to encompass almost a fifth of all stock trades and a tenth of total share volume. (Schwab leads with a 25% share, while Fidelity ties TD Waterhouse for third with 12% each.) E Trade's recent acquisition of Telebank, with $2 billion in deposits, makes Cotsakos the head of both an internet brokerage and a bank. Stakes in an electronic mortgage broker, an online investment bank and other services suggest that Cotsakos plans to offer everything that Schwab, Wells Fargo and other giants provide through their stores and staff. But he'll do it solely through the internet.

Cotsakos knows his marketing. He was a co-CEO of A.C. Nielsen before joining E Trade. And he knows self-directed investing. No planners or private bankers for him, insists the 51-year-old executive. "You find the time because it's worth the time," Cotsakos says. Not all of his customers will be purists, he concedes, estimating that half the do-it-yourself crowd will want some human advice. It'll be delivered through interactive video or pay-per-view sessions with star advisers. Cotsakos is happy to compromise. "This is," he figures, "a trillion-dollar market."

American Express's David Hubers. He started at

American Express Financial Advisors 35 years ago, a pup right out of college. Today, he's the big dog running the fastest-growing profit engine at parent company American Express, generating more than $800 million in annual earnings. Guess who employs more certified financial planners than anyone? Guess whose people create more financial plans than any other company? Hubers, CEO of the Minneapolis-based adviser unit since 1993, sure knows the answers, and sees more green ahead. "We believe that do-it-yourselfers will migrate to face-to-face advice," says Hubers, noting that baby boomers will have increasingly complex financial lives as their portfolios grow and they approach retirement.

American Express charges between $400 and $15,000 for a plan. But that's not where the money is. "Financial planning," Hubers explains, "captures greater share of wallet." Clients who go through the planning process buy two to three times more products than clients who don't. "With financial planning," he adds, "you focus on building a relationship as opposed to being transaction-oriented, as some of our competitors have built their businesses. This results in fewer transactions and less churning." For example, annual redemption rates for the company's mutual funds are 10%, half the average for the industry. That steadiness makes the typical American Express client more profitable than customers at many competing firms.

While Intuit and E Trade work to render financial planners obsolete, Hubers hopes to double his force of 10,000 advisers. "Five years down the road," he predicts, "the industry will be dominated by one or two dozen major brands. Such global companies offer the attributes of confidence, trust, security, quality and the like. It's sort of self-fulfilling. In order to compete and invest in new technology, you have to have size and scale. Those that don't have that are at a disadvantage."

American Express almost certainly will be one of the advantaged. Its adviser division has 2.3 million clients, manages $232 billion of their money and has a brand name that's in the stratosphere of marketing. To Hubers, 56, technology is a servant. "It allows us to increase the productivity of financial advisers," he says. "Routine transactions can be done online, and they can serve a greater client base. It allows companies to access a greater part of the marketplace." You can't imagine Cotsakos talking like that. Then, again, Cotsakos and his company aren't yet earning $800 million a year. If Hubers is right, then American Express will be among those that dominate the new century.

❧ Our Hall of Fame & Shame Awards

When you think about it, the key financial trend spanning virtually the entire 20th century was the democratization of finance. This trend has made you as important a player in the market as any Wall Street hedge fund manager. Early in the last century, the market was unapologetically an insider's game, with small investors serving mostly as lambs to be fleeced. But gradually this changed. Crucial turning points include the creation of the SEC in 1934, the rise of the great wire houses like Merrill Lynch, the outlawing of insider practices that were once common, the invention of money-market funds and mutual funds, the unfixing of commission rates and the creation of discounters such as Charles Schwab, and the rise of the internet as a vehicle to convey stock information and trade shares. All of these events, and many others, helped shift the balance of power between Wall Street and Main Street. While it's impossible to count the many incredible things that have happened in the financial world in the last 100 years, we've highlighted some of the most notable winners and sinners below.

The century's best investor. There were many of them during the 20th century, ranging from Wall Street trailblazers like Bernard Baruch and Benjamin Graham to modern-day gurus such as Warren Buffett. But our nominee is someone who's never gotten his due as an investor. Would you believe Ty Cobb? Yes, that Ty Cobb, the ornery baseball great who retired from the game in 1928 with the astonishing lifetime batting average of .367. What has never been truly appreciated is that Cobb was a star investor too. Though his annual salary never topped five digits, he became a millionaire even before he hung up his sharpened spikes. And that was back when a million bucks was considered real money.

Cobb took his 1909 World Series money and bought a piece of a copper mine for $3 a share. When he sold the shares just a year later, they were worth $1,000 apiece. But his greatest triumph was his prescient purchase of two stocks. The first was Coca-Cola, which he began accumulating in 1908 after signing an endorsement contract with the company. The second was a small car company that was eventually purchased by General Motors. In both cases, Cobb showed real vision. Coke at the time was a mere upstart, competing against much more entrenched brands. And as for GM, you can imagine what the car industry was like at the beginning of the century. Thanks to his shrewd stock picking, Cobb was that rare thing, an individual investor who thrived during the Depression. In fact, by the end of the 1930s, he was wealthier than he'd been at the beginning of the decade.

The century's top financial book title. The winner is an obscure book that was published in 1940 and called *Where Are the Customers' Yachts?* Written by a disenchanted ex-broker named Fred Schwed, it amounted to the first full-scale broadside aimed at the brokerage industry. The title, of course, comes from a now famous anecdote, recounted in the book, about a broker showing off his big, new yacht, only to have the other person ask, "Where are the customers' yachts?" Lo, these many years later, variations of this question are still being asked. Schwed's book, by the way, is still in print.

The century's savviest financial prediction. This goes to a now deceased futurist named Herman Kahn. In the early 1980s, please recall, inflation was rampant, interest rates were off the charts, and the stock market was nowhere. Kahn wrote a little book entitled *The Coming Boom.* It is an amazingly prescient work. Kahn not only predicted that we were about to enter an era of unparalleled prosperity. He also foresaw that it would be driven by the technology industry. He even predicted that computer networks (that is, the internet) would become an important trend. Alas, he also claimed that we would soon enter a new era of suburban mass transportation. But even the great ones cannot be expected to get them all right.

The century's dumbest financial prediction. Yale University professor Irving Fisher declared in September 1929: "Stock prices have reached what looks like a permanently high plateau." John Kenneth Galbraith would later describe Fisher as "the most innovative economist of his time," a man who made serious contributions to monetary theory. But it is this unfortunate utterance for which he will always be remembered.

The century's worst market timing. Our nomination goes to Gerry Tsai's 1965 decision to leave fund manager Fidelity and strike out on his own. Do you remember Gerry Tsai? He was the first money manager to get the kind of press normally reserved for rock stars. As a young man at Fidelity in the early 1960s, he turned in dazzling numbers and came to exemplify the "go-go years," as that era was later dubbed. In 1965, after being told he would not become the next head of Fidelity, he quit in a huff and started his own mutual fund, the Manhattan Fund. Hoping to raise $25 million, Tsai was so hot he got nearly 10 times that amount. You can guess what happened next. In February 1966, the same month that Tsai began his fund, the market peaked. By the summer of 1968, the fund ranked 294th out of the nation's 300 largest funds. Tsai bailed out that summer, selling to an insurance company. He later joined American Can, which he turned into a financial services company and renamed Primerica. Even then, however, the Manhattan Fund debacle dogged him. "We had one bad year, in 1968, and I've been killed in the press ever since," he growled years later. "Like a ballplayer, right? If you have 10 good games and one lousy game, you're a bum."

The century's best stock pick. Mutual funds were so tarnished in the wake of the go-go years that they seemed headed for extinction until the 1980s bull market brought them back. The man most responsible for their revival was Fidelity's Peter Lynch during his time as the skipper of Magellan Fund. That's why we think Lynch deserves the award for the century's most important stock pick—Chrysler. He began accumulating the stock in the early 1980s at the very time the car company was on the edge of bankruptcy. Betting heavily that the government would not let Chrysler go under and that Lee Iacocca would find a way to return the company to profitability, Lynch began buying up the stock until it was the largest position in Magellan's portfolio. Bingo. Magellan in the early 1980s grew 70% in 1980, 16% in 1981, 48% in 1982 and so on—thanks in no small part to Lynch's having bet the ranch on Chrysler.

There have been stock picks that made people richer. There have been gutsier calls too. But there has never been a more important pick. When small investors began to take notice of the 1980s bull market and started looking for ways to participate in it, they found Peter Lynch and his spectacular record. Thus began the great triumph of the mutual fund in the modern era.

Chapter 2

Your Best Investments In 2000

*T*he current economic expansion has gone on so long that it's poised to set an all-time record this year. Growth stocks have soared to seemingly unsustainable heights. And yet, each time it looks like the stock market finally has to pull back, it rises even higher. Stock market forecasters aren't the only ones who keep being confounded. Economists have the same problem. It seems every time they project the next quarter's growth, they underestimate not by a fraction but by more than a percentage point. This endless stream of positive surprises provokes the questions that contrarians keep asking. Will tech stocks crack? Will value stocks perk up? Will the market return to traditional levels? Or are we really in a much-heralded New Era?

✒ *Our Market and Economic Forecast*

We at MONEY are convinced that historical patterns inevitably reassert themselves if you look beyond specific questions to more general ones. Many specifics about investing have changed since the 1982 recession. But long-term market trends haven't altered much. The secret to making stock market profits safely over the next year or two depends on your being able to distinguish between transient market behavior and permanent shifts.

The U.S. economy really is almost as dynamic as it appears. Although stocks won't be able to keep up the fantastic pace of the 1990s, odds are they'll keep rising for at least another year or so. Nonetheless, there are far more risks for investors than there were three years ago. Inflation is rising slowly. Another danger is recession. While a slump isn't in sight, it can't be ruled out entirely. There are less dire risks too. Federal Reserve chairman Alan Greenspan has kept interest rates as much as a percentage point too high for most of the past five years. Greenspan's high-rate bias hurts but has a positive side too. The market will get a new energy jolt when he finally lets rates come down.

All these crosscurrents demand a more refined portfolio strategy than investors needed in the '90s. Let's first examine the key questions. What are the sources of the economy's stunning growth? Why hasn't inflation been more of a problem? What does Alan Greenspan think he's doing? And how healthy is today's market overall?

Corporate profits will keep climbing. Share prices follow corporate profit growth over the long haul. Investors can expect companies to keep boosting earnings, though not at quite the same rate they have achieved over the past five years (see the top chart in "More Fodder for Bulls in 2000" on the next page). Factors driving this expansion include productivity gains, globalization and the rising use of credit. "In corporate America, productivity has risen more rapidly in the 1990s than in any cycle on record," says Merrill Lynch chief economist Bruce Steinberg. Productivity gains averaged less than 1.5% a year in the 1970s and less than 2.5% in the 1980s. They have topped 3% annually in the past few years. "The productivity trend of the 1990s was even better than previously reported, and I think that it's still being underestimated," Steinberg adds.

The current economic boom isn't confined to the U.S. The rise of Asia, the fall of the Berlin Wall and the spread of democracy in Latin America have improved the prospects for growth in almost every region. Even Europe is showing renewed vigor. Whereas the world's young and restless once looked to Che Guevara for inspiration, they now prefer Bill Gates as a model for personal success. (For more on Gates, see "The Outlook for Besieged Microsoft" later in this chapter.) Many U.S. blue chips are growing faster overseas than they are at home. So a robust global economy feeds back into the profits of U.S. multinationals, including big tech stocks like Cisco, Intel and Microsoft.

Since the 1987 crash, inflation has plunged and earnings of blue chips have climbed. Low inflation and rising profits are the key ingredients for a bull market. So stocks have soared over the past decade. And this boom doesn't look as though it's over yet. Inflation is creeping up. But it isn't likely to get a lot worse. And blue chips' earnings seem likely to keep rising, albeit a bit more slowly than they did in the 1990s.

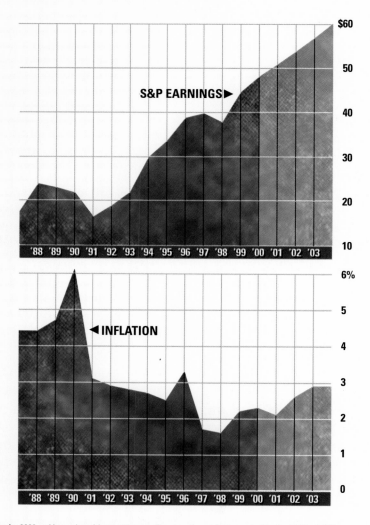

Note: Figures for 2000 and beyond are MONEY estimates. **Sources:** Bernstein Research, Standard & Poor's DRI.

Only one major trend that has fueled U.S. corporate profit growth looks worrisome. That's the rapid rise in borrowing by American consumers. Consider net saving. That's the difference between the income of U.S. households and corporations and their spending on consumption and investment. Since 1995, net saving has swung into negative territory. The personal savings rate is at a postwar low chiefly because of credit-card use, says Prudential Securities chief economist Richard Rippe.

Open-handed spending is justified. Americans have fat profits on their stock portfolios and their real estate, and they can afford to enjoy their profits. But it's impossible to keep overspending at today's breakneck pace. The risk for investors is that a sudden decline in credit growth could reduce consumer spending so much that it would cause a recession. That, in turn, could trigger a major drop in stock prices on the order of 30% or more. As we see it, though, consumer borrowing will probably slow more gradually. As long as any slackening of the economy is mild, it could actually be good news for stocks. Inflationary pressures would dissipate, and interest rates could fall.

Inflation will slowly trend up. The outlook for inflation is another crucial issue for investors. A recent 12-month spurt in oil prices, from $11 to $26 a barrel, may conjure up a return to the double-digit inflation that followed the oil crisis of the early '70s. But volatile food and fuel prices aren't what economists worry about most. At $11 a barrel, oil was unusually cheap, and the price isn't likely to keep surging. If anything, the cost of crude could come down a few dollars a barrel. More important, a one-time jump in oil prices won't lead to a sustained increase in inflation unless rising labor costs have already got an inflation spiral going.

Inflation psychology becomes dangerous when workers demand higher wages and consumers rush to buy as soon as possible, fearing that prices will be even higher in the future. In that sort of climate, a sudden hike in oil prices can permanently shift inflation into a higher gear. You might think just such a wage-price spiral would be under way now, given that the U.S. economy is white hot and unemployment is down to a scant 4.1%. But there's no sign any such thing is happening. Why not? Phenomenal gains in productivity are part of the reason. If workers make more widgets an hour, then manufacturers don't have to charge more for widgets even if they raise wages. And while inflation is rising, it isn't going up very fast. Forecasters typically see the annual rate below 3% for five years or longer (see the bottom chart in "More Fodder for Bulls in 2000" on page 36).

Two other factors have helped restrain price increases. First, the Asian financial crisis caused a temporary slowdown in global economic growth and slashed demand for many raw materials, which helped dissipate inflationary pressures in the U.S. Thus we enjoyed the benefits of a recession that happened in other countries. Second, price increases have been held down by momentum. The inflation-bashing by Fed chairman Paul Volcker in 1979 caused a brutal recession in 1982 and also ended the inflation psychology of the 1970s. Interest rates as high as 14% and massive job losses made Americans far more conscious of security and less inclined to push for big wage boosts.

Those reduced inflation expectations have become a self-fulfilling prophecy. As workers demanded less, prices went up less. Alan Greenspan is fully aware that this spiral could start running in the opposite direction if annual inflation reaches the 3% threshold. Indeed, much of the Fed's policy since 1994 has aimed at preventing exactly that from happening.

Interest rates will head back down. Greenspan has kept interest rates quite high relative to prevailing inflation for much of the past five years. As a result, he has room to cut rates enough to lower yields on both Treasury bills and bonds by at least half a percentage point, and perhaps even a full point, if the economy slows within the next year or so. Lower rates, of course, would likely give the stock market an extra kick. The expected range for Treasury bill yields is shown in the top chart in "Interest Rates Have Room to Fall" on the right. That range is no more than 1.5 percentage points above the inflation rate. The bottom chart shows the range for bond yields is 2.0 to 3.5 percentage points above average inflation over the previous three years. As both charts illustrate, Greenspan pushed up both short-term and long-term interest rates in 1994. For most of the time since then, rates have been as much as a full percentage point higher than inflation would lead you to expect.

Interest Rates Have Room to Fall

Fed chairman Alan Greenspan has kept interest rates quite high relative to prevailing inflation for much of the past five years. As a result, he has room to cut rates, which would lower yields on both Treasury bills and bonds by at least half a percentage point if the economy slows within the next year or so. Lower rates would likely give the stock market an extra kick. The expected range for T-bill yields shown in the top chart is no more than 1.5 percentage points above the current inflation rate. The range for T-bond yields is 2 to 3.5 percentage points above average inflation over the previous three years.

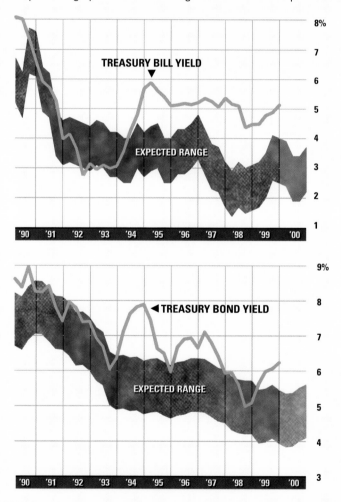

Note: Figures for 2000 and beyond are MONEY estimates. **Sources:** Bernstein Research, Standard & Poor's DRI.

If there's a warning sign, it's that a shrinking number of stocks are carrying the market averages higher. The top chart shows how tech stock PEs have been soaring. (To represent tech, we've plotted the average PE for Cisco, Intel, Microsoft and Oracle. But the gains are even greater for dotcom shares that have little in the way of earnings.) Meanwhile, the average PE of the blue chips in the S&P 500 is up only moderately, while the median PE of all the stocks with earnings has hardly changed. The bottom chart shows more and more stocks have gained less than the S&P 500. The chart shows the percentage of stocks that are at least 15% behind the index for the previous 12 months. Such divergences signal that a bull market is running out of gas.

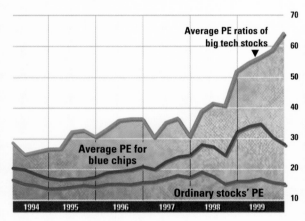

Sources: Standard & Poor's, Value Line.

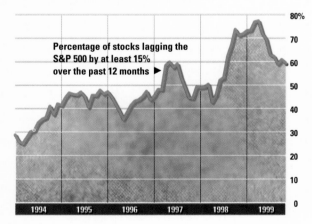

Source: Salomon Smith Barney.

Greenspan has simply been following the level of interest rates set by the money markets. But he does have some discretion. Whenever Greenspan has had a choice between standing pat or nudging rates up, he has gone for the rate hike, particularly during the past year. To a large extent, this bias is part of a pre-emptive campaign against a return of inflationary psychology. Greenspan believes that by the time inflation becomes evident, it requires painful measures to stop it from spiraling out of control.

There's an important piece of good news to discuss here. Greenspan has room to let interest rates come down once he sees the economy is slowing or decides that inflation pressures are dissipating for other reasons. In that particular scenario, both short-term and long-term interest rates could fall by at least half a percentage point and possibly by as much as a full point.

Fewer stocks will lead the advance. The most popular stock groups continue to post impressive gains. But the rest of the stock market isn't nearly so dynamic. In fact, the divergence among stock valuations since 1997 has been extraordinary. While the PE (price-earnings) ratio of the median stock with earnings has declined slightly, to 15.2, roughly in line with historical norms, the PEs of growth stocks have soared (see the top chart in "The Market's Unsettling Divergences" at left). The average PE of the S&P 500 index, which is skewed toward growth companies, has trended higher over the past five years. And the PEs of top tech stocks have exploded. There's no way to show internet stocks on this chart; most have no PEs because they have no earnings.

If tech stocks are rocketing and the average has hardly changed, then something else must be going down. And value stocks sure are. The cheapest 10% of publicly traded companies have lagged expensive stocks by 27% over 18 months. That's the worst and longest relative decline for cheap stocks in 40 years. "The market is sending a message that the economy is going to slow," says First Albany strategist Hugh Johnson. "Cyclical stocks such as automakers, home builders and retailers have all generally been performing poorly." Because it would bring down inflation and interest rates, such a slowdown would be good news for the long-term health of the economy and the stock market, provided it didn't turn into an outright recession.

Market volatility will continue to rise. So you might think it would be smart to sell everything and keep your money in bonds. From today's levels, stocks are statistically likely to earn only single-digit returns. If you can get 8%, say, on select income investments, why bother owning stocks? That's a fair question, particularly when it comes to putting new money to work. But there are compelling arguments against a headlong flight to safety. First, market timing never pays off down the line. It's simply too hard to call market turns with accuracy. Any successful investment that you sell in a taxable account will most likely be subject to capital gains taxes, which will reduce your working capital going forward. Most important, with a little effort you can always find a few great stocks in any market.

Your real goal should be to get your share of whatever further gains the averages earn, take advantage of any pockets of opportunity and hold down your overall level of risk. You can do this with individual investments or with mutual funds. We cite a number of specific investments later in this chapter.

Risk-reducing strategies will rule. Look for chances to buy top growth stocks on major dips. You should always have a buy list of a couple of dozen blue-chip growth stocks that you would jump at if their prices came down. Balance growth investments with value and small-caps. There's no question that both value stocks and many small-company shares are cheap statistically. Just remember that those stocks may take three to five years to pay off. Also be sure to have some exposure to international economies. You don't have to buy shares in the Trashcanistan Fund to be a global investor. Many U.S. multinationals have sizable involvement in the most attractive foreign economies.

In addition, shift some money to income investments such as tax-free municipal bonds. And don't assume that indexing is a no-brainer. When the stock market is fairly cheap across the board, you can buy anything reasonable and end up doing well. But the more stock sectors diverge, the more important selectivity becomes. For new investments, ask yourself what you can buy that would most improve the balance of your portfolio.

Keep in mind that the stock market returns an average of 10% to 12% a year over long stretches of time. When the market has had a period of outsize gains, it's inevitable that a subpar period will follow. That doesn't have to happen in 2000 any more than tossing a coin and getting 10 tails in a row means that the next toss has to come up heads. But don't expect that stocks will turn in 20% a year forever. If you can crank out 9% or 10% a year with below-average risk, you'll be doing very well. With inflation below 3%, that works out to quite a high real return. This is the kind of market that rewards the disciplined and patient but slaughters the giddy and sloppy.

❧ Why Wal-Mart Is Our No. 1 Pick

What name first comes to mind when you think of the great blue-chip growth stocks of the past quarter century? Coke? General Electric? Merck? Well, Wal-Mart has crushed them all. Since 1977, the stock has returned an amazing 35% annually, turning a hypothetical $10,000 investment into around $6.9 million (see the chart "Striking It Rich With Wal-Mart" on page 44). In the 21st century, it also figures to outstrip most of today's crop of silicon startups and dotcoms over the long term.

Wal-Mart isn't in a sexy industry, isn't run by a young entrepreneurial millionaire and doesn't woo workers with promises of stock options. It's simply a juggernaut, built on a combination of solid technology, smiley-face service and old-fashioned business skill. Wal-Mart has figured out how to pile up billions of dollars in profit by selling staggering quantities of low-margin goods. Its $147 billion in sales over a recent 12-month period are double those of Sears and K Mart combined. Its $4.9 billion profit in that period is nearly triple their total.

Relentless execution of its basic business model has helped Wal-Mart stock soar even as other retailers have been battered by fears of rising interest rates and declining consumer spending. Can Wal-Mart keep going? To answer that question, we interviewed Wal-Mart execs, Wall Street analysts, major shareholders, retail consultants, rivals and customers. We started in the small town of Bentonville, Ark., where Wal-Mart runs its far-flung operations from a converted warehouse building located on Walton Boulevard. In a series of interviews, chairman Rob Walton (son

Striking It Rich With Wal-Mart

Wal-Mart's stock has been an awesome investment. Here's what you would have lately if you had invested $10,000 in the stock and nine other blue chips in 1977.

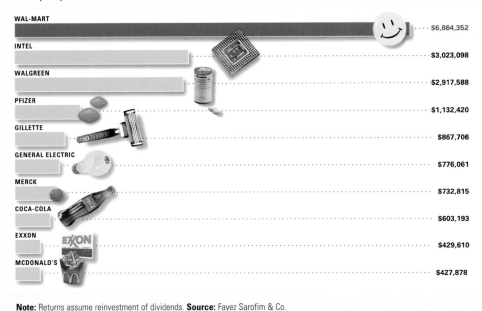

WAL-MART	$6,864,352
INTEL	$3,023,098
WALGREEN	$2,917,588
PFIZER	$1,132,420
GILLETTE	$867,706
GENERAL ELECTRIC	$776,061
MERCK	$732,815
COCA-COLA	$603,193
EXXON	$429,610
MCDONALD'S	$427,878

Note: Returns assume reinvestment of dividends. **Source:** Fayez Sarofim & Co.

of founder Sam), CEO David Glass and other top executives gave us a detailed picture of the company's strategy. They are planning growth on a mind-boggling scale for a company this big. Their projections call for boosting both revenues and profits at least 15% a year (excluding any potential acquisitions), which would push sales past $200 billion in just two years. To hit those numbers, Wal-Mart is steamrolling ahead on three main fronts—the grocery business, foreign markets and the internet.

Has Wal-Mart reached the point where it's just too big to keep growing rapidly? Perhaps. But the company's history is one of proving the naysayers wrong. "Our prospects are better today than at any point in our history," contends Glass. "We can be anything we want to be. Any limits are self-imposed because we can do whatever we want."

Mr. Sam's spirit remains strong. If Glass' comments sound more like an inspirational spiel from Tony Robbins than a dispassionate assessment of business prospects, that's simply the Wal-Mart way. At the firm's shareholder meeting last year, 20,000 investors and employees descended on the local university's Bud Walton stadium for a morning of chatting and cheering. "It's like a cult," says Jerry Rascona, who runs the lawn-and-garden department in Wal-Mart's Middle Island, N.Y. store and owns some 700 shares of the stock. Wal-Mart remains imbued with the spirit of Sam Walton, who died in 1992. Photos of Mr. Sam line the walls of the corporate headquarters. The hokey customs he initiated, like "people greeters" at the stores' entrances, endure. But don't let the folksiness fool you. Like its founder, Wal-Mart is one big, tough, shrewd operator. It uses its size to wring the best deals from suppliers. It carefully calibrates the price and placement of every item it sells, using reams of computer-generated data on the buying patterns of the 100 million people who come to its stores each week.

How tech changed a mundane business. The backbone of the company's success is not the products or the stores but its massive computer system. The company claims it is the second most powerful in the world, surpassed only by the Pentagon's. By analyzing the constantly updated information, Wal-Mart executives and store managers can track customer behavior with startling precision and to great effect.

At Wal-Mart No. 0001 in Rogers, Ark., store manager Mike Walker points a hand-held scanner at a package of Kraft American cheese singles on special for $1.98. With the click of a button, the machine shows how many have been sold in the store that day and how many are in transit, in the warehouse and on order. Click again, and the handheld pulls up the price Wal-Mart paid for the cheese and tallies its profit margin. "We know everything about every item," Walker says. "We can get more sales and make more money based on what we know."

What are the bestsellers in each store by total dollars? By profits? By volume? Wal-Mart knows and can position its hottest items in the best locations for boosting sales. How well did a new product fare on its first day of introduction? Wal-Mart knows and can tweak the color or size or flavor of the product with the supplier immediately. Are golf balls flying out of one Florida store but languishing in another? Wal-Mart knows and can move the sluggish product to the place where it will sell, rather than having to mark it down.

What Wal-Mart is now learning to do with the data, however, goes beyond traditional inventory management. By looking into the shopping baskets of its customers, the chain is learning which items to stock near one another (bananas close to cereal, alarm clocks with suitcases). And by working closely with more than 7,000 vendors who have access over the internet to the company's data on all of their products, Wal-Mart can hammer out deals for special flavors and sizes and instantly nix products that don't sell in early tests. By learning what works and what doesn't, in real time, Wal-Mart can shift gears faster than many small merchants, let alone other giants. The payoff from all this number crunching? Wal-Mart has sliced its inventory costs (because goods sit on the shelves for less time) and increased its sales per square foot (to $374 vs. $222 for K Mart).

Let the supermarket food fights begin. If you don't think of Wal-Mart as a grocery store, you will soon. Across the country, it's creating enormous 200,000-square-foot supercenters that offer all the usual items but also devote about a fifth of their floor space to groceries. Wal-Mart's foray into food will turn it into the country's No. 1 supermarket within five years, some analysts predict, catapulting it ahead of Kroger and Safeway and pummeling many of the smaller chains.

Why would Wal-Mart move into a field with even lower margins, fiercer competition and more vexing distribution difficulties than the discount business? For starters, filling America's shopping carts is an annual $450 billion business, dwarfing the discount sector. And Wal-Mart executives see it as a field where the company's unparalleled skill at pushing large volumes of cheap goods will give it an unbeatable edge. People shop for food twice as often as for hard goods. So food brings more shoppers to Wal-Mart's supercenters, creating more potential buyers for the chain's higher-margin items, like books, CDs and computers. And tracking food purchases gives Wal-Mart information on its

Crushing Rivals Sears and K Mart

How Wal-Mart stacks up against its biggest competitors on key financial measures.

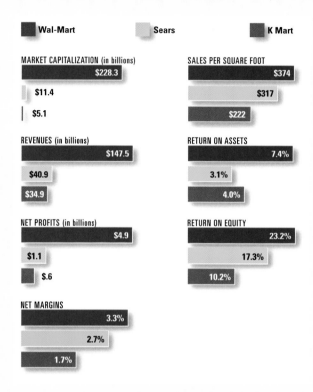

■ Wal-Mart   ■ Sears   ■ K Mart

MARKET CAPITALIZATION (in billions)
- Wal-Mart: $228.3
- Sears: $11.4
- K Mart: $5.1

SALES PER SQUARE FOOT
- Wal-Mart: $374
- Sears: $317
- K Mart: $222

REVENUES (in billions)
- Wal-Mart: $147.5
- Sears: $40.9
- K Mart: $34.9

RETURN ON ASSETS
- Wal-Mart: 7.4%
- Sears: 3.1%
- K Mart: 4.0%

NET PROFITS (in billions)
- Wal-Mart: $4.9
- Sears: $1.1
- K Mart: $.6

RETURN ON EQUITY
- Wal-Mart: 23.2%
- Sears: 17.3%
- K Mart: 10.2%

NET MARGINS
- Wal-Mart: 3.3%
- Sears: 2.7%
- K Mart: 1.7%

Notes: All numbers are for latest 12 months except sales per square foot, which is for 1998. **Sources:** Baseline, company reports.

---

customers' ethnicity and demographics that it can't get any other way, letting it fine-tune its merchandising efforts even further. "Everything we do is a driver of volume," says Lee Scott, a 20-year Wal-Mart veteran who was tapped as chief operating officer last year and is expected to become the next CEO. "Additional customers let us lower the price, and lower prices draw additional customers."

Moreover, Wal-Mart sees the food sector as ripe for conquest. It is extremely fragmented. The top two chains, Kroger and Safeway, account for just 12% of sales. While many of the country's grocers are preoccupied with the problems of integrating acquisitions, Wal-Mart is simply rolling out new stores. (Wal-Mart prefers not to buy existing chains because it wants to sell food and its traditional merchandise under one roof.) There are upwards of 650 supercenters, and this year alone, Wal-Mart figures on adding at least 160 new ones, mostly by knocking down the walls of existing discount stores to create space for food.

At the same time, Wal-Mart is testing a new concept called the Neighborhood Market in a handful of locations in Arkansas. Dubbed "small-marts," these green-and-white stores are stocked with fresh fruits and vegetables, a drive-up pharmacy, a 24-hour photo shop and a selection of classic Wal-Mart hard goods. The company is moving slowly on this concept, planning to open no more than 10 this year. The goal is to ring its superstores with these smaller offshoots, keeping them close enough to be served by the same distribution centers, to attract customers who may be in a hurry or want only a few items.

Isn't the nation already saturated with nearly 3,000 Wal-Marts and membership-only Sam's Clubs? Won't building so many new stores simply shuffle customers from one Wal-Mart to another? "We've been willing to cannibalize our stores rather than going into a defensive mode where we insist each store has to make a certain amount of profit," explains COO Scott. His reasoning rests on the simple advantages of size. He figures that the overall increase in market share and corporate profitability more than offsets the negatives of cannibalization.

Targeting shoppers around the world. While most of Wal-Mart's growth over the next few years will come in the U.S., the company eventually will run out of room here. But Wal-Mart has made many costly mistakes since it first ventured out of the U.S. in 1991 with a store in Mexico City. Time after time it sold the wrong products and even bollixed up entire efforts (it pulled out of a loss-plagued Indonesian venture in 1998).

To that end, Wal-Mart recently altered its strategy. Instead of scattering stores around the globe, it's concentrating on becoming a major player in Europe. In December 1997, the company snapped up the 21-store Wertkauf chain in Germany. A year later, it grabbed 74 more Interspar stores there. Last year, in a blockbuster deal that shook up the once sleepy European market, Wal-Mart shelled out $10.8 billion to buy Britain's Asda, a 229-store Wal-Mart wannabe. "We've been a little too spread out," admits John Menzer, Wal-Mart's head of international sales. "We're going to try to fill in regions."

The response in Europe to Wal-Mart's incursion was immediate and dramatic. Competitors scrambled to match Wal-Mart's low prices, long hours and friendly service. Then, before summer was out, France's Carrefour chain of hypermarkets had combined forces with its smaller competitor, Promodès, in a $16.5 billion deal. Rumors are flying about who will be next.

It's often easier for Wal-Mart to buy existing stores in Europe than to build new ones because of stubborn local regulations. But it still plans to put up lots of bricks and mortar in Europe and elsewhere around the globe. Menzer says he will open 90 to 100 stores a year overseas for the next three to five years. His target is to double sales this year. International stores recently provided just 9% of Wal-Mart's total sales. Analysts say that figure should reach 20% by 2001. Looking further, Menzer has his sights set on hitting the $100 billion mark by 2010.

Figuring out what works on the web. The company would certainly seem to be far behind Amazon.com and other online retailers racing to become "the Wal-Mart of the web." But Wal-Mart may be better positioned to claim that title than the upstarts. It recently struck a deal with America Online in which AOL's Compuserve unit will provide a low-cost internet access service that carries the Wal-Mart brand. The retailer will promote the service and AOL in its stores and through television advertising. AOL, in turn, will use its audience of 19 million users to promote Wal-Mart's web store. The potential market could be huge as more of the middle-American shoppers who frequent Wal-Marts go online. Consulting firm Forrester Research figures that sales on the net will soar to $184 billion by 2004, a more than ninefold increase over last year's estimated $20 billion. Seema Williams, the analyst who wrote the Forrester report, thinks that Wal-Mart will "sweep the market in categories it is strong in."

Wal-Mart seems to have all the key ingredients for online success. It has one of the most recognizable brand names, pric-

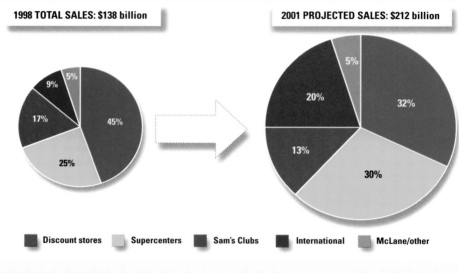

Charting Future Engines of Growth

Supercenters and foreign stores will contribute a bigger share of Wal-Mart's sales.

1998 TOTAL SALES: $138 billion

5%
9%
17%
45%
25%

2001 PROJECTED SALES: $212 billion

5%
20%
32%
13%
30%

Discount stores   Supercenters   Sam's Clubs   International   McLane/other

Note: 1998 totals 101% because of rounding. **Sources:** Wal-Mart financial statements, Morgan Stanley Dean Witter estimates.

ing power and unparalleled distribution capacity. So far, however, Wal-Mart is moving slowly. CEO Glass explains: "You have to offer convenience at a price that is competitive, and I don't think anyone has figured out how to do that and make a decent return on the investment."

Glass is working hard to solve the riddle. For two years, without fanfare or heavy advertising, the company has been testing wal-mart.com, gathering data about who's buying and what products they want. The online store offers roughly 42,000 items (vs. 100,000 in a typical supercenter). As in its stores, Wal-Mart slashes prices to draw customers. Some online-only specials are designed to undercut the prices of well-known etailers. Later this year Wal-Mart will offer an astounding 600,000 items—far more than any existing Wal-Mart carries. Net shoppers will also be able to buy airline tickets, make rental car reservations, fill prescriptions and send digital photos. In what's called a "clicks and mortar" strategy, Wal-Mart will use its stores to bolster its online operations and vice versa. Customers can already shop online and then pick up their goods, prepacked, at the closest Wal-Mart. And the company is testing a program that introduces its traditional shoppers to the internet through store kiosks. There, for example, they can order computers not stocked in the store.

Placing your bet next to the Waltons' 38% stake. If you buy the stock today, you're basically betting that Wal-Mart can sustain its remarkable growth record. The firm is known for its operational skills. But continued expansion for a company already so huge is fraught with uncertainty, if only because no store has ever been this big before. Although Wal-Mart's execs say they aren't worried about oversaturation in the U.S., finding places to put new stores has been getting tougher as communities fight to keep Wal-Mart out. And the company still has plenty of competition. K Mart, now on the mend, has begun opening its own superstores. Overseas, companies like Carrefour don't roll over easily. The internet remains a big unknown. And while Wal-Mart is less vulnerable to economic swings than most retailers, it would still suffer in a recession.

Perhaps the biggest risk is the lofty valuation of Wal-Mart shares, which recently traded around $63 on the New York Stock Exchange. The stock consistently commands a premium over other retailers and the S&P 500 index. It's priced at 53 times latest 12-month earnings, vs. 28 for the S&P 500, and 45 times this fiscal year's consensus earnings estimate of $1.40 a share. That's near the top of its historical PE range and certainly seems like a lot to pay for a company with 3.3% profit margins and a 15% earnings growth rate. Wal-Mart's high PE increases the danger for investors should the company simply fail to expand as fast as Wall Street expects it to. Those are issues you should consider before investing.

The case for buying Wal-Mart sounds a lot like the argument for buying so-called New Economy stocks like America Online, Lucent Technologies and Microsoft. Wal-Mart is the dominant company in its business; it has one of the most consistent track records of earnings growth; and its profitability on most key measures keeps getting better. This may not be the glitziest company in America. But it is well run. "Wal-Mart is a good example of a company that should carry a high earnings multiple," says Tim Ghriskey, a Dreyfus portfolio manager who owns the stock. "It is a dominating company and thus is worth a premium to the market and to its group."

It's also worth noting that the people with the most riding on Wal-Mart are confident. Wal-Mart chairman Rob Walton says that he, his mother and three siblings, who collectively own 38% of the company, haven't pared that stake since Sam Walton's death in 1992 and have no plans to start. "I feel really good about where Wal-Mart is," he says. A lot of smaller shareholders would have to agree.

✒ Top U.S. Stocks and Funds to Buy

When we sat down to discuss the best investments for 2000, the historically high price of the stock market was much on our minds. Is the moment near when unloved value stocks will rise again? Should we tell readers to stay out of the market? Alas, we kept coming round to the same crucial point. The U.S. economy continues to perform admirably and will likely do so in the near future. To us, this means that considerable opportunity still exists for investors, particularly in those areas that are driving our economic expansion. Thus we chose to focus our research on three key forces that seem likely to dominate American business for at least the next several years.

The first is the march of technology. In the 1990s, technology stocks outpaced the S&P 500's heady 400% return by a multiple of three. Much of that gain came from the personal computer industry and the rise of corporate networking. Looking ahead, the build-out of the internet will propel the sector. Credit Suisse First Boston estimates that we're just halfway through a cycle of telecom equipment upgrades leading to a global network that will handle data and video as deftly as voice, over phone or cable lines or via wireless devices.

The second is the aging of the population. Retailers and leisure companies have courted baby boomers for decades. But healthcare companies are just beginning to feel the wave of demand generated by the 77 million Americans born between 1946 and 1965. Four out of five drugs are prescribed to the over-50 crowd. In the next 15 years that group will grow by 30%. Thus the companies supplying drugs and medical equipment seem poised to prosper.

The third is deregulation. The dismantling of government protections in American business isn't new. But it's still big. We've focused on two industries, financial services and power utilities, where the pace of change is especially rapid, and the stakes, as well as the opportunities, are particularly large

How we selected our picks. Taking those three trends as our starting point, we began digging into companies, crunching numbers, debating valuations and testing our hypotheses with analysts and stock pickers. In the end, we identified both individual stocks and mutual funds that we believe can take best advantage of the growth forces in our society. We didn't stop at the U.S. shoreline, however. The global economy is stronger and more dynamic than it's been in years. So we recommend two stock funds that give you a way to invest in the powerful trends driving world growth (see "Timely Bets for Overseas Profits" on page 65). For income-minded investors, we suggest two bond funds that figure to thrive in today's financial climate (see "Great Ways to Earn High Income" on page 64).

Note that some of our healthcare picks and most of our technology favorites sport sky-high valuations. Tech stocks are particularly dear because earnings growth in the sector is much faster than that of the market as a whole. When stock prices reach such lofty altitudes, however, there's always the possibility of a big pullback. So if you decide to buy some of our richly priced recommendations, consider using a strategy called dollar cost averaging. That way you invest a set amount each month until you've put in all you want. By averaging in, you will end up with a lower cost basis on your overall stake. You might also consider spreading your risk by investing in the tech-laden Nasdaq Index 100 Tracking Stock, which tracks the performance of the biggest Nasdaq stocks. The remainder of our picks for 2000 are listed by relative valuation, from lowest to highest. The last two, Qualcomm and Broadcom, carry extremely high PEs that are appropriate only for aggressive investors.

Buy Duke Energy. Once it became clear in the late 1980s that power generation would be deregulated, managers of utilities knew that their basic product would become a cheap commodity. Thus they started cutting costs and stopped building new plants. In response, the country's capacity reserve margin (the amount of extra energy available to handle peak demand) has shrunk from 40% in 1986 to less than 12% today. That's part of the reason you suffer through brownouts in summer. It's also why you can expect power prices to start rising.

Dave Kiefer, manager of the Prudential Utility Fund, explains that this shortage should benefit companies that had the foresight to acquire and run power plants outside of their regulated territories. They can sell their juice to other utilities or trade it like pork bellies. Duke Energy, the Carolinas-based utility, is a leader among these new growth-driven power producers and is one of the country's biggest utilities. "We saw this coming 10 years ago," says CEO Rick Priory. "We saw that if we stood still it would erode our business." After shaving costs, Duke began to acquire, acquire, acquire. "Our board has reviewed $16 billion in deals over the past 2.5 years, a total of 32 transactions," notes Priory. Duke now runs power plants from California to New York and gets 5% of its operating earnings from power trading. In addition, it has natural gas pipelines and pipeline construction projects along the eastern seaboard and into the Midwest. This is critical because, for the first time in 15 years, power plants are being built again. Most of them will run on gas.

Recently traded on the NYSE around $48, Duke sells for a modest 12 times estimated 2000 earnings. That's a bargain given its projected long-term earnings growth of 9% a year and a 4.6% dividend yield.

Buy Citigroup. Over the past five years, more than 1,700 commercial banks were snapped up by bigger rivals, making consolidation seem like old news in U.S. financial services. Then in late 1998 Citigroup all but forced the death of the Glass-Steagall Act that long separated banking and investment banking firms. Citigroup redefined how financial services would work by combining Citibank with the Salomon Smith Barney brokerage and the Travelers and Primerica insurance groups before such a merger was technically legal. Without banking reform, Citi would have had to undo the deal. Now the question is, can Citigroup make its 54 million client relationships more valuable? Investors' lack of conviction is keeping the stock's price down relative to other multiservice financial firms such as American Express. There's your opportunity.

The key to Citi's future is cross-selling. On the institutional side, Salomon investment bankers are generating an extra 60 to 65 underwriting deals per quarter by leveraging off Citibank relationships. Retail cross-selling may be tougher. "A lot of this is still to come on the consumer side," concedes Ted Paluszek, co-manager of Scudder Financial Services fund, which holds Citigroup. Yet Salomon brokers already are selling mortgages to wealthy clients. Citi tellers and branch managers are studying to become licensed insurance agents and brokers. Therefore, once Citigroup gets a customer in the door, there's a chance that he will walk out with three or four financial products. If the strategy works, Citigroup's earnings should compound 15% annually over the next five years. That's about 25% above the sector norm.

Lately traded on the NYSE around $56, or 18 times 2000 earnings, Citigroup's stock is more expensive than other banks. But it isn't just a bank and shouldn't be valued as such. In our view, the stock looks almost cheap next to the PEs of closer cousins like American Express (27 times 2000 profits) and insurance giant AIG (31 times).

Buy Cardinal Health. Value plays in the drug industry are hard to find. That's why we like Cardinal Health. The company is best known as a distributor, the middleman between drugmakers and pharmacies and hospitals. But distribution now accounts for only 38% of operating profits. Largely via acquisitions, Cardinal has become the country's No. 1 manufacturer of latex gloves, caps and gowns, drug packaging and gel-cap technologies.

In the age of the internet direct-sales model, middlemen look more and more endangered. But Cardinal is tying itself more closely to its clients. For example, when Merck got government approval for its migraine drug Maxalt, Cardinal's divisions put the compound into quick-dissolve tablets, printed the inserts, cartons and labels, packaged the pills and then distributed them within 48 hours. "We've accumulated market-leading companies with products that are in high demand," says CEO Bob Walters. "We have breadth, depth and scale."

What about the stock, which recently traded on the NYSE around $47? Investors seem to be waiting for Cardinal Health to stumble again following a Y2K-related sales slump for its Pyxis machines, which dispense drugs at hospitals. We think this skepticism is probably overdone, creating an opportunity for patient investors. Cardinal's 19 PE is less than its expected profit growth of 22% annually. "We've been adding to our position over the past six months," says GE Investments analyst John Schaetzl.

Buy Bristol-Myers Squibb. Heart disease and cancer are the biggest killers in the developed world, especially among people over 50. They're also the targets of more of Bristol-Myers Squibb's drug lineup than any other maker's. The company already is the No. 1 manufacturer of cancer drugs and is expected to increase revenues from such therapies almost 50% over the next three years to $5 billion, according to Merrill Lynch estimates. In the works are a melanoma vaccine, an oral chemotherapy drug and improvements for blockbuster breast cancer drug Taxol. Over the same period, the company's cardiovascular sales figure to almost double to $6.8 billion. "Bristol-Myers has the broadest pipeline of singles and doubles in the next five years," says Babson Growth manager Jim Gribbel, a large holder of the stock.

The drugmaker could hit a few home runs in heart treatments. The hypertension drug Vanlev, expected to be released this year, appears more effective than other drugs at lowering both systolic and diastolic blood pressure. Wall Street analysts predict that sales could pass $2 billion by 2003. Bristol-Myers and its competitors carry near-term risks, however. Democrats seem poised to make the high cost of drugs a major campaign issue. In the worst case, drug companies would have to roll back prices a bit. Even if that happens, the cuts would be more than offset by the increased volume brought on by the aging population, says Lehman Brothers analyst Kim Wallace.

Lately around $68 on the NYSE, the stock trades at roughly 30 times estimated 2000 earnings. That's slightly higher than its historic average but in line with its peers. Earnings growth should average an above-par 14% a year.

Buy Medtronic. Drugs aren't the only defense against heart disease. Both Medtronic and its biggest competitor, Guidant, are developing pacemakers and defibrillators that control and improve heart conditions. Take congestive heart failure (CHF), which occurs when the heart's pumping ability weakens. Now there are implants that stimulate the heart's contraction. "CHF is potentially the biggest growth area we have," explains Medtronic CEO Bill George. "These devices are already in Europe and should be coming to the U.S. in early 2001." J.P. Morgan analyst Mike Weinstein says that the market for such implants could exceed $1 billion.

Medtronic and Guidant dominate their fields. Each spends about twice as much on research as other device companies. Medtronic, however, is more diversified, with 25% of revenue growth coming from neurological and spinal products, which are used to control everything from tremors to back pain. It's also less vulnerable to pricing pressures in the now mature market for coronary stents (implants that keep arteries open following angioplasty). The stock, recently around $36 on the NYSE, trades at a rather expensive PE of 39. Earnings, however, are on track to grow 20% in 2000 and are expected to maintain that pace long term. That makes the stock a buy, in our view.

Buy Invesco Health Sciences Fund. No healthcare portfolio would be complete without exposure to biotechnology. Drug companies traditionally have used chemistry to treat what ails us. But many of the newest, most exciting drugs are coming out of the study of genetics. In the past year alone biotech has given us new treatments for arthritis, breast cancer, influenza and Parkinson's disease. But most biotech companies are still small, with just one or two drugs in their pipelines. So they're risky investments. You can pass this portion of your portfolio to an expert, such as John Schroer, manager of Invesco Health Sciences Fund, which returned around 20% annually over the past three years. Besides mainstream holdings like Bristol-Myers and Medtronic, his fund typically holds about a fifth of its assets in biotechnology companies. That makes the fund a good way to play biotech even if you like to buy individual stocks. And it gives fund investors exposure to the healthcare industry.

Buy Lucent Technologies. The market for telecom equipment is expected to reach $800 billion in 2003, up from $450 billion last year. Given that kind of growth, industry leaders like Cisco, Ericsson, Lucent and Nortel have excellent prospects. But if your portfolio lacks such a stock, Lucent looks like the best value at a recent price of around $80 on the NYSE. The company's $5 billion in research and development has earned it the leading positions in almost every area of telecom infrastructure-wireless, fiber optics, communication chips and software, service and support. "You have a management that is making the right moves," says Ned Brines, telecom analyst and co-manager of the Phoenix-Ingeman Focus Growth fund, which recently owned 8 million Lucent shares.

Lucent is increasing revenues about 18% a year, four percentage points faster than the industry average. The company also expects to hike profits at an industry-leading 25%. Yet its PEG ratio, or its PE divided by its rate of expected earnings growth, is at least 25% lower than the other giants'.

Buy Qualcomm. Wireless communication is exploding. Goldman Sachs estimates worldwide wireless subscribers will reach 820 million in a couple of years, up from 475 million in 1999. Mobile-phone penetration in the U.S. will double by 2005, with more mobile devices than PCs connected to the internet. No company is better positioned to exploit this boom than Qualcomm, which is emerging as a wireless hybrid of Microsoft and Intel. It owns the operating system known as CDMA (code division multiaccess) that's becoming the industry's digital standard, and it also controls the market for CDMA chips.

CDMA was first developed by the U.S. military during the 1970s. Its major advantage over earlier technology is that wireless providers can fit eight times more calls on their radio frequencies than they could with analog-based systems. (Sprint PCS and Bell Atlantic Mobile use CDMA.) Further, CDMA is expected to be the standard for what's known as 3G (third generation) wireless, in which broadband will allow your mobile phone to handle voice, data and video. "A number of companies looked at CDMA in research labs, but everybody thought it was too complicated," says Qualcomm CEO Irwin Jacobs. "But the fact that it works exceedingly well has become obvious."

Qualcomm collects a royalty from every company using CDMA, including all the major handset sellers and telecom-equipment makers. After Qualcomm finishes unloading its own money-losing equipment business and its unevenly profitable handset operation, the company will start sporting software-like profit margins. J.P. Morgan's Gregory Geiling figures that Qualcomm's operating margins will go from the low teens last year to 45% to 50% in 2000. The stock has had a staggering run. But we think there's more to come. "Qualcomm is in an enviable position because people underestimate how much we will embrace wireless," says Chris Bonavico, manager of Transamerica's Premier Aggressive Growth Fund. Qualcomm is among the fund's five largest investments. The stock lately traded around $98 on Nasdaq. That's roughly 100 times projected earnings for 2000 or 2.8 times its expected 35% earnings growth. Bulls point to that growth, and Qualcomm's expanding margins, to justify its nosebleed PE. But keep in mind that expectations are very high.

Buy Broadcom. It's the leading supplier of chips that go into the set-top boxes and cable modems that will let cable companies sell phone service. "Broadcom has beaten people to the punch and is driving the standard in cable," says Kevin Landis, manager of the Firsthand Funds. But it's Broadcom's positioning in the internet-everywhere world of the near future that has investors really excited. In that world, your refrigerator will keep inventory of your groceries and talk to your home PC or television, which will then send a message to your cell phone to tell you to buy milk. Broadcom will produce the chips that make this communications stream flow inside and outside the home, whether your internet service comes via a traditional phone line, coaxial cable or wireless network. "Whatever bullet that high-speed telecom providers want to shoot, Broadcom should have one. It will be cheaper and more powerful than the rest," says

Trent Nevills, co-manager of the Federated Communications Technology fund. The stock recently made up about 1.5% of his fund's holdings.

Broadcom's edge lies in its research staff, 70% of whom have advanced degrees. Another big advantage is its design library, which allows it to quickly layer new functions on top of existing chips. Analysts project that the company will increase earnings 48% annually over the next five years. Recently traded around $218 on Nasdaq, Broadcom carries what Nevills calls "an intense valuation"—roughly 175 times estimated 2000 earnings. "It's the very early stage for Broadcom's markets," concludes Nevills. "And I've never seen a company this good."

❧ The Outlook for Besieged Microsoft

Soon after a federal judge denounced Microsoft as a predatory monopolist, the *New York Times* ran a long analysis of the company's legal prospects on the front page of the business section. Back in the paper's tech section that same day was a review of a kitchen countertop computer that gathers your email, news and local weather. It could someday be used as a family calendar and planner or an online connection to your grocer. If you're a tech investor, it's the second story that really matters.

How come? In all likelihood, Microsoft eventually will settle with the government for remedies less drastic than breaking up the company. But that kitchen computer doesn't use Windows, the PC operating system that gave Microsoft its monopoly strength. And it's the onslaught of similar internet "appliances" that threatens Microsoft's future. Bill Gates knows this and has his troops pumped up about the net. But Microsoft's success is hardly assured. Here are key issues that the company has going against it and for it in the battle for the web.

PCs will be less dominant on the net. In a few years your phone, car and fridge will be connected to the internet and have little specialized computers inside that retrieve email, draw maps and plan your purchases. "PCs are becoming legacy systems," says Ransom Love, CEO of Caldera Systems. His company

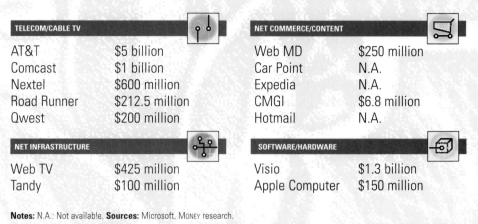

Where Microsoft Invests Its Billions

The company has spent more than $10 billion to prepare for the day when the PC is no longer the center of computing. Microsoft's largest stakes include the following:

TELECOM/CABLE TV

AT&T	$5 billion
Comcast	$1 billion
Nextel	$600 million
Road Runner	$212.5 million
Qwest	$200 million

NET COMMERCE/CONTENT

Web MD	$250 million
Car Point	N.A.
Expedia	N.A.
CMGI	$6.8 million
Hotmail	N.A.

NET INFRASTRUCTURE

Web TV	$425 million
Tandy	$100 million

SOFTWARE/HARDWARE

Visio	$1.3 billion
Apple Computer	$150 million

Notes: N.A.: Not available. **Sources:** Microsoft, MONEY research.

sells a business version of the Linux operating system, the free Windows alternative that runs that kitchen computer. "In a couple of years we'll have about 2 billion devices connected to the net, of which a mere 700 million will be PCs," adds Jean-Louis Gassée, CEO of Be Inc., another rival operating system company.

Windows CE for net devices is a clunker. Since its debut in 1996, Microsoft's scaled-down operating system has failed to gain traction with makers of cell phones, set-top cable boxes and palm computers. Critics charge that it's clunky and hogs too much memory. Five of the biggest cell phone makers have formed a consortium called Symbian to develop an operating system for tomorrow's phones, which will incorporate mini-browsers to hook them up to the net. Nokia has already opted to use Symbian's operating system and one developed by 3Com's Palm Computing, rather than Windows CE. And palm-size PCs from Compaq and Hewlett-Packard that use Windows CE haven't had the runaway sales success of the Palm Pilot. Microsoft's Phil

Holden, group product manager for Windows CE, responds that his software allows hand-held devices to do more. "The Palm Pilot is great for writing up quick notes," he says "But its data input is not the best, and it can't do long emails."

Microsoft's legacy hurts the company. Even in the event that Microsoft improves its product, consumer electronics manufacturers are wary of falling under the company's control the way PC makers did. "Everyone is so afraid of Microsoft's muscle that Windows CE might do better without that name attached to it," says Kevin Landis, manager of Firsthand Funds. Thanks to the antitrust case, Microsoft won't use its power to (as a company official said in an infamous email about Netscape) "cut off the air supply" of a competitor in the market for web device operating systems. Microsoft's Holden maintains that the company isn't trying to hold device makers to a single standard. "We're not offering a one-size-fits-all approach," he explains. "We enable the vendors to pick and choose the components they need. We don't necessarily control the end experience."

Reports of the PC's demise are premature. Microsoft argues that the PC will retain its place in the home. "We don't think of it as the post-PC era," says Holden. "Internally we refer to it as the PC-plus era, where the PC is supplemented by any number of additional devices." Perhaps. But even if Holden is wrong, the home PC won't begin to lose ground for at least two or three years. And certainly the machine that replaces the PC on your work desk over the next few years is going to be another PC. "Even if we assume that we're in a new era, and we're calling PCs old world, the mistaken assumption is that the old world disappears," says Michael Kwatinetz, an analyst at Credit Suisse First Boston who's followed Microsoft for a decade. "People are still buying mainframes, which supposedly died 30 years ago!"

The remaining life cycle of PCs, plus this year's launch of Windows 2000, means Microsoft shouldn't have any trouble cranking out robust earnings growth for several more years. Jeffrey Maxick, director of research for Madison Securities, projects that Microsoft's earnings will grow more than 20% this year, based on Windows and Office software alone.

Microsoft invests heavily in the internet. The cash flow that Windows generates today is being put to good use. Microsoft has invested in telecom including broadband technology and internet infrastructure companies. It holds major stakes in AT&T and Comcast and owns Web TV. The telecom investments alone have shown annualized returns of 78% and are now worth $12 billion, according to the company. Microsoft also continues to develop its own web content and its internet service provider, the Microsoft Network. And it invests in or acquires small companies that create content and online technology. Max Katcher, manager of Ameritor Security Trust, recently had 20% of his fund's assets in the stock. He believes the company "has made enough acquisitions to get into any business it needs to."

Investors overlook the company's net stakes. Let's say that Microsoft's web businesses made up a stand-alone stock that the market afforded a high-flying internet valuation of 43 times revenues (the average for sector leaders AOL and Yahoo). That stock would carry a market capitalization of about $38 billion. Instead, money losers such as Microsoft Network, online magazine Slate and email service Hotmail are perceived mainly as a drag on the whole company's earnings. "I don't think they're getting any credit in their stock price for these investments," says Kwatinetz. Microsoft is aware of this; it recently spun off its Expedia online travel service. The stock, offered at $14, quadrupled to $57 on its first day of trading. More financial engineering is likely down the road if net stocks continue to carry rich valuations. That could mean big payoffs for Microsoft shareholders.

What shareholders should do now. A comparison with the IBM of the mid-1980s is instructive. Microsoft is facing a technology transition that could make or break its business, just as IBM did when the hot spot in computing moved from mainframes to PCs. It took IBM 10 painful years to adjust even though it had developed the first PC. On the other hand, IBM in 1984 was a hidebound organization that couldn't, or wouldn't, see the future. The Microsoft of Bill Gates and his right-hand man, Steve Ballmer, sees the battle ahead and will remain a fierce competitor no matter how its antitrust case is resolved.

If Microsoft makes up a big portion of your technology portfolio, we recommend putting any new money to work in companies that are more clearly positioned for the internet era today. We analyze some of them in the preceding section, "Top U.S. Stocks and Funds to Buy." Also consider other big-name stocks such as Sun Microsystems and Oracle. If you're just starting to invest in technology stocks, don't build your portfolio around Microsoft. Instead, diversify your holdings to include networking, telecom and chip stocks. Microsoft is too big and smart to bet against. But you're not buying the monopoly of the future anymore.

❧ Great Ways to Earn High Income

With interest rates ticking up last year, it was the wrong time to have been clinging to the "safety" of bonds. Investors in the bellwether long-term Treasury bond were down around 7.7% in 1999. But if you agree with our forecast for falling rates in 2000, now is a great time to grab some big yields. Remember that as rates fall, bond prices rise, as depicted in the chart "How Bond Prices Seesaw With Rates" at right. The best opportunities appear to be in mutual funds that invest in high-yield junk bonds and municipal bonds.

Buy Fidelity High-Income. We like this fund for investors who want an aggressive junk bond play. Over the past three years, Fidelity High-Income has earned a juicy 9.5% annually. "In general, bond funds that have the lowest quality credits did awfully last year," says Morningstar junk fund analyst Sarah Bush. "But Fidelity holds a lot of low-quality credits and did very well. They have a topflight research team." Although default rates have risen on high-yield bonds, junk funds had positive gains last year.

Buy Vanguard Intermediate Term Tax-Exempt. This low-cost fund holds higher-quality municipal bonds that lately yielded around 5.1%. That's the taxable equivalent of about 8.5% a year for someone in the highest federal tax bracket. Municipal bond funds didn't fare well in 1999 in part because insurers, typically big muni buyers, had lower profits and thus less money to

How Bond Prices Seesaw With Rates

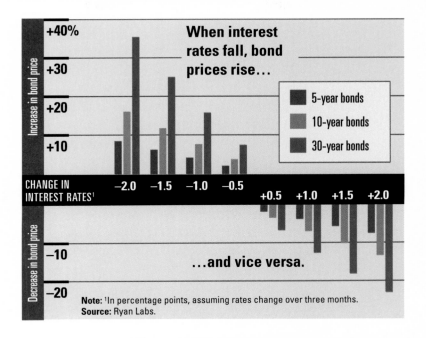

When interest rates fall, bond prices rise...

Increase in bond price

+40%
+30
+20
+10

Legend:
- 5-year bonds
- 10-year bonds
- 30-year bonds

CHANGE IN INTEREST RATES[1]   −2.0   −1.5   −1.0   −0.5   +0.5   +1.0   +1.5   +2.0

Decrease in bond price

−10
−20

...and vice versa.

Note: [1]In percentage points, assuming rates change over three months.
Source: Ryan Labs.

invest. Now tax-equivalent yields are close to what you get from a corporate junk bond if you're in the top bracket. The best way to get this embarrassment of tax-free riches is to buy bonds directly. But for investors with less than about $25,000 on hand, Vanguard Intermediate Term Tax-Exempt is the way to go in our view.

✒ Timely Bets for Overseas Profits

We've had an amazing run in U.S. markets over the past decade as our economy has undergone a series of radical transformations. Perhaps we can take that ride again with European and Japanese companies, which are just beginning to make all the investor-friendly changes U.S corporations did back in the 1980s. Merger activity abroad is frenetic. There were more deals in

Europe in the third quarter of 1999 than in the U.S. "Just open up the *Financial Times* of London," says Mark Yockey, manager of Artisan International Fund. "There must be five or six restructurings a day." Meanwhile, European and Japanese banks and manufacturers are starting to modernize their information technology infrastructures and build out internet capability. And as government bond yields drop, the everyday European saver should start pumping money into the stock market. "The Italian guy who was used to getting 8.5% on bonds is now getting 4%," notes Montgomery Global Opportunities manager Oscar Castro.

Trouble is, some of the most intriguing plays abroad aren't easily accessible to U.S. investors. Take Italy's Banca Popolare di Brescia, or Bipop. Its strong internet presence and big fund management and distribution businesses make Bipop sort of the Charles Schwab of southern Europe. Unfortunately, Bipop does not have an ADR (American Depositary Receipt) trading on U.S. exchanges. And good luck getting reliable information about it in English on these shores. You're better off finding a fund manager with a good track record picking such growth stories.

Buy Scudder Greater Europe Growth.
The fund, led by Carol Franklin, is divided between older large-cap names that are aggressively restructuring, such as Siemens, and innovators like Bipop. The fund is up about 26% annually over the past five years.

Buy Artisan International Fund.
It's our choice for a global play. Under manager Yockey, Artisan is up 28% annually over the past three years, whipping its benchmark index by 16 percentage points. In addition to innovative European tech stocks such as Swedish Information Superhighway, Yockey recently had a 17% stake in Japan. He's passed over the banks and industrials in favor of the likes of Asatsu, an advertising firm partially owned by Saatchi & Saatchi, and Toyo Information Systems, which provides technology services to banks.

Chapter 3

Secrets of Savvy Fund Investors

*T*he perfect mutal fund offers terrific long-term gains, bountiful dividends and never, ever loses money. Alas, such a paragon doesn't really exist. No fund can deliver both high returns and safety over a meaningful period of time. Investing always means weighing potential benefits against risks. The cardinal rule is that the more safety you demand, the less return you can expect, and vice versa. That means you cannot search intelligently for the best funds without some soul searching first. Where to begin? We suggest that you glean insights from the following profile of Bill Miller, the most successful fund manager of the past decade.

Tips From Today's Top Manager

Talk about an amazing track record. In an era when most fund managers have had trouble keeping pace with the S&P 500 index, Bill Miller has beaten that benchmark every year since 1990. No other fund manager came close to duplicating that feat. In fact, in the 1990s Miller's Legg Mason Value Trust gained nearly 21% annually, easily outdistancing the S&P 500's 18% rise.

So why isn't Miller as famous and revered as superstars like Peter Lynch, the long retired skipper of Fidelity's Magellan? During Lynch's 1980s heyday, most investors bought into the Great Man theory of fund managing. That is, we accepted as gospel the idea that a great fund manager could beat the market.

In the 1990s, however, that faith has been shaken, and the adulation Lynch received as a matter of course has been replaced by suspicion. As index funds have outperformed the vast majority of actively managed funds, and as more and more star managers have crashed and burned, many investors have become leery of even the best-performing fund managers.

In the case of Miller, these suspicions are heightened by what appears to be a glaring contradiction. He runs a value fund, but his two biggest holdings are highfliers America Online and Dell—hardly what one would call value stocks. So instead of basking in 1980s-style praise, Miller has had to face 1990s-style skepticism. Is he taking too much risk? Is he somehow cheating on style to attain his performance? Is he really the value investor he purports to be? Here's what we found.

Return on capital is the key to success. The first point Miller wants to make is that, no matter what you think of the stocks in his portfolio, he's a value guy through and through. "I've never really understood the typical growth investor," he says cheerily. "I've always wanted to get the best value when I buy a suit or go to the grocery store. And I have the same temperament when it comes to buying stocks." In fact, it was this approach that first led Miller to the research department of Legg Mason back in 1981, when he was 31. The Baltimore-based firm had a value orientation. The following spring, when Legg Mason Value Trust was started up, he was made co-manager with Ernie Kiehne, one of the better-known value managers of his day.

The timing for this new fund was perfect. The first rumbling of the great bull market could be heard in the distance. There were hundreds, if not thousands, of beaten-down stocks that were poised to climb. Kiehne and Miller had a good run taking the classic approach of value investors, buying stocks with low multiples of earnings or book value and then selling once these ratios had risen to levels suggesting that the stocks were fully valued.

Then came the October 1987 market crash. For the next three years value funds struggled mightily. "I did awful during that period," recalls Miller. But it was during this time that he gained the insights that would guide his thinking in the 1990s.

Unwilling to accept the idea that value investing was something that went in and out of style, Miller began to look back at his picks over the years to try to figure out what characteristics his winners had in common. "It became clear to me," he says now, "that low PE and low price-to-book were not the best predictors of return." After all, he adds, crummy valuations don't automatically signal that a stock is undervalued. Sometimes they mean that "the underlying business is crummy." The measure that best predicted whether a stock would be a winner, according to his research, was return on capital. That is, the companies that did the best job of creating new value by reinvesting their capital were most likely to be rewarded with high stock prices.

Emulate the Buffett principle. Miller had a second insight that might be called the Buffett principle. Warren Buffett is widely heralded as a great value investor. Yet many of his longtime holdings have become very expensive stocks. Still, Buffett doesn't sell them. He believes in the power of the businesses, and he believes they can create additional value. Most value investors don't follow his lead. At a certain point, they sell their winners on the theory that once a stock has, say, doubled, it is no longer a value stock. As a result, value investors often settle for doubles when others are holding on for those elusive ten-baggers.

Did Miller still care about PE and other fundamentals? Sure he did. But under his new formulation, he had to look beyond the PE before he bought a stock. For instance, for most of the early 1990s, IBM was a statistically cheap stock in Miller's view. He resisted buying it, however, because its return on capital was poor. Then Lou Gerstner became CEO and began emphasizing return on capital. Miller bought the stock in 1994. It doubled within two years, prompting many other value managers to take their profits. But Miller has kept IBM in his portfolio, and it has been a ten-bagger for him.

Believe it or not, the same is true of AOL and Dell. People forget now how beaten down these stocks were just three or four years ago. Many investors thought that AOL would be obliterated by the rise of the internet and that Dell would be hurt as computers became increasingly "commoditized." Miller bought the two stocks because they were cheap but also because he thought both companies had superior business models that the market would eventually recognize. They were, in other words, value plays in his view.

What people question, of course, is that Miller hasn't sold AOL or Dell. Though he has recently lightened up on both stocks, they still represent the largest positions in his portfolio. Miller is unapologetic. In response, he notes the Buffett principle. He also relies on his own complex models based on projected profitability and his beloved return on capital. These give him a sense of what fair value is for the stocks he holds. And just as a low PE doesn't necessarily signal an undervalued stock, he says, "a high PE doesn't necessarily signal that a stock is overvalued." He adds, "So long as Dell is generating superior returns on capital and its superior business model is intact, I won't sell."

Of course, Miller's record is his strongest defense. You can't say that he is simply riding a hot streak, not after nine straight years of beating the market. He is plainly doing something right. And he's certainly not trying to hide his methodology. In a sense, what Miller has done is adapt old-fashioned value investing to a long-running bull market. And he's done it with surprising rigor and discipline.

ꙮ Key Issues Investors Must Resolve

Our forecast of a volatile stock market this year serves as a reminder that share prices don't always rise steadily. This basic fact of life has been easy to forget during the market's unprecedented bull run. A sturdy portfolio of funds must be diversified among different asset categories in a way that balances your expected returns with your tolerance for risk. Consider how one recent study found that roughly 90% of long-term investment results can be explained purely by your asset mix. That's the proportions of your portfolio dedicated to broad investments like stocks, bonds and cash. Other factors that many investors view as crucial, such as the choice of specific securities and the timing of purchases and sales, accounted for only 9% of the results.

Say that two investors choose the same asset allocation and put 60% of their money into stocks and 40% into bonds. They will tend to end up with pretty much the same results in the long run, regardless of the particular bonds and stocks they choose. Meanwhile, an investor with 80% in stocks and 20% in bonds will fare differently from the 60-40 investors. Your choice of funds matters, of course. But before you dwell on selecting individual funds, you should step back and look at your overall portfolio. There's no point asking, "Should I buy this fund?" unless you have first asked yourself, "Do I have too much money, or too little, in stocks?" Below we ask other key questions.

Are you seeking growth, income or safety? You're a growth investor if your key need is to build capital for a major future expense that's five or more years away, such as your kids' college education or your own retirement. Funds invested mainly for capital appreciation are best for you. Such funds have a strong record of appreciation over long periods but are the most prone to harsh short-term setbacks. As a result, you shouldn't consider yourself a growth investor unless you can endure painful stretches when your fund is down 20% or more. If you want your funds to help you pay ongoing expenses, such as your living costs in retirement, you're an income investor. Look at funds invested partly in bonds and sporting above-average yields. If you need money for an expense you will incur within a few years, what you need from your funds is safety. Your best choices are ultrasafe money-market funds.

Are you comfortable with risk? Think of risk as the entry fee you pay to invest. You can choose to take a lot or a little. But you can never avoid it entirely. The payback for assuming risk is potential return. The most aggressive stock funds, for example, have suffered precipitous falls of 20% or so in their worst years. But their long-term returns, which lately averaged close to 12% annually, make a compelling case for investing in them anyway. Stocks almost always beat bonds in the long run. This has been true for most of this century despite wars, economic crises and global change.

How soon do you need the money? The longer you're planning to hold on to your fund shares, the more you can afford to shoot for the stock market's higher returns. Say you had invested in the S&P 500 index at the start of any calendar year since 1926 and pulled out after 12 months. You would have made money two out of three times. Had you held on for five years, your odds of making a profit would have improved to four out of five. And if you stood by your stocks for 10 years, you would have finished in the black 96% of the time.

How much could you bear to lose? No matter how great a fund's long-term record may be, you won't score big if you bail out when the fund turns temporarily cold. So ask yourself how much you could stand to see your investment plunge in a given year before pulling the ripcord. If you're willing to stomach losses of 10% or more in a year, you're an aggressive investor. That suits you for high-risk, high-return funds such as those invested for aggressive growth or in small-cap stocks. A 5% threshold suggests you're interested in trading off some performance for safety in, say, growth and income funds that blend yield-rich stocks and bonds. If you can't tolerate any losses, you're too conservative for stock funds and all but the safest bond portfolios.

Do you require lots of hand holding? Funds can be sold in either of two ways. Many funds are peddled by stockbrokers, independent planners and insurance agents. You get the salesperson's advice in choosing your fund. But the fund will deduct a commission (the load) from your investment either in an up-front fee or in some combination of redemption charges and ongoing annual charges. No-loads are sold by fund companies directly to investors without commission. Note, however, that not all no-loads are free of commissions. Many of Fidelity's directly sold funds carry low loads of 2% to 3%, which the company pockets. The low load isn't as onerous as charges that are levied by broker-sold funds. But you don't get a broker's advice for your money either. Otherwise, there's no difference in performance between load and no-load funds. So whether to go load or no-load hinges on how much you value a salesperson's fund-picking prowess and advice.

How Today's Fund Wars Affect You

You would think that most mutual fund companies were minting money in today's giddy stock market. Think again. Many are

Percentage of U.S. stock funds beating the S&P 500 index

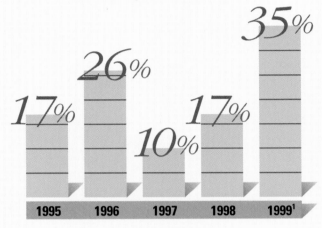

Note: [1]Through June 30, 1999. **Source:** Morningstar.

Less investor cash is coming in.

Net new investment in stock funds (in billions)

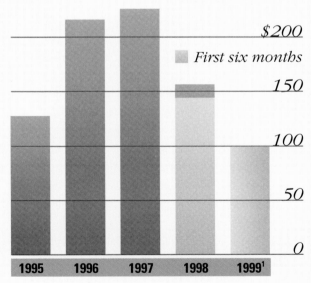

Note: [1]Through June 30, 1999. **Source:** Investment Company Institute.

struggling as trigger-happy market timers move their money in and out of the hottest funds. (For more on this subject, see "Why Market Timers Give Funds Fits" later in this chapter.) Other investors are abandoning funds altogether to speculate in high-flying internet and technology stocks. Yes, the fund business remains lucrative. But profit margins are shrinking as the sector confronts a new competitive landscape in which managers no longer can sit back and watch the bucks roll in—and stay in. Indeed, the industry's boom times seem to have ended, replaced by an ugly free-for-all for new customers.

Why should the troubles of fund managers matter to you? If a fund company is scrambling to attract cash, shareholders in its funds can end up with higher risk or lower returns or both. That's because asset-hungry fund families may choose to focus on short-term marketing over long-term investing. Fund managers are encouraged to chase the latest stock fads, while those whose styles are deemed passé are dumped like last season's fashions. Popular funds are allowed to balloon to unmanageable size. Says Neil Kauffman, a Philadelphia investment adviser: "If a fund company's main aim is to gather assets, come hell or high water, that's not where you want to be." Even if there are no visible changes in your funds, managers at weaker firms can be distracted. Imagine a heart surgeon whose practice is in financial turmoil. Would you want to go under the knife?

Your job as a fund investor is clearly more complicated. Not only must you monitor your funds, you must also keep tabs on your fund family. Later in this chapter we'll give you guidance on managing a fund portfolio today. But first, it's important to know why the fund business is facing tougher times.

Fundholders are growing restless. Most of their returns have failed to keep pace with the benchmark S&P 500 index in recent years (see the chart "After Years of Lagging the Market..." at left). In response, more investors are now abandoning active management in favor of stock index funds, which recently accounted for about 40% of new money committed to stock funds. True, the market began to broaden last year, during which the percentage of actively managed funds beating the S&P rose to 35%. But that's still a dismal record.

New fund buyers are harder to find. Total mutual fund assets have swelled during the past 15 years, from $370 billion to an estimated $6 trillion lately. The percentage of households owning funds also has soared, from 12% to an estimated 44%. For the fund industry, that may be as good as it can get. "Most people who have the money to invest in funds are already in them," says fund consultant Geoff Bobroff. Investors are continuing to put in money. Problem is, investors are pulling money out at an even faster rate. The redemption rate has risen an average of 33% annually in the past four years, according to data from the Investment Company Institute, a fund trade group.

More investors pick stocks. Easy winnings in the bull market and greater access to research online have given more armchair investors the confidence to do their own stock selection. It's not only do-it-yourselfers who are leaving funds. Investors who need advice are choosing wrap accounts, which are separately managed portfolios offered by brokers and financial advisers. "As account balances grow to $50,000 or $100,000, most investors start seeking advice," notes consultant Andrew Guillette of Cerulli Associates. About 30% of wrap accounts include mutual funds. But the rest hold mainly individual stocks.

Supermarkets are squeezing fund firms. With the rise of Schwab One Source and other one-stop fund networks, fund companies have lost control of their customers and pricing. "In a fund supermarket, investors no longer feel loyalty to one fund company," explains Bobroff. "They can switch with a phone call or a click of the mouse." Even so, many fund companies need the supermarts for a steady flow of new customers. And it gets worse. The marts are hiking the prices they charge fund companies for space on their rosters. Many fund groups are launching their own supermarkets. But financing such operations carries a big tab. "This is a mature industry, so the cost of acquiring and retaining assets will inevitably be higher," says consultant Avi Nachmany of Strategic Insight.

Profits are captives of the bull market. As stock appreciation bulks up assets under management, fees earned by fund companies also swell. Since 1995, the market's rise has accounted for as much as 68% of the growth in fund industry profits, according to Morgan Stanley analyst Henry McVey. With such a plush cushion, even companies losing assets can remain comfortable. But as cash flows continue slowing and costs keep rising, McVey expects fund companies' pretax profit margins to erode by as much as one percentage point annually over the next few years. And he's assuming a steady market. No one is predicting major bankruptcies. But you should expect to see more mergers as well as buyouts by financial services companies seeking the steady income of the asset management business. The most vulnerable fund groups may be mid-size firms (less than $50 billion in assets) that lack the clout to compete with giants like Fidelity and Vanguard in the retirement plan business.

≈ Tactics That Protect Your Portfolio

Turmoil in the mutual fund industry may offer you some benefits along with unpleasant surprises. For starters, you can expect more choices and convenience, whether you invest online or through brokers. That's because both load and no-load fund companies will be reaching out through many marketing channels. Some experts even predict that the focus on performance will eventually lead to lower average expense ratios. Says John Rekenthaler, research director at fund researcher Morningstar: "Pressure from internet-savvy investors has led to lower costs for everything from online trading to book shopping. There's no reason that pressure won't spill over to funds as well." But it won't happen overnight. Meanwhile, as fund companies struggle to maintain their margins, you face a greater risk that your funds will change for the worse. To keep your returns on track, follow these guidelines.

Choose among different fund offerings. If your main goal is consistency over the long term, you may do best with the plain-vanilla funds sold by the major families. "The largest firms take the edges off investing," says Morningstar president Don Phillips. "They're more dependable, so you're less likely to get hurt." Big firms also have more research and management depth.

As a result, companies like Vanguard, T. Rowe Price and Putnam make sure their funds stick to their investment styles and stay close to their benchmark index. The flipside is a practice commonly called style drift, in which a manager's discipline changes as the fund's assets swell. For more, see "Cut to the Chase on Inflated Returns" at right.

For a shot at index-beating returns, consider boutique firms such as Longleaf, Davis and Skyline. "Because they are smaller, these firms are better able to make contrarian bets or follow a unique investing strategy," says Kurt Brouwer, a financial adviser in Tiburon, Calif. "But boutiques can be more risky because they tend to depend on just one or two managers." For every winner like Longleaf Partners fund, a consistently top-ranked performer, you may end up with a disappointment, such as the beleaguered Yacktman Fund. Its chief has been embroiled in a boardroom battle with fund directors that was largely driven by slumping sales.

Watch your funds' weight. Fund portfolios generally thrive in an asset sweet spot—neither too fat nor too puny. With a tiny or shrinking fund, the manager may lack the cash to buy good stocks without liquidating other desirable holdings in the portfolio. And if a fund fails to grow, or starts losing assets, chances are the fund company will close it or merge it. By contrast, too much cash can spur a performance slump, especially if the fund holds less liquid small-caps or foreign shares. Or it can spark a shift in investing strategy toward more easily tradeable but premium-priced blue chips. That's no way to maintain a diversified portfolio.

Cash flows are very volatile, however. So you may not get much warning before size becomes a problem. To monitor how quickly your fund is growing or shrinking, check Morningstar and Value Line. Both regularly report asset sizes in their fund publications, and Morningstar lists that data on its website. When possible, says Morningstar research director Rekenthaler, pick funds that are likely to close if they reach a particular asset size, such as T. Rowe Price Small-Cap Value, which previously shut its doors when assets surged. Consider switching if your fund becomes bloated. Some advisers steer clear of small-cap funds that quickly grow beyond $1 billion. A more important yardstick may be a fund's cash position. More than 10% can mean the portfolio manager has more money than he or she knows what to do with.

Be skeptical of category shufflings. Fund tracker Lipper recently reorganized its groups and rankings, a move that will likely prompt more companies to change their offerings. Predicts Strategic Insight's Nachmany: "Fund groups may find they don't perform so well in one category, so they'll try to fit into a different one." If your funds start morphing, you should think about your options. "It's generally best to get out," says Lou Stanasolovich, a Pittsburgh investment adviser. "But if you will have big taxable gains, you may need to think twice."

Fund groups have engineered comebacks, of course. Janus and Fidelity, for example, began piling up returns and market share when they tossed aside their old strategies and jumped on the bandwagon of large-cap growth stocks. But if you see little reason to expect better performance from your funds, you have more freedom than ever to invest elsewhere.

✍ Cut to the Chase on Inflated Returns

To see why so many investors are frustrated with funds, you need look no further than the Chase Vista family. In promoting this 14-fund, $10 billion group over the internet, banker Chase Manhattan claims that "our portfolio managers count on a disciplined investment process developed and proven over many years" and declares that "nothing can replace consistency."

Well, almost nothing. Chase Vista's management team, more than 30 investment professionals led by veteran David Klassen, was recently replaced to "strengthen our asset management capabilities and to better serve clients." Klassen's and his team's track record had been decent but not overwhelming. Their replacement is another group of Chase portfolio managers based in Houston and led by Henry Lartigue, whose record is outstanding but is built on a different approach to picking stocks.

From their inception to this latest switcheroo, the Chase Vista funds have been a textbook example of how fund track records are not always what they appear to be. A few years back, Chase

Vista's flagship fund, Growth & Income, was extremely hot. In fact, from its inception in September 1987 through June 1992, Growth & Income was the No. 1 stock fund in the country. In its ads, Chase Vista boasted of the "unmatched consistency" of Growth & Income's returns. Thanks to the fund's performance and the fact that in late 1990 Chase began paying brokers a 4.75% commission to push its funds, Growth & Income mushroomed from just $19 million in assets at the end of 1990 to $1.5 billion by the end of 1994. It lately was around $2.1 billion.

Better to be lucky than smart. There's more to the story, of course. While a string of good managers helped, the fund was also born lucky. It was launched on September 23, 1987, right before the crash of October 19, that Black Monday when the S&P 500 index lost 23%. Since the fund was still in diapers, it was 100% in cash. While the crash pulverized competing funds, Vista's cash cushion kept it from losing a cent. You cannot lose money on stocks if you don't own any.

Heading into a market crash with 100% cash accounts for about half of Growth & Income's cumulative edge over the market in the fund's first five years. Thanks to that cash hoard, not only did the fund dodge the losses of Black Monday, it was also perfectly positioned to profit from what followed. The fund's first manager, James Manley, left Chase in 1991 and now runs $250 million for institutional investors at Manley Fuller Asset Management in New York City. He says he intentionally kept the fund out of the market at the start, believing that stocks were overpriced. But it's hard to believe he'd have gone to 100% cash if the fund had not been less than a month old, and Manley agrees that the fund's biggest advantage at the start was "having all that cash to take advantage of values right at the bottom."

Enhancing profits in a fund's infancy. Along with good timing, the fund employed several strategies that managers often use to get new money flowing into a fund. One is to waive expenses. Running a newborn fund can cost as much as 2.5% in annual expenses. When those costs are subtracted from a young fund's return, as they normally are, they take a big bite out of performance. But for Growth & Income's first five years, Chase ate the fund's costs. This temporary giveaway, we estimate, increased the fund's annual returns from an average of 31% to 32% from 1988 to 1992. That's just when the fund was building the three-year and five-year track records that are so vital to luring customers.

Another ploy is to keep a fund tiny in its fledgling years, enabling it to invest in hot little companies, to trade rapidly and to sink plenty of the portfolio into the stock pickers' best ideas. Even after its first two years of spectacular returns, during which the fund gained 121% vs. the S&P 500's 54% rise, Growth & Income still had only $9 million and barely 800 shareholders. Manley loved the flexibility of running such a wee fund. His buying or selling wouldn't move stock prices, and he could always get enough of a stock he liked. "There's no question that size makes a difference," he says. Only in the fall of 1990, when Growth & Income had a three-year track record, did Chase begin to market it aggressively. Nearly a billion dollars gushed in over the next four years. Note, however, that the fund has not beaten the S&P 500 in any calendar year since its assets passed $1 billion in 1993. On the other hand, the fund's robust performance in its early years has kept it well ahead of the S&P 500 since inception (see the chart "Revealing Views of Vista's Gains" on the next page).

Switching styles as assets swell. When money pours in, many small funds change into something different. "Our style was small-cap value," says Manley. "If I had continued to manage the fund, it would have stayed a small-cap value portfolio." Instead, Manley left in 1991. His successor, Mark Tincher, who ran the fund from 1991 through 1995, invested in stocks of all sizes, ending up with a portfolio of medium-size stocks on average. "That made sense as the fund grew bigger," says Tincher. More recently, Klassen ran the fund as a basket of large, value-oriented stocks. In other words, each manager followed a different discipline. "We can't change what the history is," acknowledges new manager Lartigue. "When the fund was smaller, they used small-cap and mid-cap stocks. For the last three to five years, the fund has been implanted in the large-cap value box. And that is where we expect it to stay."

Perhaps the fund has run out of styles to adopt. No one disputes Lartigue's ability. Top fund headhunter George Wilbanks

Revealing Views of Vista's Gains

Here's how $10,000 grew in Chase Vista Growth & Income (red line) and in the S&P 500 (blue line). The tan line shows how $10,000 would have grown in the Chase fund if it had not been 100% in cash during the 1987 crash and if it had not waived its early expenses.

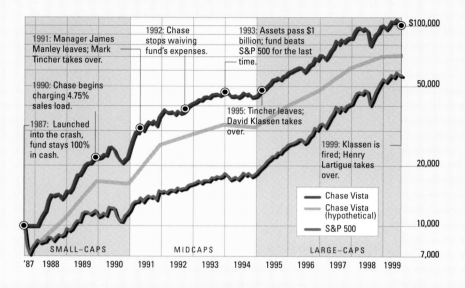

of Russell Reynolds Associates in New York City calls Lartigue a "wonderful manager with a great track record." Lartigue's flagship Chase Core Equity Fund has returned nearly 20% annually since its launch in 1993, beating growth-and-income funds as a group by three percentage points a year. But, as Lartigue concedes, he specializes in technology, healthcare and telecommunications growth stocks, not the value-minded, more diversified approach that Vista Growth & Income had followed.

Lartigue hastens to add that his group of 42 managers runs more than $10 billion in large-cap value portfolios. Its Equity Income Fund has outperformed its peers by nearly a percentage point annually over the past decade, showing that his group is amply qualified to run a large-cap value fund like Growth & Income. But this fund's history shows that "consistency" had little to do with its returns and that figuring out how a fund will be run can be terribly tricky.

So what are the lessons here? Luck matters. When portfolio managers look brilliant, at least part of that brilliance may be luck. And good luck rarely lasts very long. Size also matters. We tend to ignore any portion of a track record that was earned before a fund had at least $25 million in assets. Cost matters as well. If you're considering an investment in one of the more than 2,700 stock funds that are currently waiving some of their expenses, look in the footnotes of the prospectus to find out what the fund would cost if the manager weren't eating the fees. Sooner or later the manager will make you pay up.

✍ *Why Market Timers Give Funds Fits*

You've probably never heard of Markman Capital Management in Minnesota or Merriman Capital Management in Seattle. These two low-profile firms specialize in market timing using mutual funds and control upwards of $750 million worth of fund assets between them. Yet the two companies and hundreds of similar outfits lately have become the fund industry's worst nightmare.

These market-timing firms pool money from their individual and corporate clients, then use that bulk buying power to trade giant blocks of fund shares through discount brokers like Charles Schwab, Fidelity and Waterhouse. It's routine for them to whip millions of dollars in and out of a single fund, often without warning and in a matter of days. Many funds are never invaded by timers. But at funds where timers have struck, managers say this hot money disrupts their investment strategies, raises costs for you as a fund shareholder and often creates sudden tax bills.

For their part, the fast-trading advisers make no apologies for what they do, insisting that they are only protecting their clients from volatile markets and inconsistent fund managers. They add that the fund companies are only too happy to take their business in bull markets and whine about hot money only when the advisers take it away. Even though the timers rarely park in any fund for more than a few months, their money easily generates more than $250 million in annual fees for the fund industry. That helps explain why so many leading fund companies have spent millions of dollars on promotion to attract the big bucks from timers.

With advisers heaving such giant sums in and out of funds, small investors are in constant peril. It's important to emphasize that none of this activity threatens to destroy your fund or wipe out your investments. But the activities of timers can take a real bite out of your returns and make it that much harder for your fund manager to pursue his or her strategy. Here's why.

Timers can raise your fund's taxes. Fast-trading advisers yanked about $400 million, or a fourth of the total assets, out of one value-oriented small-stock fund over roughly a five-month period. That mass redemption forced the fund manager to sell huge amounts of stock that he would have preferred to keep. Those sales created large capital gains for the fund. As a result, an extra $50 million in taxable capital gains had to be paid out to the fund's loyal long-term shareholders. That money would otherwise have compounded tax deferred for years to come. By our estimate, these stampeding advisers cost this fund's typical shareholder $165 in federal tax for each $10,000 invested in the fund.

Timers can increase your fund's costs. When a fund sells securities to meet a redemption, its trading costs are paid not by the redeeming shareholder but by those who stay. That's why the timers we interviewed say they prefer trading no-load funds, which they pay nothing to buy or sell, to trading stocks, for which they would incur costs on every order. But you may have to pay whenever big timers force a fund to sell some of its holdings. According to the trading consultants at Plexus Group in Los Angeles, it often costs a fund at least 1% of the proceeds when it sells a stock. That's a direct hit to your return. "If I have to sell into a falling market," complains one fund manager, "and my loyal shareholders have to pay the freight for the market timers who leave, that really hurts."

Timers can lower your fund's returns. The golden rule of investing is to buy low, sell high. But hot money makes it harder for fund managers to do that. Martin Whitman of Third Avenue Value Fund sums it up: "These people take money away

When to Abandon a Sinking Ship

Deciding when to sell a pet fund is among the most difficult tasks of investing. It's easy to be rational in evaluating a fund's characteristics before you buy it. But once your money is committed, your emotions come into play, alternately tempting you to hold on to winners long after they have peaked and to jettison losers just before they bounce back. To spot the right time to sell or switch to a more promising fund, you must continually compare the ones you own with others and with your personal financial goals. As long as a fund is meeting your objectives, you should strive to hold on to it. But you shouldn't hesitate to move your money if another fund seems likely to do the job better. You should consider selling or switching under each of the following circumstances.

Your investment goals mature. As you get older and closer to your objectives, your needs and your tolerance for risk will inevitably change. When your children near college age, for example, you should stop taking risks with your investments for their tuition because you can't afford to lose a chunk of it in a last-minute market dip. When they are in high school, begin switching some of the college money from growth stock funds to short-term bond and money funds.

The fund assumes a new personality. Think back to the reasons that initially led you to invest in a fund. If it no longer fits those criteria, you should consider looking for a replacement. For example, your growth fund's assets may have grown so large that you fear the manager has lost the flexibility that helped him or her get high returns. Or your fund may have increased its annual fees beyond what you are willing to pay. You might also decide to switch if the manager responsible for the fund's past success retires or quits. Fund groups may not be in a hurry to notify investors that the manager has left. But if you notice changes in performance, volatility or the fund's investment style, a new hand may be at the helm. To find out for sure, ask the fund.

Your returns are consistently lackluster. If a fund turns out to be a subpar performer, you obviously will want to replace it. But you should give a fund at least a year to prove itself. If you are in a conservative stock fund, you might even give it two years. After two years, however, it's time to take your money out of the fund if it still languishes relative to its group or benchmarks like the S&P 500 index.

from us when we could most use it, and they give us money when we have no good place to put it." In addition, many fund managers say they are forced to "keep their powder dry." Since they never know when an adviser may snatch a few million dollars out of a fund, they are compelled to keep more cash on hand than they otherwise would. That cushion dampens your return whenever stocks and bonds outperform cash, which is most of the time. Many managers also say they must concentrate more of their money in the most frequently traded securities so that they can readily raise cash to meet a rash of redemptions from big timers. The need to favor more active issues, though, can prevent a manager from investing in less popular securities that, over time, may well generate higher returns.

How to avoid timer-induced whiplash. You can shield your portfolio by owning funds that do not participate in the "no transaction fee" networks of discount brokerages. Such holdouts include Vanguard, T. Rowe Price, Acorn and Longleaf Partners. Timers also tend to shun funds with redemption fees—sales charges levied on people who hold a fund for less than a minimum period, often 180 days. Hot performance streaks, which typically are enjoyed by funds buying more volatile investments like small tech stocks, quickly grab timers' attention. When you buy a hot fund, you face not only the traditional danger that it will go cold but also the new danger that timers will rampage through it, wrecking your investment return and inflaming your tax return. Conversely, funds with a history of generating consistent, moderate returns rarely attract the hot-money crowd. Ditto index funds based on broad benchmarks like the S&P 500, the Wilshire 5000 or the Russell 2000.

❧ *Blunt the Taxman's Bite of Profits*

Investors' lives are greatly simplified by funds except at tax time. That's partly because tax law requires funds to pay out, or distribute, virtually all their income from interest, dividends and net capital gains each year. That means you often owe taxes on capital gains from your fund even if you didn't sell any of your shares. Things get more confounding when you do sell shares. If you're like most investors, you have your funds reinvest your distributions. From a tax standpoint, each reinvestment counts as a separate purchase. Thus you're confronted with a mess when you sit down to calculate your taxable gains. Included might be a large clump of shares you bought at one price (your initial investment); dozens of tiny lots acquired at different prices (shares purchased with reinvested distributions); and a further raft of small chunks each bought at yet another price (the regular purchases you made). Each lot of fund shares that you bought produces a different capital gain or loss, which means that much extra calculator punching to figure out what you owe Uncle Sam. Here are tips that can spare you some headaches.

Buy fund shares at the right time. Most stock funds distribute capital gains once a year, and some funds pay out income quarterly. (To learn your fund's distribution dates, just call its toll-free number.) If you're contemplating a purchase close to a distribution date, don't act until after the date passes. Otherwise, you'll receive a taxable payout of all the capital gains or income the fund booked since its last payout even if you've owned your stake for only a week. In effect, the fund hands you back part of your principal in the form of a distribution. But now you owe tax on it.

Watch out for embedded gains. When you're considering whether to buy a fund, check the changes in net assets in the fund's annual report. The number to look for is the "change in unrealized appreciation on investments." That represents capital gains embedded in the fund's portfolio. When the fund sells its winners, those gains must be distributed to shareholders. To judge how big the payout could be, divide the unrealized appreciation by the fund's net assets. A result of more than 0.2 suggests that a walloping big payout is possible. While the potential for a big distribution shouldn't rule out a promising fund, it could decide a close call between competitors. In contrast, realized losses are a plus. The fund can use prior losses to offset gains.

Capitalize on your mistakes. If a fund is down for the year, consider selling it and taking the tax write-off. The loss can offset capital gains plus as much as $3,000 of other income. In fact, it often makes tax sense to move out of a losing no-load fund temporarily even if you still like its prospects. The IRS will disqualify the loss if you repurchase shares within 31 days. But nothing prevents you from hopping into a similar fund for a little longer than that and then switching back to your favorite.

Strive to sell in the same tax year. While you don't want to overrule your investment sense just to streamline your taxes, here's something to think about. If you sell a fund's shares over a number of years, you have to keep records of each sale and decide which of the four IRS approved accounting methods (described below) yields the lowest tax. If you sell all at once, all four methods will give you the same tax. So you can use the simplest method called *average cost, single category*. It allows you to figure the average cost of all your shares, regardless of when you bought them. And that work will be done for you if the fund you're selling belongs to one of the growing number of families that calculate tax costs for redeeming shareholders. Keep in mind, however, that if you're not unloading all your shares, the single category method may cost you more in taxes than the alternatives described below.

Choose the best formula. Unless you elect otherwise, the IRS assumes that the fund shares you sold first were the ones you bought first. That method is called *first in, first out*. It's fine if your fund has been a loser. But the oldest shares may have the biggest gains. So they are the ones on which you're better off postponing taxes. You can do that using a method called *specific identification*. It permits you to sell whichever shares will minimize your taxes. You might pick only shares on which you have a loss, offsetting gains from a different investment. Another method, *average cost, double category*, requires you to distinguish between shares you've held for more than a year and those you bought more recently and to calculate a separate average cost for each. That way you take advantage of the difference in tax rates on long- and short-term gains. Long-term gains (on shares held more than a year) are taxed at a maximum of 20%. Short-term gains are taxed as ordinary income at rates as high as 39.6%. Here's a final caveat, however. Once you decide to use either single or double category for a given fund, you're stuck with that method for the fund. You are not permitted to change the tax treatment without written permission from the IRS.

Chapter 4

Cut Your Taxes From 2000 On

*F*iling your income taxes isn't exactly what most people would call a favorite rite of spring. Worse, many recent changes in the tax laws are complicated in the extreme. That's where this chapter can help you. Whether you do your taxes yourself or use a professional preparer, we can walk you through strategies that are most likely to reduce the tax on your return. We also include guidance on what to do now to keep your taxes low in 2000 and subsequent years. In the sections below, we mention whenever you need to file a special form with your return to claim a particular tax break. You can download forms from the Internal Revenue Service website (irs.gov) or order them by telephone (800-TAX-FORM) or by fax (703-368-9694).

❧ *Reduce Your Adjusted Gross Income*

To claim the full amount of many new tax write-offs, your adjusted gross income must fall below certain limits. As your AGI exceeds the limits, the write-offs phase out and eventually disappear. To complicate matters, the AGI thresholds vary depending on the tax break. For example, on a 1999 return, joint filers qualify for the $500 per-child credit if their AGI is $110,000 or less. But to claim the full $1,500 HOPE tuition credit, joint AGI must be $80,000 or less. In addition, on your 1999 return, many of your itemized deductions will be cut by an amount equal to 3% of every dollar by which your AGI exceeds $126,600. The itemized deductions include mortgage interest, state and local taxes and miscellaneous expenses. To help you keep your AGI low enough to preserve valuable tax benefits, consider two moves that can reduce the AGI you report.

Fund a deductible IRA, Keogh or SEP. If you're covered by an employer's retirement plan but your spouse is not, the non-covered spouse can make a deductible $2,000 contribution to an IRA, provided that your joint AGI is $150,000 or less. If neither you nor your spouse is covered, you can each fund a $2,000 deductible IRA no matter how high your AGI is. You have until the time you file your '99 return to open an IRA, but no later than April 15. If you've already filed your '99 return and would like to open and deduct an IRA for 1999, you must file a new 1999 Form 1040 before April 15. Be sure to attach a cover letter to the revised return explaining that it's a substitute for the original.

If you have earnings from self-employment, fund a Keogh or SEP (simplified employee pension). The most popular varieties of these retirement plans let you contribute and deduct up to 13% of your net earnings from self-employment. To fund a Keogh for '99, you must have established the account by December 31 of last year. You can still open a SEP for 1999, but no later than April 15. For both plans, you have until the time you file your return (including extensions) to fund the account. You don't need to file any special paperwork to fund your Keogh. If you're setting up a SEP, you need to fill out Form 5305-SEP or Form 5305A-SEP and keep it with your records. Ask the plan's custodian or a tax adviser which forms apply to you.

ꙮ Grab Any College Tuition Credits

The HOPE tuition credit can slash your taxes by up to $1,500 for tuition you pay for yourself, your spouse or your dependents during the first two years of college. The lifetime learning credit lets you subtract up to $1,000 from your taxes for post-secondary classes in any year that you don't also claim the HOPE credit for the same student's tuition. To be eligible for the maximum credits, your AGI must be $80,000 or less for joint filers; $40,000 or less for singles. The credits phase out for couples and singles once AGI exceeds $100,000 and $50,000, respectively. File Form 8863 with your return. Here's how to capture these breaks.

Use the credits even if your child pays the tuition. As long as you claim your child as your dependent on your return, you can take the applicable college tax credit against tuition payments he or she makes from student loans, a campus job or other income. Don't feel as if you're stealing the credit from your child. As your dependent, he or she is prohibited from claiming the credits.

Let Uncle Sam help you pay off student loans. On your '99 return, the tax law grants a write-off of up to $1,500 for interest that was due and paid in 1999 on student loans, such as Staffords for undergraduates and PLUS loans for parents. You can even deduct the interest on a personal loan you used to pay for college, provided the loan is not from a family member and you can show that the entire loan was used to pay tuition bills. "Under proposed IRS regulations, personal-loan proceeds against which you claim an interest deduction should be received 60 days before the classes begin to 60 days after they end," says Martin Nissenbaum, the national director of personal income tax planning at Ernst & Young in New York City.

To qualify for the full $1,500 deduction, your AGI must not exceed $60,000 for joint filers, $40,000 for singles. The break phases out completely at AGI levels above $75,000 and $55,000, respectively. In addition, the deduction is allowed only for interest paid during the first 60 months of the loan payback. You don't have to itemize to claim the write-off. Just enter the amount on your 1040.

❧ Prep for the Dreaded Schedule D

Securities that you own for more than a year before selling qualify for the long-term capital gains rate of 20%, or 10% if you're in the 15% tax bracket. If you sell securities you've owned for 12 months or less, your gain is taxed at your top marginal income tax rate. What if you didn't sell any investments but have only distributions from a stock or bond fund? If so, don't overlook the requirement to file Schedule D, Capital Gains and Losses. "That's a miserable 54 lines that the IRS estimates will take you four hours and 20 minutes to complete," says Jim Jenkins, a certified public accountant in Southfield, Mich. The upshot? If the dreaded D is in your future, you should consider using a tax pro to do your return.

Don't mistakenly overstate your gains. To figure out your gain on a stock, you reduce the amount of your sales proceeds by your basis, which is taxspeak for your cost to acquire the shares. But there are as many ways to compute basis as there are ways to acquire stock. For example, to calculate the basis of a stock you bought directly, you tack on to the share price any fees or commissions you paid when you bought the shares. (And you subtract fees or commissions on the sale from the sales proceeds.) The computation can get more complicated, however, if you acquired your stock some other way, such as buying it through a dividend reinvestment plan, inheriting it or exercising a stock option. Unless you're supremely confident about preparing your tax return, check with a tax pro before you inadvertently overstate your gains.

Write off your high-tech investing tools. If you use a computer and software to manage your investments, you should try to write off some of the costs as miscellaneous itemized deductions. Here are the main obstacles. Only the portion of the item's cost that is attributable to your investment-related activity can be counted toward your write-off. So if you spend half your time on your computer for day trading and the other half in a Star Wars chat room, only one-half of your allowable computer costs are deductible. The other hurdle is that only miscellaneous expenses that exceed 2% of your AGI are deductible. So you must add up all of your miscellaneous write-offs, such as unreimbursed employee expenses, tax-preparation fees and investment-related costs, and deduct only the portion that exceeds the 2% of AGI. If you can't write off your miscellaneous expenses because they don't total more than 2% of your AGI, try to double up on your deductible expenses every other year.

Here's how to tally your high-tech write-offs correctly. A portion of the purchase price of a computer you use for investing can be depreciated over five years. You would be wise to ask a tax pro for help with the gnarly calculation, which is filed on Form 4562. For example, if you bought a $3,000 computer in 1999 and used it 20% of the time for investing, your depreciation comes to $60 in 1999 and a total of $540 in subsequent years.

The purchase price of investment software can be depreciated over three years, if its so-called useful life is greater than one year. If the software will be obsolete within a year, however, you can write off the entire purchase price in the year you buy it. But be careful. "Software is not obsolete just because there's a new version out," says Kristi Mathisen, a C.P.A. at Bader Martin Ross & Smith in Seattle. "It's obsolete when it no longer computes accurate results or when your right to use it expires." The calculation is also included on Form 4562.

Be sure to keep bullet-proof records. To help substantiate your write-offs, you need to have a contemporaneous written record showing your log-on and log-off times and noting which programs you were using or sites you were visiting in every given time period. What if shoddy record keeping prevents you from claiming investment-related deductions on your '99 return? Act now to put an adequate tracking system in place for this year. Laurence Zuckerman, a C.P.A. and software expert at Micro Vision Software in Hauppauge, N.Y., suggests using a computer spreadsheet to record and tabulate your online investment activity.

🦢 Nail Down Home Sale Exclusions

Tax law changes let joint filers exclude from tax up to $500,000 ($250,000 for singles) in capital gains on the sale of their home if the house was their primary residence for at least two of the five years before the sale. What if you sell before meeting the law's two-year residency requirement? The answer is very complicated.

If you sold a home in 1998 that you owned on August 5, 1997, you could shield a portion of the gain if you bail out early. Say you sold after owning the house for only one year. Since

Lower Your Odds of Being Audited

IRS computers are trained to look for irregularities in certain areas of a return. If you claim unreimbursed employee business expenses, are self-employed or inflated your income when you applied for a mortgage, you stand a greater than average chance of getting an IRS audit notice. If you have legitimate deductions in any of the frequently scrutinized areas, don't cheat yourself by skipping the write-offs. Just make certain your records are impeccable. And always attach to your return an explanation of deductions that might raise questions. Here are audit attractors.

Claiming unreimbursed business expenses. Auditing employee business deductions provides a windfall of extra taxes for the IRS. The chief reason is that in order to claim them, you must be able to prove they were legitimate business expenses and your employer didn't cover them. And the record-keeping requirements for entertainment and travel expenses are among the tax law's strictest. Employees who deduct personal computers used at home are also audit targets.

Filing a Schedule C. Submitting one for your unincorporated small business sends a red flag to IRS auditors. Documentation is very important here. For example, if you claim a theft loss you should attach a statement describing the items stolen from your company and how you arrived at the amount of the deduction. Schedule C filers are also more vulnerable to so-called lifestyle audits, in which the IRS investigates your standard of living to make sure it fits with the income you report.

Taking long-term care deductions. Keep a copy of any contract you sign for such care, as well as receipts or canceled checks for medical services and expenses not covered by insurance. Get a copy of the caregiver's professional license.

Making certain IRA withdrawals. You don't pay a penalty if you tap your IRA, prior to turning age 59.5, to pay for medical insurance while you are unemployed. You must be unemployed for at least 12 consecutive weeks. Save copies of your unemployment checks, the Form 1099-R from your IRA sponsor showing your distribution and canceled checks or receipts for your health insurance premiums.

Deducting losses on rental property. To claim a loss, you must be able to prove that you actively manage your rental property by doing substantially all of the work on it. Make sure you have records showing that you took an active part in such management decisions as approving tenants and authorizing repairs on the property.

Fudging on loan applications. The IRS compares income on mortgage and small business loan applications with the amount borrowers show on their tax returns. One compliance study triggered nearly 500 audits.

that's one half of the two-year residency requirement, you get to shield from tax an amount equal to one half of the full exclusion. So if you're a married joint filer, you could shelter up to $250,000 in gains. If you're single, you can shield up to $125,000. If you sold a home in 1998 that you bought on or after August 6, 1997, you could shield a portion of the gain only if you moved because of unexpected circumstances, such as a job transfer or ill health.

If you sold your home in 1999, the rules for claiming a partial exclusion are also a tad convoluted. If you owned your home on August 5, 1997 and you sold before August 5, 1999, you can claim a pro rata share of the exclusion no matter why you sold. If you bought your home after August 5, 1997 and you sold before living there for two years, you can claim a portion of the exclusion only if unexpected circumstances required you to move.

✎ Plan Ahead for Plum 2000 Breaks

If you didn't reap all the tax savings you had hoped for on your 1999 return, you're not alone. The tax code is now crammed with credits, deductions and other juicy benefits. But to qualify for them, either in full or in part, your adjusted gross income must not exceed certain limits. So what's a beleaguered taxpayer to do? Make less money? Of course not. If you forfeited tax breaks on your 1999 return, or see that you're on track to do so this year, you have to take steps now to control how and when you receive your income. There are perfectly legal ways to delay collecting income until a later year or to shift income onto your child's tax return. But unlike deductions you can grab at the last minute, controlling your income requires you to put a plan in place before you make the money.

Sell property on installment. If you have a taxable profit on the sale of real estate, business property or personal effects, the tax law allows you to be paid in installments that may stretch out over years. The main advantage is that you don't have to report the gain on your tax return until you receive the money, so the sale won't push you into a higher tax bracket or boost your AGI to a level where you lose tax benefits. The disadvantage is that you don't get all of the money right away, and thus can't spend or reinvest it immediately. Still, the ability to preserve tax breaks takes the edge off that sacrifice.

Say, for example, that you and your spouse have two children and an AGI of $75,000 but that selling your rental property this year would add another $60,000. With an AGI of $135,000 in 2000, you would kiss good-bye a $500 tax credit for each of your children, the $1,500 HOPE tuition credit and the $1,000 lifetime learning credit. Moreover, your itemized deductions would be clipped by $252. However, if you were paid in three $20,000 annual installments, you would be eligible for the full per-child credit and for partial HOPE and lifetime learning credits. You would also get the full benefit of your itemized deductions.

Exchange your investment real estate. With a "like-kind exchange," you trade one piece of investment property for a similar one. This maneuver allows you to postpone reporting the profit realized from the first property until you sell the newly acquired property sometime in the future. "If you plan on reinvesting the proceeds from the sale in another property, you shouldn't pay any tax right away," says Ed Slott, a C.P.A. in Rockville Centre, N.Y. "And if an exchange allows you to keep your AGI low enough to qualify for some other tax benefits, all the better." A like-kind exchange is exceedingly complex, so consult a tax pro before attempting to execute one.

Defer your 2000 annual bonus. If you're expecting an AGI-bloating bonus, talk to your boss about receiving the windfall in 2001. If you ask for a deferral after you've done the work or achieved the goal on which the bonus will be based (or after your boss has announced that you'll be getting a bonus), the IRS may argue that you're attempting to delay taxes on income that was actually payable, and taxable, this year.

Pump up your 401(k) plan. Every dollar you put in your 401(k) reduces your AGI by a dollar. So before you insist you can't afford to fund your 401(k) to the maximum allowed by your plan, you need to re-examine how you spend and save. You may find, for example, that you have earnings on investments outside your 401(k) that can be used for everyday cash outlays, thus freeing up more of your salary for 401(k) contributions. Say you're single and making $45,000 a year, of which you put $1,500 in your 401(k). Also assume that you earn and reinvest about $100 a month from the savings accounts you have outside of your 401(k). If you used those earnings for your routine spending, you could afford to divert another $1,200 a year into your 401(k). And if you're paying off a student loan, an additional $1,200 cut in your AGI would allow you to write off an extra $120 in loan interest on your tax return.

Shift assets to your children age 14 or older. When

you give interest- or dividend-paying assets to your kids who are at least 14, the income shows up on their returns, not yours. So if you're planning to pay for their college costs in a few years anyway, why not give some money to them now to preserve your tax breaks? Say that assets you've given to your 16-year-old son earn $3,000. That's three grand that won't be included in your AGI. Even better, your son's federal income tax on the amount would come to just $345, assuming he has no other income. To compare, if the $3,000 had been reported on your tax return, the tax on that amount would have come to $930, assuming you're in the 31% tax bracket. If you're ready to sell appreciated stock, also consider giving it to children who are at least age 14. They can then sell the stock and report the profit on their return. And you avoid including the gain in your AGI. As an added plus, children will pay tax at their rate, presumably just 10% on a long-term gain, vs. 20% for you.

The easiest way to funnel money to your kids is to put the assets in no-fee custodial accounts that you can open for each of your children at a bank, brokerage or mutual fund. You can give as much as $10,000 a year ($20,000 if you and your spouse make the gift together) without incurring a gift tax. The child gains full control of the assets at age 18 or 21, depending on your state law. Think twice, however, before giving assets to children younger than 14. The so-called kiddie tax will require them to pay tax at your top rate on investment income over $1,400. Also, when children are very young, it's difficult to gauge whether they will be mature enough at age 18 or so to handle the money. By the time your child is a teenager, it should be easier to assess whether he or she can eventually be trusted with the stash.

❧ Being Charitable Cuts Your Bill

A burst of generosity is a popular way to reduce your taxes, since you can deduct gifts to charity as long as you itemize. But don't wait for year-end if you have assets other than cash or securities to donate. The rules are tricky for determining how much you can deduct for nonfinancial contributions. To ensure the biggest possible write-off, you should take the time to consult a tax pro before you make a gift, especially if your donation is sizable. Here's a tax primer on three common charitable gifts.

Write off your old wheels. You can deduct the fair market value of a used car that you give to charity. As a starting point for determining that figure, use the value given in the Kelley Blue Book used-car guide or the National Automobile Dealers Association's NADA Official Used Car Guide. But remember that fair market value is what you could get for the car if you were to sell it on the date of donation. So if your car is a real clunker, you can't claim the Blue Book value as a deduction. Conversely, if you think your car is worth more than the used-car guides indicate, document your deduction by keeping a written record of the attributes your car had that the guides didn't account for. If you plan to deduct an amount that's much higher than average, get a mechanic's appraisal.

Give away pricey art and collectibles. When you donate tangible personal property that has increased in value, the size of your write-off will depend on how long you have owned the asset and how the charity uses it. If you owned the item for more than a year before donating it, or if you inherited it from someone who had owned it for more than a year, you can deduct the fair market value if the charity uses the item to further its stated tax-exempt purpose. Say you donate a painting you've owned for many years to a museum. The painting cost you $5,000 but is now worth $20,000. If the museum adds the painting to its collection, you can deduct $20,000. But if the museum sells the painting, your deduction is limited to $5,000, the price you paid for it. Those are the rules even if the museum buys another painting for its collection with the proceeds from selling yours. So to get a write-off for your gift's full fair market value, ask the charity for a letter stating that it intends to use your donation in a way that is directly related to the charity's mission. Keep the letter in your records.If you donate an appreciated item you've owned for a year or less, the tax law generally limits the deduction to the price you paid for the item.

Bequeath appreciated real estate. You can also write off the fair market value of land or buildings that you donate to charity, as long as you've owned the property for more than a year or inherited it from someone who owned it for more than a year. But real estate would usually result in either a capital loss or a capital gain if it were sold rather than given away—a fact that has important tax repercussions. For example, if you have a loss on your real estate, you're better off selling the property and giving the proceeds to charity. That way, you can deduct the loss on your tax return and claim a deduction for the charitable contribution. If selling your real estate would result in a long-term capital gain, however, you get a double tax benefit by simply giving it away. That's because you avoid tax on the gain and you get a write-off for the property's fair market value. It's just the tax code's way of saying that giving doesn't have to hurt.

Breaking Up Is Hard on Returns

Last year some 48 million married couples signed joint tax returns. In so doing, each spouse swore that "to the best of my knowledge and belief, [the return was] true, correct and complete." It's an oath that some spouses will live to regret. That's because signing a joint tax return still makes each spouse liable for back taxes, interest and penalties the IRS may later assess in an audit. You are on the hook for the entire amount even if your spouse earned all of the income and claimed all of the write-offs. True, recent changes in the law make it somewhat easier to get out from under your spouse's or your ex-spouse's tax debts. For starters, the law relaxed some of the requirements to qualify as a so-called innocent spouse, a designation that essentially absolves you of your spouse's tax sins. They also created two new levels of indulgence, known inelegantly as equitable relief and separate liability. As welcome as the new protections are, however, it's important to note that they can be very limited and are inherently complex. Below are the three options you face when your spouse's tax mess lands in your lap.

Innocent spouse relief. Under the new rules, you can apply for innocent spouse relief for any item that is challenged on a joint return. In contrast, the old law let you seek such relief only for "grossly erroneous" entries that had generally resulted in a tax understatement of more than $500. But the new rules do not repeal the highest, and often insurmountable, hurdle if you claim to be an innocent spouse. The burden of proof is on you to show that you did not know and had no reason to know of your spouse's tax hijinks. Say the IRS asserts that a married couple failed to report income on a joint return and attempts to collect back taxes, interest and penalties from the now ex-wife. The woman may be able to prove that she did not know her ex-husband was hiding income. But her claim for innocent spouse relief is likely to be rejected if her lifestyle was out of line with the income shown on the returns. That's because a reasonably educated person is expected to know that an elaborate lifestyle is impossible to maintain on a modest income.

Equitable relief. This category was established for a spouse who is not clueless enough to be "innocent" but can nevertheless make the case that being faulted for the other spouse's misdeeds would be unfair. Moreover, equitable relief is intended for filers who reported their taxes correctly but did not pay the balance due. Let's assume, for example, that you filed a joint return showing that you owed $15,000. Also assume that you and your spouse paid half of the bill and took out a loan to cover the remaining $7,500. If, without your knowledge, your spouse then blew the loan proceeds at the blackjack table, the IRS could agree not to come after you for the debt.

Separate liability. If you are divorced or legally separated or have been living apart from your spouse for at least the past 12 months, you can cut your tax ties to your (soon-to-be) ex by reworking your prior joint returns to specify which income and write-offs belonged to you alone. The task can be very tricky and thus would require the help of a tax pro if your taxes are even somewhat complicated. You must file an election with the IRS stating that you are requesting separate liability. And your assertions are subject to challenge by your ex-spouse and the IRS. If all parties agree that you've correctly divvied up the returns, the IRS can't hit you up for the tax on an item attributable to your ex unless it proves you had "actual knowledge" of the issue. That's a very tough standard.

For example, if the IRS wanted you to pay back taxes on unreported income from one of your ex's accounts, it would need evidence such as bank records showing that you withdrew money from the hidden stash. Even if you manage to extricate yourself from the responsibility for a joint return, you're likely to pay a high price, emotionally and financially. Your best course of action is not to rely on the new rules to help you out but to go into joint filing as you should go into marriage itself—with your eyes wide open.

If you have doubts about your spouse's tax moves, you should not hesitate to ask for a complete explanation. If you're not satisfied with the answer, you can file your own return using the status known as "married, filing separately." Bear in mind that separate filing usually results in a higher overall tax bill than joint filing. But look on the bright side. If you iron out your differences with your spouse, you have three years from the time you file to amend a separate return to a joint return.

✒ *Four Tax Code Snafus to Avoid*

You could end up paying Uncle Sam much more than you owe if your tax pro isn't up to speed on today's fast-changing rules. That's the conclusion of our latest tax preparer test in which we sent a financial profile of a hypothetical family to 60 such pros. No two contestants who completed the test came up with the same bottom line. Worse, no one turned in an error-free form.

The test's author, C.P.A. Mark Castellucci, calculated the lowest legal tax at $37,105. Castellucci acknowledges that his computation is not the only possible correct answer because the tax law itself is ambiguous in some areas. Still, you can't blame ambiguity for the fact that the contestants' answers ranged from $34,240 to $68,912—a chasm of about 100%. That means our fictional family could have underpaid its tax by nearly $3,000 or paid nearly double what they owed.

Pitfalls that tripped up our pros may surface as you prepare your taxes. Before we review them, meet our fictional family. Ken Johnson, 60, is a self-employed computer consultant, and Barbara, 45, is an architect. They have two children—Joy, 20, a full-time college student who lives away from home, and Craig, 12. In addition to Ken's wages and self-employment income of $72,775, he received a $142,000 payout from his 401(k) when he took early retirement in 1999. Barbara rolled over a $127,000 retirement payout when she decided to switch jobs last year. These were the pros' most common mistakes.

Handling tricky 401(k) withdrawals. Because Ken was 59.5 when he took his $142,000 distribution for early retirement, he was eligible for special tax treatment known as five-year averaging. This technique lets you pay tax on your payout as if you had received the money over five years instead of all at once. (Note, however, that this tax break expired on December 31, 1999.) Four preparers didn't realize Ken could use five-year averaging even though his birth date was clearly given on the first page of the test. They thus kneecapped him with an additional $26,558 in tax. Another 14 contestants flubbed the averaging calculation by using an out-of-date rate, resulting in a tax overstatement of $420. Two pros erred in favor of the Johnsons by wrongly applying a 10-year average calculation, which lowballed Ken's tax by $1,010. The problem is that 10-year averaging applies only to taxpayers born before 1936.

Assessing penalties on 401(k) loans. When Barbara switched jobs last year, she still owed $15,300 on a loan taken from her 401(k) years earlier. So her former employer simply deducted that amount from her account before rolling over the

Take Our Taxpayer Aptitude Quiz

Completing the test below will help you decide whether you need a professional to prepare your next tax return or whether you are tax-savvy enough to go solo.

1. From the date of purchase, how long must you own stock before selling for your gain to be considered long term?
   A. 12 months
   B. More than 12 months
   C. More than 18 months

2. Fees or commissions you pay to buy stock are:
   A. Deductible in the year you pay them
   B. Added to your cost basis
   C. Neither a nor b

3. Fees or commissions you pay to sell stock are:
   A. Deductible in the year you pay them
   B. Subtracted from your sales proceeds
   C. Neither a nor b

4. This year you sold stockholdings from your portfolio, incurring roughly a $3,000 capital loss, and your spouse also sold stock for a $4,000 capital loss. Assume that neither of you had any capital gains. On a joint return, you can deduct:
   A. $3,000
   B. $6,000
   C. $7,000

5. An excess capital loss may be carried forward:
   A. For three years
   B. For five years
   C. Until used up

6. In 1999, you refinanced your mortgage for the amount remaining on your old mortgage and paid points. You must:
   A. Deduct all of the points on your 1999 return
   B. Deduct the points over the life of the loan
   C. Not deduct the points on a refinancing

7. In 1996, you bought a new primary residence. In 1999, you finally sold your old house, which was your main home from 1980 to 1996, for a $125,000 profit. Do you owe tax on the gain?
   A. Yes
   B. No
   C. Only if you were 55 or older when you sold.

8. To qualify for the new lifetime learning credit for classes to improve your job skills (worth up to $1,000 annually), you, your spouse or your dependents must take post-secondary courses:
   A. Full time
   B. At least half time
   C. There is no course load requirement.

9. If a bona fide loan to a family member is deemed to be uncollectible, can you write the loan off as a bad debt?
   A. No
   B. Yes, on Schedule A
   C. Yes, on Schedule D

10. Mutual fund distributions are taxable in the year that they're declared by the fund even if they were reinvested.
    A. True
    B. False

HOW TO SCORE: Give yourself one point for each correct answer. Don't take credit for lucky guesses. **3 or fewer points:** Run, don't walk, to a good tax pro. **4 to 7 points:** Commendable. But without a pro, you may miss out on tax breaks you deserve. **8 to 10 points:** You can try doing your return yourself. On the other hand, if you're so up on the tax law, your taxes are probably complicated enough to warrant using a pro.

Answers: 1. B, 2. B, 3. B, 4. A, 5. C, 6. B, 7. B, 8. C, 9. C, 10. True stash to an IRA. Unfortunately, that maneuver exposed Barbara to tax and a 10% penalty on the $15,300. That's because you have 60 days from a rollover to add an amount to the IRA that is equal to an outstanding loan balance withheld by your employer. If you don't—and Barbara didn't—the amount is deemed a premature withdrawal subject to tax and penalty.

What most test takers didn't know is that this is a case where Uncle Sam has a heart. If you have a medical deduction and a premature 401(k) withdrawal in the same year, you can reduce the penalty for early withdrawal by an amount equal to 10% of your deduction. The Johnsons' medical write-off came to $5,066. So they qualified for a $507 exception to the penalty. This reduced the hit from $1,530 to $1,023. All but three of our test takers made the Johnsons pay the full penalty. There are similar exceptions to the fine for early withdrawals from IRAs. For example, you may avoid a penalty if you take an early IRA withdrawal to pay for medical insurance during unemployment. Such leniency shouldn't encourage you to tap your tax-deferred accounts early. But if you have to dip into the money, make sure you don't pay an unnecessary penalty.

Calculating capital gains on home sales. In 1997, when the Johnsons bought and moved into their current home, they were unable to sell their former residence, where they had lived for nine years. So they rented out the house for two years, finally selling it in June 1999 for a gain of $35,727. Under the tax law passed in 1997, a couple who sell a primary residence can completely avoid tax on up to $500,000 of profit, provided they had lived in the house for at least two out of the five years before the sale. The Johnsons clearly met that requirement. Yet eight preparers didn't know that the new law applied in the Johnsons' case and thus wrongly counted the gains as taxable, for a painful overstatement of $8,718.

Figuring the tax bite on stock options. In January 1999, Ken exercised nonqualified stock options from his former employer. The difference between the option price and the stock's fair market value came to $8,000. This amount was correctly reported on Ken's W-2 form. But seven professional preparers didn't realize that the $8,000 was already included in Ken's taxable wages. So they taxed the amount twice—once as ordinary income and again as a short-term capital gain. The tax overstatement totaled $2,408.

❧ Make the Most of Tax Preparers

Many people find the tax filing process less daunting if they hire a professional preparer. Don't think you've done your part by handing your accountant a stack of receipts. Your tax pro won't ace your return unless you're an active partner in the process. That doesn't mean you need to master the tax law or second-guess your pro's every move. But you do need to take the steps detailed below to help educate your pro on your tax situation. (To see whether you can go solo or need a pro, take our tax aptitude quiz on page 104.) The taxpayer who is organized and informed gets the most accurate return and the biggest tax savings. Here is what it means to be a good client.

Prepare in advance for your preparer. Filling out the questionnaire that tax pros provide is not enough. Before you meet with a preparer, check your previous two or three returns to review the deductions you've been taking. Note the ones you think you still qualify for and jot down a reminder to ask about any other tax breaks that might apply to you. If you're using a new preparer, you'll need to provide a copy of last year's return. It may contain such valuable information as losses you can carry over. A preparer who has done your taxes in the past should have copies of your prior years' returns on file.

Next, review your income statements, including W-2s from employers and 1099s from banks, mutual funds and other payers. It's up to you to examine them carefully and request any necessary corrections from the issuer. Your pro will assume that these documents are accurate. Then organize your records for your deductible expenses. That involves grouping receipts and canceled checks in categories that mirror the entries on a tax form. Itemized deductions on Schedule A include medical, taxes, interest, charitable gifts and miscellaneous expenses. Be sure to tally the expenses for each category. Some preparers want a list of your totals only. Others will just flip through your receipts to make sure you haven't included any questionable items.

Raise issues pertinent to your return. You can research current tax rules and how they might apply to you by visiting the IRS website at www.irs.gov. You can also use the interview of a software program such as Tax Cut or Turbo Tax (see "Top Software for Do-It-Yourselfers" on page 108). Your input is especially crucial during filing season, when your pro has limited time to ask questions. The proper treatment of some tax items is open to interpretation. Can you accelerate deductions for software by saying it will soon become obsolete? Did you really need to travel to a distant city for medical care? If the legitimacy of a write-off comes down to a judgment call, your pro should tell you. You, in turn, must be clear about whether you want to take the write-off, even at the risk of audit, or whether you want to err on the side of caution.

Bare your personal as well as financial life. You will obviously want to tell your pro about any big financial moves you made during the year. But personal events can also affect your taxes. Open up about events in your personal life even if you're not sure they're relevant. Make sure that you mention a marriage (your own, your ex's or your child's); a divorce (impending or finalized); deaths in the family; support you gave an elderly parent; and debts you collected or failed to collect. And let your pro know if you heard from the IRS or a state tax agency last year. If you blow a tax-cutting opportunity during the year, there's little corrective action you can take when you file. Get your pro's opinion before taking such steps as buying business equipment, taking money from a tax-favored retirement plan or selling a large block of stock.

What your tax preparer owes you. An ethical one will pay any interest or penalty caused by errors he or she makes on your return. But, of course, it's better to avoid mistakes in the first place. And the best way to do that is to be the most valuable player on your tax team.

✒ Top Software for Do-It-Yourselfers

The federal 1040 return had more than 175 new or revamped tax forms at last count. That is a job for a computer if you feel comfortable doing your own taxes. To help you choose the software, we recently reviewed three widely available tax preparation packages. They are Block Financial's Kiplinger Tax Cut, Intuit's Turbo Tax and a newcomer, Second Story Software's Tax Act. Each comes in basic and deluxe versions. We focused mainly on the more expensive deluxe editions, which offer more guidance than their bare-bones counterparts. We then checked out four tax preparation sites that are accessible on the internet—Web Turbo Tax (turbotax.com); Kiplinger Tax Cut Online (taxcut.com); Secure Tax (securetax.com) and Thomson One Tax (onetax.com).

Tax Cut and Turbo Tax lead the pack. Both programs feature a lengthy question-and-answer format that records your data directly onto tax forms, guidance through difficult sections and explanations of recent tax changes. Both offer free electronic filing (Tax Cut in basic and deluxe versions; Turbo Tax in deluxe only). In contrast, the basic edition of Tax Act can be downloaded free from the company's website (taxact.com). But the developer doesn't guarantee the accuracy of its calculations. Deluxe Tax Act is guaranteed but isn't as user-friendly or comprehensive as its competitors.

Why Tax Cut is more user friendly. Although both programs are standouts, our preference is Tax Cut. Its spare but intuitive navigation makes it easier to use than its Turbo Tax rival. Consider how the two programs take you through the vital tax interview. Tax Cut lets you choose "full interview" or "fast lane." This lets neophytes take a cautious approach, while experienced filers select from a checklist only the parts of the program they know apply to them. Turbo Tax, on the other hand, relies on a one-size-fits-all interview that essentially puts all users in the fast lane. This eliminates multiple screens and repetitive questions. But the pace may seem too brisk, especially for novices.

The difference is especially apparent when you're trying to figure out which credits apply to you. Tax Cut's full interview typically offers one tax deduction per screen and asks you whether you think you qualify. Turbo Tax presents a bulleted list of credits with checkmarks next to those you can take based on information you've provided. The program then asks you to check any other credits you think may apply. We were left with the unsettling feeling that we might blow past something we would catch under Tax Cut's more methodical questioning.

We also prefer Tax Cut's help features. If you type "medical expenses," the program links you to a set of tax tips, a video clip or a mini-worksheet for computing the deduction. Search for "medical expenses" in Turbo Tax, and you're sent to one written tax tip, with no links to other relevant resources. It's not that Turbo Tax doesn't offer more information. You just have to do more searching to find it.

The drawbacks of online filing. If you just want to fill out your tax forms on the computer, you can easily find a suitable online site. And you'll probably pay less than you would to buy software. For example, Web Turbo Tax charges $10 to $20 for a federal return and $10 to $20 for a state return. Kiplinger Tax Cut Online is free but offers Form 1040EZ only. But none of the sites are as instructive as the best of the software. You also have to cope with slow downloads and other snafus inherent in being online for a long time. That said, among the sites, Web Turbo Tax is the easiest to use and the most helpful.

Shrewd Moves at Retirement

As you approach the finale of your working life, it's time to ponder how best to pull money out of the IRAs, 401(k)s, Keoghs or other retirement accounts that you built up so industriously over the years. Uncle Sam, who abstained from taxing your savings while they were growing, now wants his piece of the action. Make one false move, and he will grab for more. Withdraw money before you turn 59.5, and you may have to pay a 10% penalty on top of your regular taxes. Take out too little after age 70.5, and you're bludgeoned with a 50% penalty. Don't despair, however. Buried deep within the U.S. tax code are ways to ease the pain. To that end, we consulted accountants, tax attorneys and financial planners. We recommend that you too seek out experienced professional advice before you make final decisions on the following questions.

The no-brainer withdrawal strategy. If simplicity is what you are after, the easiest way to get what's coming to you from your company retirement plan is to roll over your lump-sum payment into an annuity with an insurance company. Make that one decision now, and the toughest choice you'll have to make is where to cash your monthly check. But simplicity comes at a very high price. Most annuities pay interest of about 6% annually, plus a small return of capital. For a 65-year-old man with a retirement kitty of $500,000, that translates into an annual payout of about $48,600. That's not so bad in today's dollars. Yet over the course of the next 21 years—his expected lifetime—inflation would cut the real value of that payout in half. Worse, from the standpoint of your heirs, annuity payments typically stop upon your death. True, many annuities offer the option of having your payments continue for 10 or 20 years even if you don't make it that far. But you pay for the privilege by getting lower payments.

The lump sum advantage. People who aren't particularly good at controlling their spending are better served by a steady stream of income from an annuity. But most people are going to want to handle the lump sum themselves. With the freedom comes responsibility for picking your way through a tax code studded with land mines. Here are your choices.

If you don't need the money right away, your best move is to leave your tax-deferred savings untouched as long as possible. Why? Any distribution you take from such retirement plans will be taxed as ordinary income, whereas money from other parts of your portfolio may include lightly taxed capital gains or nontaxable returns of capital. By taking money from those sources, you are using funds that are taxed at lower rates. Equally important, waiting to tap your tax-deferred accounts allows your nest egg to keep building without being taxed. Over time, there is no better way to help your money grow.

If your company has a strong 401(k) plan, you may want to leave the money there, assuming the plan allows it. Otherwise, you should roll over your lump sum payout into an IRA. Make sure to ask your employer to transfer the money directly into your IRA. If you take the cash yourself, the IRS will require your employer to keep 20% as withholding.

Your options if you decide to retire early. In that case, it's even more important to keep that tax-deferred account growing. Just ask Ken and Marilynn Nemeroff of San Diego. Three years ago, Ken accepted a buyout package from his employer, Pacific Bell, to take early retirement. A 28-year Pac Bell veteran, Ken, then just 55, had always dreamed of retiring early to travel while he and Marilynn were still young enough to enjoy it. But even with $130,000 in a 401(k) plan and nearly $300,000 in a qualified pension, he figured it was still too early to cash out and head for the islands. With the help of a financial planner, Ken opted to roll his pension over into an IRA and to leave his 401(k) untouched in the plan at Pac Bell. That choice knocked roughly $60,000 off the Nemeroff's tax bill, which with penalties thrown in could have topped $150,000. In the meantime, Ken is happily back on the job at Pac Bell as a contract employee. He and Marilynn, an adult education teacher, plan to retire for good when Ken hits 60.

Your choices after you reach age 70.5. Just when you thought that you were too old to have to play by anyone else's rules, along comes the government with a harsh reality check. Whether you need the money or not, you have to start tapping your 401(k), IRA or other tax-deferred retirement plans by April 1 of the year after you turn 70.5. If you don't, the IRS will simply calculate the minimum you have to withdraw and tax it at a 50% rate. If this sounds like tough love, you'll be happy to know the government has softened its stance. You no longer have to start tapping your 401(k) at age 70.5, provided you still work for the employer who is sponsoring it and you don't own more than 5% of the company. What if you're retired? You'll have to choose between two formulas for determining your minimum annual withdrawal.

The first is called the *term-certain method*. To figure out just how much you need to withdraw using this approach, look up your life expectancy, or the joint life expectancy of you and your beneficiary, in IRS Publication No. 590. For a copy, call 800-829-3676 or consult the IRS website (irs.gov.) Unless the beneficiary is your spouse, the IRS limits the age difference between beneficiaries to 10 years for computing a joint life expectancy. That means you can't stretch out the withdrawals by naming your five-year-old grandson as beneficiary. Next, divide the total value of your retirement accounts by your life expectancy. Say you're 70 years old and have an account balance of $500,000. Using a single life expectancy of 16 years, you would have to pull out one-sixteenth of the money in your plan, or $31,250. The next year, you'd have to take out one-fifteenth, and so on down the line until you turn 86 and clean out the balance.

The second formula is the *recalculation method*. This is one of the few places where the statistical odds are actually stacked in your favor. The older you get, the longer you're expected to live. At age 75, the IRS assumes you'll live to 87.5. That's more than a year and a half longer than they thought you'd live when you were 70. So if longevity runs in your family, use the recalculation method to make sure you don't run out of cash too soon.

Here's how it works. Each year you recalculate the minimum withdrawal based on your new life expectancy. At 71, for example, the IRS expects you to live for another 15.3 years, so you divide your balance by 15.3 to come up with the amount you have to take out. A year later, your life expectancy will have dropped only nine months, meaning you divide the balance by 14.6. The good news is, the IRS life expectancy tables go to age 115. The bad news? If you've still got money in your tax-deferred accounts when you're 115, there probably isn't any bad news.

Chapter 5

Managing Your Money Online

*I*n this chapter, we've searched the internet to find leading websites in every major personal finance category. We ventured to the farthest reaches of the web, visiting nearly 1,000 sites in all. We emerged with a smorgasbord of online addresses that no person who cares about money can afford to ignore. They are a diverse collection. Some, like Microsoft's MSN Money Central, are backed by the richest corporations in the world. Others are the passion of one person, like the Superstar Investor directory that Terry Silver runs from his home in San Ramon, Calif. But they all have this trait in common—they're the best financial sites that the internet has to offer.

Later in this chapter we also tackle the daunting task of ranking today's top online brokerages. These firms have made buying and selling stocks cheaper, faster, easier and more fun. There's just one problem. With so many electronic brokers vying for your business, how do you choose among them? Most are trying to be all things to all people. Others are going after special niches like day traders. But such segmentation is good news only if you know exactly what you need and which net brokers have it. To help guide investors through the confusion, we measure what the online brokers have to offer.

The Top Personal Finance Supersites

There are more than a dozen megasites vying to be your one-stop financial portal. But Yahoo Finance, Microsoft's MSN Money

Central and Intuit's Quicken.com run circles around the rest. All three deliver quotes, research, news and other investing essentials and can help you with additional personal finance tasks like shopping for a mortgage or estimating taxes. Of course, no single site can do it all, and each of the supersites has features that will appeal to some users more than others. We recommend you give all three a test drive. You'll likely find that one becomes your first stop whenever you hit the web.

Yahoo Finance (finance.yahoo.com) excels at no-frills design and nonstop delivery of data. Thus it is the pinnacle of utility and the best place to go when you need factual financial information fast. Want to check out a particular stock that has caught your fancy? Punch in its ticker at the top of the home page (or look it up by name). Volumes of additional info are just another link away. From the first screen you can also see how the Dow and other indexes are doing or head for breaking stories from Reuters and the Associated Press. The site is organized into broad categories such as research and world markets. And while Yahoo hosts its own information centers and marketplaces for products like loans, insurance and real estate, it's also one of the best directories on the net. If it can't give you what you need, it will point you to the sites that can. Yahoo's message boards are the biggest, baddest investor discussions on the web. But hype, rumor and incivility run wild, making this one Yahoo area not worth most serious investors' time.

MSN Money Central (moneycentral.com) offers lots of sections that place a greater emphasis on editorial content and step-by-step guides than Yahoo does. But Money Central's real strength lies in its wide range of interactive tools and investing research. The only hitch is that you have to download a small program to your hard drive upon your first visit to the site to take full advantage of the tools. But they are well worth this inconvenience. The Research Wizard (which walks you through the basics of fundamental analysis) makes the site accessible to newcomers. In contrast, its stock screener, charting capabilities and other free onscreen gadgets are among the most sophisticated available anywhere.

Quicken (quicken.com) provides broad coverage and consistency. You can get the scoop on all personal finance topics without having to dig far. The site is logically laid out, with major categories tabbed at the top of every page, allowing easy access from virtually any other part of the site. And each area is complete in itself with bulletin boards, reference materials, solid (if generic) advice and, in many cases, a marketplace where you can shop for financial products like insurance and mortgages.

✍ *The Best Addresses in 15 Categories*

Fixed-income securities. If you're not as familiar with bonds as you are with stocks, a great place to start is Investing in Bonds (investinginbonds.com), brought to you by the Bond Market Association. The site not only explains how bonds work, it gives advice on identifying investing objectives and finding the right mix of stocks, bonds and cash. Our top destination for buying and selling bonds is Bond Center at E Trade (etrade.com). Offerings include muni bonds, corporates, zero coupons and Treasuries, among others. There's a $40 fee for trades of fewer than 20 Treasuries or 10 munis or corporates. As with all bonds, the commission is embedded in the selling price. E Trade's searchable database organizes bonds according to price, yield, credit rating and maturity. Bonds are not as liquid as stocks. But the broker's quick-pick feature calls up lists of all bonds that are available for immediate purchase.

Home buying and selling. No real estate site promises to let you do everything online. But many let you tour thousands of homes, hundreds of miles away, any time of day. Realtor (realtor.com), the official site of the National Association of Realtors, is the biggest home-search site out there, with 1.3 million listings nationwide. The site walks you through every stage of buying or selling a home, including advice on moving. You can hunt for a house by clicking on a map or typing in an address or a zip code. Or you can screen neighborhoods on such attributes as school quality, average home costs or crime statistics. If you don't find a listing you like, Realtor will email you possible matches as they come on the market. Sellers can save on broker fees with Owners (owners.com), a marketplace with about 20,000 listings

Where These Financial Pros Go Online

We asked these experts to share their favorite personal finance destinations on the web.

🐭 **Tom Marsico, Manager of Marsico Focus Fund.** With only 30 or so holdings in his fund, Marsico must pick his stocks carefully. And he uses the web to aid his research, usually heading straight for a company's site. "The quality of corporate sites just gets better, especially product and investor information," he says, naming Cisco and Microsoft (both of which his fund holds) as having particularly informative websites. A stake in the biotech firm Genentech also leads him to the National Institutes of Health (nih.gov). "We'll search there to see how different people are using the company's drugs."

🐭 **Amy Domini, Manager of Domini Social Investments.** When not hunting for Italian postcards from the 1920s on E Bay, Domini searches the web for the latest news on progressive, socially conscious companies. "There's a saying that the trade press has the story three months before the financial press," she says. "But specialty websites have the story before anyone else." She checks out the Gay Financial Network (gfn.com), for example, to learn about corporate policies on benefits for same-sex couples and heads to the Pesticide Action Network North America (igc.org/panna) for the latest on food safety.

🐭 **Mark Mobius, Manager of Templeton Developing Markets.** Traveling the world (often to countries with pricey net access fees) limits Mobius' browsing time. So he sticks mainly to news sites like those of CNN (cnn.com) and the Financial Times (ft.com). He also visits international economic organizations like the Institute of International Finance (iif.com) and The Organisation for Economic Co-operation and Development (oecd.org). But the internet has been instrumental to his efforts in other ways. "Investors can now look at the companies in which we are investing and become interested themselves," he says. "Ten years ago it would have been difficult to convince someone of the opportunities in Africa. But now you can access any number of sites and learn what is going on in virtually any country."

🐭 **Andrew Tobias, personal finance author.** The author of *The Only Investment Guide You'll Ever Need* lives on the web. Besides tending to his own site, Demystifying Finance (andrewtobias.com) and visiting major money sites like Quicken and Morningstar, he buys most of his groceries and office supplies online. "You should see all the miniature pickled corn I've laid up for Y2K," he says. He starts every day at a site called Quickbrowse (quickbrowse.com). "My friend Marc Fest cooked this up in his garage. It combines everything I want to see, from newspapers to the message boards on stocks I follow, into a single long page that I can scroll up and down at will."

by homeowners. The cost of showcasing a house ranges from zero for a basic listing to $139 for a three-month premier package, which lets you post several pictures online and gives your listing the best placement. The home value tool at Yahoo Real Estate (realestate.yahoo.com) can be especially useful. Type in an address and you can check out the most recent selling price for that property. Note that not every house is listed. But it's a great gadget if you're pricing real estate or if you're just wondering how much your neighbor paid for the dump across the street.

Home mortgages. Shopping for a home loan online can save you money (many virtual brokers will waive the application fee). Or it can simply help you to track down the best rates, take that information to your local banker and close the loan the old-fashioned way. Start at E Loan (eloan.com), which has more than 70 mortgage partners and is licensed to do business in 45 states as either a broker or lender. In addition to its extensive network, E Loan offers an easy way to compare different products, apply for a loan and track its status. Although its network of lenders is smaller, I Own (iown.com) also reels in competitive rates and lets you lock them in online.

Initial public offerings (IPOs). Are you looking for an IPO site with comprehensive data and hype-free news stories? Go to IPO Central (ipocentral.com) for the scoop on postponed offerings, recent pricings and the first-day trading details of new issues. You can search for articles by a company's name or the date of its offering. The site's four-part beginner's guide also explains how an IPO actually works. Missed out on a hot IPO and want to pick up shares after the trading begins? Try IPO Edge (quote.com/ipo), part of the Quote.com supersite, which tracks aftermarket performance for every company that's gone public over the past 18 months. It rates each new issue on 36 criteria, including the quality of a firm's underwriter and buying habits of executives.

Insurance coverage. For life, home, car and even pet insurance, head to Insweb (insweb.com), the most complete insurance marketplace online. Request specific coverage and

Insweb attempts to offer guaranteed, instant quotes from multiple insurers. Its success rate varies, depending on where you live and what kind of insurance you're seeking. When quotes aren't available online, you can choose to receive no-obligation quotes from participating firms over the phone or in the mail. Even if you ultimately choose not to buy via Insweb, it's often an invaluable shopping tool. Quicken Insurance (quickeninsurance.com) is another good place to hunt for deals among home, life or car policies. If you're new to a category of insurance, you'll appreciate a feature of the online applications here that lets you click a button to learn why you are being asked a particular question and how your answer might affect your quote.

Investing directories. If there's an investing destination worth your time, you'll probably find it at Superstar Investor (superstarinvestor.com). It contains 7,500 links organized by topics (ranging from annual reports to technical analysis) and provides thumbnail reviews of leading sites in key categories. Other directories may rival Superstar in size. But many are cluttered with paid links, and none is so smartly organized. If you prefer to spend less time vetting sites, critics at Dow Jones Business Directory (businessdirectory.dowjones.com) offer up only those they consider best of breed, and they add new reviews every week. Although the directory is designed primarily as a business resource, it has sections spanning most personal finance topics.

Investment news. Need timely updates on the day's top news plus in-depth articles on specific industries or trends? Your best bets today are CBS Market Watch (marketwatch.com) and CNNfn (cnnfn.com). CNNfn, like MONEY, is owned by Time Warner and is particularly diligent about supplementing stories with links to company profiles or previous articles. Market Watch isn't as well organized, making it harder to navigate than CNNfn. But it does offer a broader collection of stock market and financial data. And it features lively commentary written by a stable of regular columnists.

Mutual fund advice and news. The must-have bookmark for every fund investor is Morningstar (morningstar.com). Access its massive database to compare funds' performances, holdings

Make the Most of Edgar's Disclosures

Obtaining a company's annual report or latest earnings release was a chore before the internet became widely accessible. You would have to call the investor relations department, then wait a week or so before your document arrived in the mail. Since 1996, however, the SEC has required that all publicly traded firms, as well as mutual funds, file financial disclosure documents online. Anyone with a modem can read them on the web or download them for free. Easy, right? Not quite.

Edgar is a bit of a klutz. Like most things government, the website that houses all those financial filings is user-unfriendly. It's called Edgar, or Electronic Data Gathering, Analysis & Retrieval (sec.gov/edgar). If you want to read up on a stock or fund, you'll have to make do with a limited search function that returns documents marred by jumbled formatting and unreadable tables, if it returns them at all.

Luckily, there are websites that clean up these filings and give you powerful tools to help find the information you're looking for. There are about a dozen sites in all; two thirds of them charge for access to their basic services (most of the free sites have for-pay bells and whistles too). The main difference between free and paid sites is their search functions. You can search the documents of one company at a time on free sites. Paid services allow you to call up filings of more than one stock.

Free Edgar is a big improvement. The best of the free sites is Free Edgar (freeedgar.com). It gives you access to company filings only minutes after they've been sent to the SEC. You'll pay for real-time access at other ostensibly free sites. Free Edgar also highlights the significant sections of each filing. So if you're examining, say, a company's annual report, you can jump from the balance sheet to a list of directors to an overview of the business with ease. You can even download tables into an Excel spreadsheet. Free Edgar allows you to set up a watchlist and will alert you by email when one of your companies files with the SEC.

Edgar Online is tops for seaches. The only subscription site you should consider is Edgar Online (edgar-online.com). It's a bit annoying that this service charges $10 a month yet restricts you to 25 real-time filings. After all, Free Edgar offers unlimited access gratis. But Edgar Online's search and watchlist capabilities are the best on the web, allowing you to combine multiple criteria such as type of filing, geographic location and industry. Say you want to see how the semiconductor stock you own stacks up against the competition. You can easily pull up all the quarterly reports filed by semiconductor companies over the past year without having to know all those companies by name. Or, if you're an investor who likes to follow the ventures of a certain entrepreneurial CEO, you could run a search to find out which boards he sits on and in which companies he's a top shareholder.

and historic returns. Cool extras include a portfolio X-ray, which lets you see the extent to which your funds hold some of the same stocks, and Q&As with fund managers and analysts. Fund Alarm (fundalarm.com) is not just the place to go for a gossipy inside look at the fund industry. It's also a great source of info on foundering funds. The site maintains a list of "3-Alarm" funds that have underperformed their benchmarks for the past 12 months, three years and five years.

Portfolio tracking and analysis. Virtually all financial sites feature portfolio trackers that let you follow a group of stocks. The top ones are easy to set up, include cost-basis comparisons (so you can see how much money you've made or lost), offer tools to help identify asset-allocation weaknesses and alert you to news that affects your holdings. CNBC (cnbc.com) has an outstanding tracker for active investors, with real-time quotes, alerts that notify you when a stock hits a price you specify and a customizable ticker tape that, like the cable network's, scrolls across the bottom of the screen. The site also has a bunch of flashy, graphical valuation tools that can help you decide whether to adjust any of your holdings. The tracker at Quicken (quicken.com) alerts you whenever an analyst upgrades or downgrades one of your stocks. More useful for mainstream investors is its portfolio analyzer, which can pinpoint diversification shortfalls, using easy-to-read pie charts.

Retirement planning. Retirement and Workplace Services, an area at American Express (americanexpress.com), offers a good general overview of various planning issues along with clever interactive features. You can, for example, calculate the impact that any habit (be it smoking or eating out) will have on your retirement savings. If you're a few years from retirement, head to the money section of Third Age (thirdage.com), a community site that's designed for "active older adults." Everything here is tailored for the over-50 set, from chats to news articles to links to other resources.

Stock charting services. The best online programs let you draw charts easily and compare many stocks on one page over multiple time periods. MSN Money Central (moneycentral.com) serves up informative charts that download in a jiffy and update on the fly. You can choose among 10 time periods or pick your own dates, and get high, low, close and volume stats for any date with a point of your cursor. Big Charts (bigcharts.com) is a close contender to MSN. And it's a top choice for Macintosh users because MSN's best charting functions work only on PCs. You can choose among several styles (such as bar, candlestick or fever line) and plenty of backgrounds. There's one minor drawback. You must hit a button to reload the page every time you make a change in your chart.

Stock message boards. For a relatively civilized stock chat environment, check out Raging Bull (ragingbull.com). The site is only loosely monitored, but the community polices itself fairly well. You can report bad posts with the click of a button, while the "ignore" button allows you to screen out posters you don't like. Silicon Investor (siliconinvestor.com) is the place to talk tech stocks. SI attracts a serious clientele, and many members post using their names rather than a handle. You have to pay $60 for the first six months to post messages. But you can read for free. Participants at the Motley Fool (fool.com) generally espouse a long-term, large-cap investing philosophy. They encourage newcomers to join in discussions, creating a more welcoming atmosphere than at the other board sites.

Stock quotes and research. Our hands-down favorite quote site is Yahoo Finance (finance.yahoo.com). It offers the best place for quick access to stock price, PE, volume and other fundamental information. Company profiles, news, charts, insider trades, analyst ratings and SEC filings are then just one more click away. MSN Money Central (moneycentral.com) serves up much of the same data in a format that's slightly less easy to use. It does, however, offer a few notable research extras, such as its "advisor fyi alerts," which supplement your quote with significant company developments, such as analyst recommendation changes, earnings filings dates and unusual trading volumes. Thomson Investors Network (thomsoninvest.net) is partly fee-based. But much of the best info is free. Examples are commentary from insider trading expert Bob Gabele; a weekly earnings newsletter from First Call;

and I-Watch, which tracks institutional trading activity. The site's Tip Sheets give quotes a new dimension. Enter a ticker and get a handy one-page overview of the company that includes charts, earnings estimates and tables comparing its key ratios to its competitors'. Quarterly and annual earnings reports filed with the SEC often disclose crucial corporate info not available anywhere else. 10K Wizard (10kwizard.com) is the best place to get them. Search here for filings by company name, ticker or any other keyword.

Stock screening tools. The Investment Finder section of MSN Money Central (moneycentral.com) is the most powerful free screening tool on the web. Using its Custom Search, you can choose among hundreds of criteria, from basics like market cap to arcana like short interest ratios, to find exactly the right stock for you. Offering a more manageable set of 33 criteria, the Stock Search section of Quicken (quicken.com) is better suited for people who want to perform basic searches quickly.

Tax planning. Use the tools provided by MSN Money Central (moneycentral.com) to estimate next year's taxes or to find out what deductions you might be missing. The site has sections devoted to topics like audits and property tax, with up-to-date information and tips, plus links to IRS publications and forms. To make sure the taxman doesn't eat up all of your market gains, go to Fairmark Press Tax Guide (fairmark.com). This site focuses specifically on investing taxes, offering advice to beginners struggling with their IRAs, active traders looking to minimize capital gains taxes and anyone in between.

Save With These Web-Only Banks

Now that internet connections are faster and consumers are more comfortable doing business by computer, even your local bank is probably offering some form of online banking. While checking your balance at your bank's website or paying bills electronically may be convenient, you're still stuck with the same mediocre savings rates, annoying fees and high minimum balances we've come to expect from traditional banks.

Enter branchless electronic banks. Many of today's best checking and savings deals come from the half dozen banks that operate solely online. Net banks can afford to pay high rates and charge low fees because their overhead costs are a fraction of traditional banks'. Telebank (telebankonline.com), Netbank (netbank.com) and Security First Network (sfnb.com) pioneered virtual banking in the mid-1990s. Newcomers Compubank (compubank.com), US Access Bank (usaccessbank.com) and First Internet Bank of Indiana (firstib.com) were launched in recent years. Although these online banks' assets, even combined, are no match for those of giants like Citibank and Wells Fargo, deposits at all six are federally insured. And their range of financial products, customer service and sites are on a par with what the established banks offer.

Does this mean you should give your corner bank the boot? That depends on what you want from a bank. Online ones have a drawback; no branches means no ATM networks. So you're apt to pay a surcharge of at least $1.50 every time you get cash. You'll have to make deposits electronically or by mail. Still, net banks are a great way to earn top savings rates and avoid fees. Here are the best choices for your different banking needs.

You don't keep much money in the bank. Traditional banks typically require a minimum balance averaging $440 for free checking and charge $6 a month if your account falls below that threshold. Wells Fargo, for instance, tacks on $9.50 a month if you deposit less than $1,000. Among the six online banks, Compubank, First Internet Bank of Indiana and US Access Bank offer free basic checking with no minimum. Netbank's basic checking account not only requires no minimum balance but also pays 3% interest.

You want to put your cash to work. Perhaps you keep enough in the bank to get free checking but hate seeing that money earn nothing. While the typical bank pays less than 1% on interest checking and requires you to have more than $2,000 on deposit to get that paltry rate, online banks pay from 2% to 6% on interest checking accounts with much lower balances.

You're a regular at the ATM. If you consider the ATM an extension of your wallet, you may want to keep an account at a local bank or skip branchless banking altogether. Or curb your ATM use by asking for cash back when you shop with your debit card. Another option is to make a point of using an ATM at one of the dwindling number of banks that don't charge non-customers. (You can visit ibaa.org to search for surcharge-free ATMs in your area.) Our favorite online bank for ATM users is Compubank. In addition to letting you search for free ATMs by state, it reimburses you for four ATM surcharges a month (up to $1.50 each). Telebank will do the same if you open your account via Yahoo. Of course, it's worth noting that if you keep $2,000 in your account and earn 3% interest, you can pay a $1.50 surcharge three times a month and still break even.

You want the highest savings rates. Web banks are ideal if you like keeping your checking account close to home but you're willing to send your savings anywhere to earn high rates (and get deposit insurance). Netbank recently paid 5.1% on its money-market account. That's more than twice the national average of 2.1%. And Netbank lets you open the account with just $100. As long as you don't write more than three checks or make more than five withdrawals a month, you'll pay no fees. One of the best web banks for buying certificates of deposit is Telebank, which recently paid 6.4% on a one-year CD, more than a full point above the 5.1% national average. Better yet, you can invest as little as $1,000.

You like personal service too. The term internet-only bank is something of a misnomer because all of the branchless banks let you do business over the phone. At Security First, you can reach a customer service rep by phone 24 hours a day, seven days a week. Phone hours at the others range from 12 to 18 hours a day, five to seven days a week.

You prefer paperless banking. Most banks offer electronic bill paying but at a cost of $4 to $10 a month. With the exception of First Internet Bank of Indiana, these online banks offer free bill paying. (Security First caps free transactions at 20 per month, which is plenty for most people.) Although the traditional banks' sites also make it easy to keep tabs on your accounts, the branchless banks do an exceptional job in this area. Most update account activity in real time rather than at the end of the day.

While many banks are staking out turf on the net, it's the online banks that are focused on making virtual banking better than the real thing. In a ranking of all internet banks by research firm Gomez Advisors, Security First Network ranked No. 1 overall. Compubank scored first for ease of use. All six online banks have easy-to-use demos. If you're impressed enough to go branchless, you can open an account without ever having to stand in line.

✍ Point and Click Financial Planners

You'd think that the internet would provide a bounty for people looking for professional financial guidance. Think again. "It's not easy," says Felicia Hsieh, an AT&T networking specialist from San Diego who abandoned her planner quest after several fruitless hours. Starting at Alta Vista's search engine, she was overwhelmed by thousands of mostly useless links to candidates. "I found upwards of a hundred planners. And I wanted a way to choose among them, but I couldn't. I might as well have gone to the Yellow Pages." Even worse, many of the planners' sites she checked out wanted more info from her than she was willing to give, while providing little of their own. "They wanted me to fill out huge questionnaires. You know, 'We'll get back to you,'" she says. "To me, that's like a cold call."

The process of finding a topnotch planner is never as simple a task as it would seem. But searching for one on the web needn't be the bust it was for Hsieh. Here's where to look and what to look out for.

Start with accrediting institutions. Literally anyone can anoint himself a financial planner, hang out a shingle and start accepting clients. No experience, education or good intentions are required. So start your search at one of the well-established organizations that attempt to professionalize and standardize this unregulated industry. That's what Carol Smith, a publishing company logistical coordinator from Monument, Colo. did when she and her husband needed help with their 401(k). "I spent an hour online and found someone local. Her credentials looked good, and once we sat down to talk, it was clear it was going to work."

The Institute of Certified Financial Planners offers membership to only those planners who have earned the C.F.P. designation. To become a C.F.P., a planner must graduate from a C.F.P. board-approved college, have three years of experience, pass a rigorous exam and have no criminal record. The ICFP's website (icfp.org) provides background information, including advice on how to select an adviser, and offers a bare-bones search function. Specify your city or zip code and the search engine spits out a list of C.F.P.s in your area. With 10,000 names in the organization's database, you'll probably find a conveniently located planner no matter where you live. If you reside in a big city, however, you'll find yourself staring at dozens of names with little information to go on beyond address and phone number. (About one in every 10 members has furnished a link with a more detailed profile.)

The International Association of Financial Planners (planning-paysoff.org) lists only 2,000 names on its site but offers more information about each one, ranging from planning philosophy to licenses and degrees. Members of the IAFP are not required to be C.F.P.s, though most are. The two groups are slated to merge this year into the Financial Planning Association, which will combine the two websites.

The National Association of Personal Financial Advisors (napfa.org), meanwhile, considers it a conflict of interest for planners to collect commissions on the products they recommend. Unlike the ICFP and the IAFP, which accept both commission-based and fee-only planners, NAPFA requires that all of its members work only for set fees. Unfortunately, its website lets you search only by state from a list of less than 700 names and provides little supplementary information about each. Still, if you agree with the organization's philosophy, searching here may get you what you need fast. If you're concerned about maintaining your privacy, note that NAPFA requires that you punch in your name and address rather than just your city or zip code to do a search. Unless you check a box requesting otherwise, NAPFA will pass your information along to members eager to stuff your mailbox with promotional information.

Beware of financial matchmakers. A couple of sites make the promising offer to match you with an adviser, computer-dating-style, based on the responses you give to questionnaires about your goals and investing habits. Don't bother, however, with Financialpro.com. It has so few planners participating that most searches there end with an error message rather than a list of names. And tread carefully at MSN Money Central's Advisor Finder (moneycentral.com). The site uses a database maintained by Dalbar, a Boston financial services research firm, of 2,500 advisers screened to ensure they have at least five years of experience, a clean regulatory record and 100 clients or more.

Don't confuse Dalbar with the Consumers Union, though. Unlike that organization, which doesn't accept any compensation from the companies whose products it evaluates, Dalbar requires planners to shell out big bucks to be included. The cost? Planners pay $750 a year for a listing at Advisor Finder and another $750 if they want to be evaluated to receive a so-called Dalbar rating. It's not exactly payola. Dalbar checks credentials and speaks with clients before it confers its rating. But a planner with a Dalbar rating is not necessarily better than one without.

Indeed, the cost of listing seems to favor planners from institutions with deep pockets. Test searches at the site, for example, returned lots of planners from American Express Financial Advisors. Most of the 500 planners with the premium Dalbar rating work for American Express. Now, American Express has a good reputation and employs many excellent planners. But it is easy to wonder how many outstanding smaller firms or self-employed advisers go unlisted simply because they are unwilling to pay the annual toll.

Your best search strategy. Rely most heavily on the professional organizations to assemble a list of planning candidates and then head to MSN Money Central's Advisor Finder as a quick check to see who else turns up. Before you log off to start interviewing the planners on your list in person, make a trip to the Certified Financial Planner Board of Standards website (cfpboard.org) and print their brochure, "Ten Questions to Ask When Choosing a Financial Planner." The questions range from general queries on services and fees to specifics about education, experience and disciplinary history. The list includes the phone numbers of a handful of organizations you should call. These include the C.F.P. itself and the National Association of Securities Dealers (since many bad brokers simply recast themselves as planners) to check up on an adviser's credentials and record. Take the brochure with you when you go on planner interviews. It's your money, so no question is too rude or nosy to ask. If a candidate is not comfortable giving you answers, then move to the next planner on the list.

✒ *Wield Your PC to Pick Funds*

Is a small-cap fund really a mid-capper in disguise? Are your overseas funds holding lots of risky emerging market shares? Has your fund manager built up a big cash cushion? Do your supposedly diversified funds own more technology stocks than the benchmark S&P 500? Determining whether your funds offer the mix you need to reach your goals is the most important part of managing your portfolio. Trouble is, your managers' latest moves don't make the TV news. Mailings from your fund companies are too infrequent, and their prose too impenetrable, to be of much help. And then there's the prospect of sitting down with 10 shareholder reports spread out in front of you, trying to add up your holdings.

Fortunately, there's a better way. Online, you can easily find everything you need to manage your fund portfolio. Using free or inexpensive websites, you can analyze your funds for stock and bond selection and performance; gather the latest news on your holdings; learn about your fund managers; and increase your general investing knowledge.

Take an x-ray of your funds' anatomy. Start with fund researcher Morningstar (morningstar.com), which features portfolio and performance data on most funds. Once you register, go to the Your Portfolio section and enter the names of your funds with the number of shares you own. Click on portfolio x-rays, and you'll get a picture of the portfolio you've created with your funds. First, click on stock sector. You'll see how your sector allocation compares with the S&P 500's. Go to world regions to see how your holdings break down geographically. Finally, click on stock style or bond style to get a breakdown of the size and style (growth or value) of your funds' stock portfolio or the maturity and quality of the bonds they hold.

Some of this information will be out of date because fund managers are required to report their holdings only twice a year. But Morningstar has full-time researchers who report on funds' buying and selling, and that updated information goes on the site. Besides, you're interested in the direction your manager is moving, not what he or she did on any one day. Other key data include how your portfolio breaks down by asset class; what you're paying in management fees and expenses; and how your funds are performing. Morningstar is also the best place to keep tabs on any developments that affect your fund. Simply click on the news section.

Search for funds that fit your profile. If you discover a gap in your portfolio, go to Quicken Fund Finder (quicken.com). There you can specify several criteria such as investment objective, expense ratio, fees and past performance. Want a mid-cap value fund with no sales load, an expense ratio of 2% or less, a minimum investment of $1,000 or less and a five-star overall ranking by Morningstar? Quicken spits out a list of prospects. You can then run the funds that you've picked back through Morningstar to see whether they really meet your needs. For insightful profiles of many fund managers, you should check out another site called Mutual Funds Interactive (brill.com). There you will find recent interviews of popular managers. Although manager profiles are MFI's bread and butter, the site also offers a complete buffet of fund information and statistics. Its Expert's Corner page gives links to dozens of articles on investing. And MFI's bulletin board, the Mutual Fund Community Newsgroup, is a great place to hash out ideas with other fund investors.

Ready for Mutual Funds 201? Log onto the Founders Group (founders.com). Hidden among the usual features of a free fund-company site (portfolio calculator, college planning tutor, promotional material) is a terrific library section with articles on topics ranging from tax laws to exchange rates. In the essays feature, Founders fund managers offer their thoughts on everything from the psychology of investing to the Asian contagion. Of course, you should also check out your own funds' websites to see whether your manager is profiled there.

✍ *How Major Internet Brokers Rate*

We set out to evaluate and rank the best online brokers for four different types of investors—mainstream investors, active traders, wealthy investors and beginners. We focused on the 15 largest firms that control an estimated 95% of online accounts. Our team of reporters tried to replicate a typical customer's online experience. We established accounts with all 15 brokers so we could buy and sell stocks, making five or more trades in each account. We explored all the nooks and crannies of each site.

In addition, we fired off email questions to each brokerage for two weeks and assessed the speed, accuracy and helpfulness of the responses. We followed a similar regimen with telephone help lines, placing at least five and as many as 25 calls (thanks to busy signals) to each broker. Our methodology also included a focus group of more than two dozen individual investors who regularly use online brokers. They gave us in-the-trenches insights into the customer's point of view, which we used to make sure we were testing the right things and judging the relative importance of each one.

How we ranked our winners. The first step in creating our rankings was to grade each broker on multiple factors in five basic areas. They are cost; customer service; ease of use; range of products, tools and research; and the responsiveness of the online system. Because the terms of our accounts varied, we couldn't precisely measure system speeds or trade execution quality. But we did compare overall site performance and noted such concrete feedback as electronic trade confirmations and real-time balance updates, as well as trading backups like automated and broker-assisted phone orders. We then combined and weighted the five categories in different ways, based on our account tests and focus group concerns, to come up with the best firms for each of our four user types. The table "How 15 Large Net Brokers Stack Up" on the next page shows how the firms rate in each category.

The table details how the biggest net brokers rated in five crucial categories we tested. The overall rankings reflect category weightings that are geared toward mainstream investors.

Company website (www.) *telephone (800)*	User friendly	Customer service	System response	Products and tools	Cost	Overall ranking
Charles Schwab schwab.com *435-4000*	◆◆◆◆◆	◆◆◆◆	◆◆◆◆	◆◆◆◆◆	◆◆	◆◆◆◆◆
National Discount Brokers ndb.com *888-3999*	◆◆◆◆	◆◆◗	◆◆◆◆◗	◆◆◆◆	◆◆◆◗	◆◆◆◆◆
DLJ Direct dljdirect.com *825-5723*	◆◆◆◗	◆◆◗	◆◆◆◗	◆◆◆◆◗	◆◆◆◗	◆◆◆◆◗
Suretrade suretrade.com *642-6900[1]*	◆◆◆	◆◆◆	◆◆◆	◆◆◆	◆◆◆◆◆	◆◆◆◆
Datek Online datek.com *463-2835[2]*	◆◆◆◆	◆◆◗	◆◆◆◗	◆◗	◆◆◆◆◆	◆◆◆◆
E Trade etrade.com *387-2331*	◆◆◆◆	◆◆◗	◆◗	◆◆◆◆◗	◆◆◆◗	◆◆◆◆
Fidelity fidelity.com *544-7272*	◆◆◆	◆◆◆◆◗	◆◆	◆◆◆◆	◆◆	◆◆◆◗
Quick & Reilly quickwaynet.com *435-4000*	◆◆◗	◆◆	◆◆◆◆	◆◆◗	◆◆◆◗	◆◆◆
Scottrade scottrade.com *619-7283*	◆◆◗	◆◗	◆◆◆◗	◆◆	◆◆◆◆◗	◆◆◆
Waterhouse Securities waterhouse.com *555-3875*	◆◗	◆◆◗	◆◆◆	◆◆◆◗	◆◆◆◆◗	◆◆◆
Discover Brokerage discoverbrokerage.com *347-2683*	◆◆	◆◆◆◗	◆◗	◆◆◆◗	◆◆◆◗	◆◆◆
A.B. Watley abwatley.com *229-2853[2]*	◆◗	◆◆◗	◆◆◗	◆◆	◆◆◆◆◗	◆◆◗
Ameritrade ameritrade.com *454-9272*	◆◆	◆◆	◆◆	◆◆◗	◆◆◆◆◗	◆◆◆◗
Web Street Securities webstreetsecurities.com *932-8723*	◆◆	◆◆◗	◆◗	◆◗	◆◆◆◆	◆◆
Brown & Co. brownco.com *822-2021*	◆◗	◆◗	◆◆	◆◗	◆◆◆◆◆	◆◆

Notes: [1]Area code 401. [2]Area code 888.

We've concluded that a site's ease of use is more important than its range of products for mainstream investors—defined as those with less than $50,000 in investable assets. That's because all 15 firms let customers trade virtually any NYSE, Amex or Nasdaq stock, and nearly all of them offer hundreds of mutual funds. Some online brokers offer more esoteric securities, such as junk bonds or options. While an expanded product menu is laudable, we deemed it less attractive to most investing tastes.

Why price is not a major factor. We decided to under-weight price when determining our overall winner for mainstream investors. Although price is still the primary marketing angle for many net brokers, the fact is that all online commissions are low when compared with full-service alternatives. What's more, most investors don't trade that often, whether online or off. A recent survey of more than 1,200 electronic brokerage customers found that on average they made just eight trades a year. That makes the difference between, say, Suretrade's cut-rate $10 charge for a typical limit order and Schwab's $30 tab just $160 per year. We rated costs by limit rather than market orders because we feel most trades should be done that way. For most investors, we suggest it's worth paying a few dollars more for a site that's easier to move through, increases the likelihood of error-free transactions and brings you top-flight research and help services via phone and email.

Top Brokers for Mainstream Investors

There's a good reason why Charles Schwab is the biggest net broker. Schwab just makes things easy for customers. This is clear even in the multiple options for opening an account. You can apply online, over the phone, via regular mail, or simply walk into a Schwab branch office. On-screen demos and help options make it simple to get familiar with Schwab's site. And the customer service operation never closes. When we placed 10 calls to Schwab's toll-free line over the course of two weeks, our average waiting time was eight minutes. That may not sound impressive. But it's much better than the average waiting time we recorded in our trials. Many brokers routinely kept us on hold for 15 minutes or more.

The Guru of Online Brokerages

When Donald Johnson posts, people take note. Johnson is the keeper of the web's definitive database of discount broker information. Collecting and editing data for a generically named site, Online Investment Services, with a nondescript address (sonic.net/donaldj) is just Johnson's hobby. But it is serious business for the 15,000 people who visit each month. Johnson, a retired 70-year-old history teacher, says the site is a "combination of two long-term interests—investing and research." He began the list in 1996 by responding to investors' postings on an online bulletin board about which brokerage to choose. "It was just a list of 20 phone numbers, and none of them had online trading," says the Santa Rosa, Calif. resident. As online trading began to take off, Johnson created a website to help investors sift through their proliferating choices.

Don's encyclopedia of internet trading. The all-text site still isn't much to look at. And it's easy to get disoriented among the many links. But Johnson's obsessively detailed ranking of discount brokerages is a true treasure trove of data. The main report lists brokers in order of basic commission. Click on any broker's name, however, and you'll get an exhaustive list of, among other details, commission rates by various lot sizes and order methods, margin rates, IRA fees, perks, excerpts of email commentary from investors and plenty of Johnson's own unvarnished opinions. He also keeps separate reports on the best brokers for day-traders, options investors and those interested in penny stocks. "Don has done a good job for the investor community," says Kul Gupta, a physician in Milwaukee with four brokerage accounts.

Brokers daren't disappoint this watchdog. Investors aren't the only ones influenced by Johnson's pastime. When discounter Brown & Co. planned to increase rates on phone orders, CEO George Brown says the company emailed an explanation to Johnson. "He seemed indignant when another company lowered its rates and then raised them three months later," recalls Brown. "We didn't want to make him mad at us." David Corcoran of Trading Direct, the internet division of York Securities, says his firm has gotten between 2,500 and 3,000 new accounts since October 1997 from people who come to the Trading Direct site via a link at Johnson's page.

Son Robert is sprucing up the site. Johnson's son Robert Mykland, an independent software developer, knew his father had his own website. But he had no idea how popular it was until he signed up for an account at Trading Direct. There in the Where Did You Hear About Us? section of the application was dad's site, listed among such options as CNBC, Yahoo and CBS Market Watch. Mykland wants to improve the site and add a search engine and chat areas. The two recently bought the domain name brokersreport.com and plan to have the new site up this year.

Schwab's online customer center clinched the broker's top spot in our rankings. Pages download cleanly, electronic trade confirmations keep you up to date and the status of each order and trade is clearly marked. While Schwab does not offer intra-day account updates, most buy-and-hold investors won't need such a feature. What about the criticism Schwab has received for system outages and slowdowns in the past year? The company is spending heavily to upgrade its capacity and technology with the goal of handling 200,000 simultaneous log-ons.

As for investment products and tools, you just name it and Schwab has it. The comprehensive free research that's available, including Schwab's own "report card" stock and fund snapshots, is broken down by industry, company and market index. At $30 a trade, Schwab charges one of the highest commissions among discounters. Schwab also levies some high extra fees, notably a $29 annual tariff on customers with less than $10,000 in their accounts who don't trade at least twice a year or add money to their balance. Nevertheless, for the vast majority of investors, Schwab is well worth the price.

National Discount Brokers was a close dark-horse contender for the top overall rating. The brokerage recently redesigned its site, making both cosmetic and system improvements. NDB earned a nearly perfect score in our rankings for system respon-siveness. Our page downloads were quick, account balances are updated instantly, and you can see how your current positions compare with those of the previous day. Navigation is better than ever now that NDB has installed a menu that links you directly to the site's most crucial spots.

What really stands out about NDB is its new trading area, by far the best of the group we tested. You're able to open the trading frame on any screen. So you can place an order at the same time you're researching a stock or checking your balance. And the site doesn't sacrifice research and tools for speed and functionality. It provides free access to The Street.com and Briefing.com, which otherwise require paid subscriptions. There was one negative. NDB's average hold time for phone customer service during our test was an aggravating 15 minutes. On the other hand, the firm's online help service was excellent and could easily head off routine questions.

DLJ Direct has plenty to recommend it. In addition to a site that's easy to use and loaded with the full range of products, DLJ Direct turned in the best download performances we experienced in our tests. And PC owners who use the broker's Market Speed software can move even faster. It is the only firm out of the 15 that does not charge extra for automated phone or broker-assisted trades. You pay a flat $20 for trades, online or off. The broker took the prize for the best portfolio tracking tools. Its offers instant account alerts on developments in your portfolio. Price and news alerts give you a heads up on companies you own as well as those you simply want to keep your eye on.

DLJ Direct's major shortcoming, according to our tests and some members of our focus group, was its customer service for investors with account balances that are below $100,000. Online help is awkward. And when we called the toll-free phone line, we waited an average of 20 minutes to get a live rep. Once we were left on hold for 45 minutes. A spokeswoman says our findings could have been due to market volatility. In any event, she notes, DLJ Direct is hiring personnel to bring hold times down.

❧ The Best Online Bets for Active Traders

Unlike mainstream investors, frequent traders make price their main consideration. The more trade-happy you are, the greater the impact of commission costs, margin costs and extra fees. But active traders have other concerns too. How fast screens load and how often balances are updated ranked high as priorities with the active traders in our focus group. Quick and easy site navigation also mattered, as did customer service geared to heavy traders and a range of sophisticated product offerings.

Following these criteria, Datek Online leads the pack. The brokerage offers cheap commissions ($10 for a 100 share limit order of a $50 stock) without sacrificing functionality. The site's features are unlimited free real-time quotes, real-time account updates and email trade confirmations. Datek's site also boasts helpful on-screen alerts. A pulldown tab at the top of the screen allows you to check price movements for any stock quickly and with little effort. Indeed, getting around Datek is a pleasant walk. After executing a trade, you are automatically kicked back to the order-entry screen so you can keep placing orders without missing a beat. And traders in a real hurry can choose Datek's express server, which bypasses the order-confirmation page process.

Suretrade has a good mix of features for an active online trader. In fact, the broker keeps a "top gun" team on its staff devoted to meeting the needs of these customers. If you trade options, Suretrade's options desk may tip the balance in its favor. Suretrade charges among the lowest commissions in the industry—$10 for a 100 share limit order at $50. It also boasts the lowest current margin rate among the 15 brokers surveyed, lately 6% for loans under $100,000. There is no minimum balance to open an account. Within its site, Suretrade keeps the screens simple to assure quick loading times. Trade confirmations are sent via email upon execution. Navigation through the trading area, however, is somewhat of a chore. Suretrade doesn't let you get quotes or look up a ticker symbol on the order-entry screen, unlike Datek and third-place finisher NDB.

NDB also scores high for active traders, with its unlimited real-time quotes, well-designed trading screen and intraday updates. Even though its $20 commission for a standard limit order is above others' fees, NDB allows you to make an unlimited number of same-day, same-side trades in a single stock for that $20. That is, you must be either buying or selling the stock, not flipping it. It's an ideal formula for certain traders, particularly those who want to average their way into or out of a position without incurring extra commissions.

✒ *Where Wealthy Investors Find Big Perks*

At the moment, $100,000 is the magic number to qualify for extra benefits. The more you place in your account, the more you'll receive from an online broker. Deep-pocketed investors should expect personal attention from a broker, lower margin rates, advance notice of IPOs and better chances of getting shares at the offer price. Throw in a cash management account that offers direct deposit, bill payment and free checking.

Schwab, the best net broker for mainstream investors, also earns the top spot for catering to the wealthy. Those with $100,000 or more in assets with Schwab (or those who make at least 12 commission stock or fund trades a year with at least $10,000 in their account) qualify for Schwab's three-tiered Signature Services. Some key advantages are a dedicated toll-free number for phone help and free online research, including company reports and daily market calls from Credit Suisse First Boston and Hambrecht & Quist. Those with $500,000 accounts also get access to a select team of brokers, a special handling desk for large block trades and options, and daily customized email alerts. Clients at the $1 million threshold receive such perks as access to company and mutual fund presentations via conference call. They're also eligible to buy shares of IPOs handled by CSFB and H&Q.

DLJ Direct is intent on pampering clients who have $100,000 or more in their accounts. It delivers free online research from Donaldson Lufkin & Jenrette, the broker's investment banking parent. You also get access to a small team of brokers and a shot at IPOs that are underwritten by DLJ. There is one limitation, however. Only clients with accounts of at least $1 million can use a dedicated hotline to bypass the broker's inadequate general customer service lines.

NDB makes the grade, offering a number of useful perks. And it has an egalitarian approach to handing them out. Special services are available to customers with large account balances, meaning that even if you don't meet the $100,000 mark, you could merit special treatment if you simply ask. Worthwhile features include a dedicated toll-free line to the preferred services desk, institutional money market rates, free asset management accounts and advance notice of IPOs. Lower margin rates are available to customers with $250,000 or more.

❧ Net Brokers That Cater to Newbies

If you're not trading online, you might feel you've missed the boat. That's hardly the case. Only 7% of households with brokerage accounts of any kind are currently investing online. That means some 26 million investor households, representing nearly

$5 trillion in assets, have yet to try out the web. That's why the net brokers are now spending hundreds of millions of dollars on advertising and promotions, offering monetary incentives and direct-mail applications to entice prospects to give them a try.

If you're among the newbies, you probably are a first-time investor or a full-service brokerage client wary about transferring a substantial balance. The first wave of online investors were typically young, web-hip people. Today's beginners tend to be more cautious. You may prefer to open an account with as little as $1,000 before taking a deeper plunge online. Of the 15 brokerages we surveyed, three stand out as excellent for beginners. These firms offer online primers to walk you through the early stages of trading. Their websites are easy to navigate. And they have low minimum deposits to open an account.

NDB scored the highest. While several firms in our survey let you open an account without depositing money, NDB goes a step further. It offers novices a free investing course via NDB University. Lessons range from "Setting Priorities" to "Investing in IPOs." A glossary covers everything from "abandonment option" to "zero-coupon bonds." And NDB's on-screen help desk provides email, phone, fax and regular mail contact information.

Suretrade is our second-place finisher for beginners. This brokerage gives its customers research and help information quickly. While 95% of communications with customers are via email, the firm responded to user requests by introducing a toll-free customer service number. E Trade also does well by beginners, with a highly navigable site and comprehensive research offerings. It delivers round-the-clock information via E Station, its on-screen customer service and educational area. E Trade regularly holds live investor question and answer sessions moderated by licensed reps.

✍ Are You Ready for Moonlight Trading?

While institutional investors have long had access to trading after the closing bell, online brokerages now are offering after-hours access to individuals. This brave new world is rife with risks, however. Small shareholders wanting to join in need to take extra precautions to protect themselves.

The main driver in the recent push to extend market hours has been the dramatic rise, especially over the past two years, of new online marketplaces commonly called ECNs (electronic communications networks). ECNs are designed as alternatives to the Nasdaq and Big Board exchanges, which use middlemen to complete trades. ECNs match buyers to sellers electronically. The automated ECNs offer fixed-fee pricing, faster order matching and later hours than the exchanges. As a result, they've quickly become a big hit with their institutional customers not just at night but during daytime hours as well. ECNs, in fact, now account for more than 30% of Nasdaq's daily trading volume.

Not content making waves in the institutional markets, ECNs are now partnering with retail brokerages to bring after-hours trading to the individual investor. Last summer, Datek Online extended customer trading until 5:15 p.m. using its affiliate, Island ECN. Then clients of Dreyfus and Discover Brokerage got the go-ahead to trade for two hours in the evening over Market XT, a new system created exclusively for individuals.

What began as a blip in cyberspace is fast becoming the Next Big Thing as the nation's biggest brokerages scramble to let their customers in on the action. Already, Datek and Island have extended their hours even further, from 8 a.m. to 8 p.m. E Trade inked a deal with Instinet to offer its clients the ability to trade until 6:30 p.m. And agreements between AOL and Wit Capital will open the floodgates further. Hustling to catch up, even the NYSE and Nasdaq have announced plans to stay open later beginning sometime this year.

Why is this happening? In part, it's simply a leveling of the playing field. Investors, who believe they've been empowered by online trading and the constant rush of news from cable television, want to be able to make (or lose) money on late-breaking earnings releases. In part, it's the natural result of investors' migration to the internet and an accommodation of habits they've already acquired. More than 5 million Americans already trade online, according to estimates from consulting firm Gomez Advisors. And the common wisdom in the industry holds that at least 20% of online trades are already entered off-hours, only to be executed when the markets reopen the next morning. Finally, there's Wall Street's belated realization that the whole nation does not run on eastern time. West Coast investors, for example, are stuck with a hardly ideal 6:30 a.m. to 1 p.m. trading day.

For now, however, investors are paying the price for this convenience. Trading outside standard market hours is volatile and difficult to navigate. Says Muriel Siebert, whose namesake brokerage was one of the first to allow customers to trade off-hours: "It's up to us to make sure that it doesn't become the wild West." That may be, but until the West is won, there are dangers you need to be aware of before entering the after-hours fray.

Beware of illiquid markets after the bell. Liquidity is a term that conveys how many buyers and sellers there are and thus how easy it is to complete a trade. During the day, buyers and sellers of most stocks find one another readily. But at night, order volume drops dramatically, creating all sorts of problems. Instinet, the largest after-hours network, processes 20 million shares a night vs. more than 170 million during the day. Some of the upstart systems transact just a few thousand shares. In the big-cap, big-name stocks like Microsoft and Dell, you may be able to trade without a hitch. After-hours trading on many systems is currently limited to Nasdaq stocks. So there's still significantly more activity in, say, Cisco after the bell than in Coke or other Big Board shares. Many other stocks, especially small-caps and mid-caps, may not trade at all. Those that do can experience wild price swings.

Fortunately, there is one important rule already in place to protect you against such price gyrations. No matter where you trade after hours, you must place limit orders. This means that rather than trading a stock at the prevailing market price (no matter how outrageous or unstable), you instead specify the highest price at which you will buy or the lowest price you will take to sell. In that way, if someone meets your price, great, you've got a deal. If not, then your order eventually expires.

Watch out for widening spreads. The spread is the gap between what sellers are asking and what buyers are offering for a particular stock. Another drawback to a market with relatively few buyers and sellers is that the spread tends to expand, making trading more expensive. The cost here is not a middleman taking his cut. It's the disadvantageous pricing that occurs in any market where there's little competition. If, for example, you want to buy a stock, and there are only a few people looking to sell, you may be forced to re-enter your limit order at successively higher prices than you preferred until you find a seller who will take your bid. Spreads should narrow as more investors come aboard. But for now they vary widely and unpredictably.

Get used to market fragmentation. When you trade after hours, you don't have access to all ECNs. In fact, you probably have access to only the one after-hours partner that your broker has chosen. That means if you are an E Trade customer and offer 100 shares of Intel after hours on Instinet, you won't be able to trade with a willing buyer on Island. At the same time, there can be big pricing disparities among the different systems. Shares of XYZ Corp. may be offered at $10 on Island but at $10.25 on Instinet and $9.88 on Market XT. And as more ECNs come online, fragmentation will only increase, causing even more scattered pricing. Without centralized pricing data, you're unlikely even to see these disparate quotes, let alone be able to choose among them.

Such inefficiencies have given some fast-moving traders with multiple accounts an arbitrage opportunity. That's one of the games that full-time trader Halbert Uy plays. "Sometimes you can buy from Instinet and sell to Island because they cannot trade with each other," says Uy. But the 27-year-old medical school dropout, who trades from multiple computers in his Washington, D.C. basement, is not a typical investor. He figures he buys and sells up to 20,000 shares a day, including a few thousand after hours.

Inefficiencies will begin to disappear, however. Eight electronic markets have announced a preliminary agreement to share their pricing information. But the details have not been finalized, and the agreement seemed to be an incomplete solution at best. Investors would be able to see more prices but, initially at least, not every investor would be able to act on every quote. The game will likely change for the better once many of the major ECNs begin sharing pricing and actual trading access and once the exchanges themselves put their own late-hours plans into effect. Although the after-hours arena is now a place primarily for active traders, a liquid and stable extended market is, in the long term, practically inevitable. And if brokerages can attract a few million more investors interested in placing trades on their own schedule rather than on Wall Street's, then the never-ending stock market may arrive more quickly than anyone expects.

Joining an Online Investment Club

Back when they were students at Vanderbilt University, Matt Burnstein and his class of 1993 buddies shot hoops together, sipped sangria at the Rio Bravo restaurant together and even studied together. These days, although their careers have scattered them across the country, the five graduates (and two of their siblings) play the stock market together through an online investment club. "We thought it would be fun," says Burnstein, a Nashville attorney. The three-year-old Mayfield Group, named after the club's junior and senior dorm, is "also a way to diversify without being killed by brokerage commissions."

Investment clubs have been around for decades. But the internet has forged new possibilities, letting far-flung members, some of whom never meet once, debate investment strategy as easily as they would in person. "The number of clubs using the internet is taking off at an explosive pace," says Mark Robertson, contributing editor at the National Association of Investors Corporation (NAIC), a nonprofit, investment club clearinghouse. Indeed, the growth of online groups has helped fuel a boom in investment clubs. The number of NAIC-affiliated clubs is now 37,000, triple the figure five years ago.

Many people sign up for online investment clubs because they don't have to show up at regular meetings. Others, like Burnstein, join as much to stay in touch with friends and family as to make money. Shannon Sennabaum, on the other hand, joined the Cross-Country online club because she is married to an Army man who's always moving around. "I never thought I could be in an investing club," she says. "But now I can just pack up and take the computer with me."

How to start a club of one's own. The first step is to decide whether the group will consist mostly of people you know, or strangers with whom you share a common investment philosophy, or a mix. If poring over balance sheets isn't your friends' idea of a good time, you can try to drum up interest among other investors at online forums like the investment club message board at the Motley Fool (boards.fool.com.) By law, all club members must be U.S. citizens. For practical purposes, the club should have no more than 25 members.

Next you'll have to figure out some way to communicate. Many clubs simply use group emails to conduct business. But Cross-Country recently set up a private website maintained by Yahoo under a deal that's available only to NAIC members (NAIC annual membership runs $40 per club plus $14 for each individual.) A Yahoo-NAIC site (clubs.yahoo.com/naic.html) offers portfolio tools, virtual meeting rooms and an events calendar. Non-NAIC members can set up a private club site with fewer amenities at Yahoo Clubs or at Excite Communities (excite.com/communities/directory).

Once you've recruited your crew, you then have to draw up a partnership agreement. This is a legal document stating that members will pull their own weight and pay their dues but can cash out whenever they want. Clubs must then submit the agreement to regulators in one of the states where a member resides. Registration costs and hassles vary widely, so shop around. The NAIC website (better-investing.org) offers a printable model agreement as well as contact information for 110 NAIC regional chapters that can help you with local filing procedures.

How to deal with the feds. Upon formation, a club must obtain a federal tax ID number by filing an SS-4 form. Once a year thereafter, clubs need to file 1065 (Schedule K-1) forms that tell the IRS not to tax the club as a separate entity. Instead, each individual is taxed only on personal gains. Martha Moore, a spokeswoman for the NAIC, says the tax man is the main reason investment clubs get into trouble because "a lot of clubs forget to file." There are other pitfalls to avoid. Don't advertise for new members, and don't let one or two people do all the work. You could run afoul of SEC rules concerning unregistered financial advisers.

You or the unfortunate soul who is elected treasurer each year may find accounting the toughest part of running an investing club. Remember the hoopla over the Beardstown Ladies?

Those midwestern grandmas accidentally fudged their 9% annual returns up to 23% because they mistakenly counted contributions as gains. To prevent this and other errors, the NAIC sells investment club accounting software worth the hefty $160 fee.

Club members emphasize the educational and social benefits, even online, of investing as a group. That's just as well, because most clubs are mediocre performers. A study by University of California at Davis finance professors Terrance Odean and Brad Barber showed that clubs averaged 14% annual returns between 1991 and 1996, compared with 18% for a value-weighted index of all listed stocks. But that should be a small consideration when deciding whether to take the group plunge because only a small percentage of your assets will likely be tied to the club. "It's important that a club function as your financial sideshow," says Burnstein, the Vanderbilt alum. "Your primary investment vehicle is too personal a choice to entrust to a committee."

✒ How to Survive Service Meltdowns

What if you try to place a trade and it doesn't work? That seems a reasonable fear, considering that many online brokers, including Ameritrade, E Trade and Schwab, have experienced at least one major online trading outage. The chances are slim that an online snafu will hurt you if you're making only a few trades a month. And there are steps you can take to ensure that you'll be able to trade when you want. These steps give you a better chance of persuading your broker to make you whole for any losses you incurred because the firm's trading system went down.

Have a contingency plan already in place. You should make sure your broker provides reliable alternative methods of conducting business, such as touch-tone phone trading, dependable live-broker call centers or even a network of branch offices. The advantage here goes to the more established firms like Schwab, Waterhouse and Fidelity. Note also that many brokers explicitly state in their account agreements that customers must have exhausted every available way to trade before the brokerage will consider compensating them for trading losses.

Scope out the customer service. If you're attracted to the rates, amenities or on-screen feel of a newer or less well-known company, make sure its customer support is up to snuff. Place a few calls to its service line and then ask a couple of test questions. Ask technical ones like "What version of Netscape Navigator or Microsoft Internet Explorer does your site require?" Ask trading ones such as "How do I get a stock registered in my name?" or "Is it possible to cancel a market order?" You can then evaluate how well the phone reps are trained to handle sophisticated questions. Likewise, call the trading line a few times over a week or so and see how long it takes to get to a live person. Inquire in advance if your broker will charge only the online commission rate if its network goes down, no matter how you place your trade. Waterhouse and E Trade, for example, both offer such price assurances. DLJ Direct always charges identical commissions, regardless of which way you trade.

Keep your trading options open. Consider opening a second account at a smaller, less popular discount firm. It might even be a broker that still, of all things, does most of its business over the phone. Then split a few of your largest positions between the two accounts. That way you'll still have access to a trade in all but the most cataclysmic market storms.

Minimize the damage in a service outage. If you get caught in a meltdown, you should start documenting what's happening. Make printouts of computer screens showing the trade you were attempting to make and screens showing that trading was still unavailable. Try to complete the trade over the phone. If that doesn't work, start calling the general customer service line right away. It's likely to take some time to get through. If the problem isn't immediately rectifiable, send an email describing the time and nature of your problem. Keep notes and print out the email. If you receive no response or are not satisfied with the response you do receive, write a letter addressed directly to the firm's compliance department. Outline your problem succinctly and include all your documentation. Describe exactly what would satisfy you, and request a written reply within two weeks.

Ways to Shop Smarter Online

Amid all the excitement about internet retailing, what you really want to know is where you can get a good deal. Is your credit-card number safe? And what else do you need to watch out for? For answers, we compiled the following tips and warnings to help make your online shopping a little cheaper, safer and faster.

Compare prices via shopping bots. The best way to find a good deal on the net is through price comparison websites called bots. These services quickly search dozens of retail sites for the lowest price on the product you want, rank the sites by price and link you to them. The best bots also display shipping charges, taxes, availability and contact information so that you don't have to visit dozens of slow-loading sites. There are many bots out there. But we'd head to Dealpilot.com for book, CD and video price comparisons, Shopper.com for computers and electronics and Mysimon.com for a wide variety of stuff, including sports equipment, tools and toys.

Shipping charges matter. One of the reasons for using bots is that they often disclose the shipping costs. In contrast, some retail sites force you to fill out lengthy forms with your address, phone number and email before they'll factor shipping costs into the price. How much of a price difference does shipping make? On a recent search for Apple's I Mac DV computer, we found that retailers Outpost.com and Macwarehouse.com were charging virtually the same price ($1,294 vs. $1,299). Yet Macwarehouse added $88.70 for shipping, while Outpost.com had free shipping. Note, however, that some sites with free shipping charge a "handling fee" that can wipe out any savings.

Don't expect immediate gratification. When you need it overnight, the web may not deliver. Say you want a book from Amazon.com. You can select overnight shipping. But Amazon, like many other retailers, promises to deliver an order overnight from the time the item is shipped. And many net retailers don't have all their items in stock. So you may pay more for overnight delivery and still not get your item for nearly a week. If you really need a last-minute present, try a gift certificate via email. A $25 one ordered from CD Now arrived within a few hours.

Be prepared for tricky return policies. Buying online is convenient. Returning items often isn't. Some virtual stores let you return merchandise to their physical counterparts (Gap, Tower Records, Toys R Us), but many won't (Barnes & Noble, Victoria's Secret, Comp USA). And, of course, many online retailers don't even have brick-and-mortar stores. That means if you don't like what you ordered, you'll probably have to pay for return shipping. If you need to return something that was sent to you erroneously, however, don't pay for postage. When we called one retailer about a book that hadn't been ordered, they quickly sent a prepaid package in which to return it. Before you buy, also find out how much time you have to return an item. Such return windows, especially for big-ticket items like computers, have been shrinking lately.

Defend against stealth sales taxes. Charging sales tax on net purchases is a hot topic these days. Some retailers do, some don't, and legislators around the country are wrestling with setting a national standard. For now, says Seema Williams, an analyst with Forrester Research, a rule of thumb is that retailers who don't charge sales tax usually won't let you return the product to their physical stores. Many retailers will charge sales tax only if you're ordering from the company's home state. And some bots, including Dealpilot, display the tax, if there is any, and factor it into the price.

Look for watchdog approval. Some online businesses, like regular ones, aren't great when it comes to customer service and ease of use. That's why it's helpful to look for logos of watchdog groups, indicating that a third party has evaluated the site. If you see a BBB Online seal, it means the retailer is a member of the Better Business Bureau, has been in business for at least a year and responds promptly to consumer complaints. If you want to know what other buyers think, go to Bizrate.com, where consumers rate retailers based on, among other things, rvice and delivery time.

Chapter 6

Realize Your Retirement Dream

*I*t's easy to feel overwhelmed when the subject turns to planning for your future So take a deep breath. Retirement is not a race. And there are many ways of getting there. In this chapter, we'll help you set personalized goals and devise strategies for achieving them.

Start by rounding up the accounts that are clearly labeled for use in retirement. These include your 401(k) or other employer-sponsored plan, IRA and any accounts for self-employed individuals, such as Keoghs. You should also add the stocks, bonds and mutual funds in accounts that aren't tax protected but that you've earmarked for retirement. Are you one of the estimated seven million employees who include stock options among their perks? If so, count these assets only if you intend to use the gains toward your retirement. Besides, you'll probably have to exercise the options long before then.

Financial planners note that many pre-retirees assume their homes will help fund that golf-club membership. It's not a bad plan. Changes in the tax law allow you to shelter from Uncle Sam as much as $500,000 in capital gains from the sale of your primary residence. But when it comes time to sell, few actually want to abandon their home sweet home. So don't count on the cash until you've got a "for sale" sign out front. An inheritance, insurance settlement or other one-time windfalls are difficult to predict and therefore unwise to rely on. And despite all the scary talk about the system going bankrupt, you'll probably get money from Social Security and perhaps from a traditional defined-benefit pension provided by your employer.

You've probably heard that fewer retirees are actually retiring these days. According to the Bureau of Labor Statistics, more than half of men age 62 still work, and 21% of men age 70 do. But it's less likely that you'll be occupying a corner office than tending gardenias at the local nursery—with a paycheck to match. So unless you're going to work as a consultant in your former field, think of any income you might earn in retirement as unexpected spare change.

✍ *Planning for the Lifestyle You Want*

The Bureau of Labor Statistics says that the more money you live on while you're employed, the more you're likely to spend when you retire. Bureau researchers found that retirees with household income of $70,000 or more spend as much in retirement as they did when they worked. Certain expenses, of course, are likely to drop. Carrying a mortgage or paying for your kids' college education should be behind you. But other costs creep up. When you spend more time at home, utility bills climb, as do maintenance costs for wear and tear. Once you're free of the office, you're likely to spend more than ever on entertainment, hobbies and travel. You'll probably find that health insurance, including basic Medicare and Medigap policies, costs more than you shelled out for your employer's group coverage. As you age, your unreimbursed medical costs are likely to soar. According to the National Association of Chain Drug Stores, the average American age 65 and older lays out about $930 annually on prescription medicines. About 10% of retirees spend more than $1,500 a year.

You may be able to slash current costs by moving from a house to an apartment, by sharing one car with a spouse rather than maintaining two or by canceling life insurance policies. That's because you no longer have to worry about covering your kids' education or providing an income for your spouse. But maybe you dream of spending your retirement traveling around the world. Some folks need less money after retiring; others need more. And financial advisers report that nearly all retirees need to revise their budgets 12 months after they quit work because the day-to-day reality is never quite what they had anticipated.

Striving to set realistic goals. You can't let all of life's uncertainties keep you from trying to establish a goal. Many billion dollar businesses run on projections that are little more than educated guesses. Your best bet in retirement planning is to start by figuring that you'll need at least 70% of the annual income you need today. As your salary rises over time, so will your ideal retirement income. Therefore, you'll want to repeat this exercise whenever your income takes a sizable jump. And don't overlook inflation. In 10 or 20 years your salary today won't have anything like the buying power it has now. While no one can be sure what the inflation rate will be, many planners build an annual rate of 3% into their calculations. Yes, the rate was higher in the 1970s and 1980s. But in the U.S. it has averaged just 2.6% a year since 1991 and 3% a year for the past 200 years.

What if you aspire to match your current lifestyle when you're no longer earning a salary? For such ambitious planning, you can set your goal between two target numbers. Let's call them the ideal and the minimum. The worksheet "Can You Retire at Today's Income?" on the right shows you how to calculate both figures. The ideal is the amount you'd need to be fairly sure that you won't run out of money no matter how long you live. To accomplish that impressive feat, your stake must be big enough that you consume no more than 4% of it annually. This assumes an annual inflation rate of 3% and an average 7% annual after-tax return. In effect, you'll be living off your interest, dividends and capital gains, leaving your original retirement stake intact. If, however, you opt gradually to draw down your initial retirement stash for your living expenses, you need a much smaller stake. This is the minimum number in the worksheet.

Let's say you want your money to last for 20 years, which is the average life expectancy at age 65. If you keep earning an after-tax return of 7% on your portfolio while you're tapping it, you can spend 9.4% of your initial stake every year. (Thus if you have $1 million at age 65, you could spend $94,000 a year for roughly the next 20 years.) The stake you'll need to produce your desired income under this scenario should be much easier to attain. And it still should provide a comfortable retirement until you're 86. You ideally should aim to end up somewhere between the 20-year minimum and the ideal.

Can You Retire at Today's Income?

Complete this worksheet to estimate how much money you likely would need to accumulate to match your current lifestyle when you're no longer earning a salary.

Take your current annual income. $ _____

Multiply it by the inflation factor from the box below, according to how many years you have left until retirement. This is the annual pretax income you will need in retirement. $ _____

Subtract your annual projected pension income. $ _____

Subtract your expected annual Social Security income. This is your desired annual retirement income. $ _____

Your ideal stake. Divide your desired retirement income by 0.04. This is the amount you would need to live on your investment earnings indefinitely without depleting your principal at all. $ _____

Your minimum stake. Divide your desired retirement income by 0.094. This is the amount you'll need if you plan to exhaust your retirement stake over the course of 20 years. $ _____

YEARS TO RETIREMENT	FACTOR				
1	1.03	11	1.38	21	1.86
2	1.06	12	1.43	22	1.92
3	1.09	13	1.47	23	1.97
4	1.13	14	1.51	24	2.03
5	1.16	15	1.56	25	2.09
6	1.19	16	1.60	26	2.16
7	1.23	17	1.65	27	2.22
8	1.27	18	1.70	28	2.29
9	1.30	19	1.75	29	2.36
10	1.34	20	1.81	30	2.43

Source: MONEY estimates.

Putting your money to work. When it comes to investing your retirement savings, you've often heard about the critical importance of asset allocation. That's the task of spreading your money among several different types of investments to increase your returns and reduce your risk. Asset allocation doesn't have to be complicated. It basically comes down to a question of owning stocks vs. bonds.

After the stupendous gains of the 1990s bull market, no one needs to tell you that stocks are the heart of any retirement portfolio. Only stocks can give you the growth you need to stay ahead of inflation and taxes. While they are subject to wild swings, most retirement investors have the time to ride out market downturns and reap the long-term rewards that stocks promise. As a rule of thumb, most people investing with retirement as a goal should consider having at least 60% in stocks. Aggressive investors should commit an even higher percentage. But don't let the dazzling returns of the long-running bull market blind you to the benefits of bonds. By providing steady income, they can help prop up your portfolio during stock market downturns. So even gung-ho retirement investors should consider keeping at least 10% of their money in bonds.

Index funds are ideal for retirement investing. These vehicles track benchmark stock and bond indexes, produce returns remarkably close to those markets and boast such key attractions as rock-bottom cost and management consistency. When you're dealing with a long-term horizon, even fractionally higher fees can end up taking a big bite out of your ultimate returns. In addition, mutual funds that mechanically follow an index veer little if at all in their investment strategies. You'll never have to fret that your hot manager has bolted for another firm or that the fund will change its stripes.

If you would rather choose actively managed funds, you'll still want to keep the bulk of your assets in broadly diversified funds that hold large- and mid-cap stocks. But refining your portfolio with funds that specialize in small stocks, real estate companies or foreign shares gives you a shot at higher returns with fewer ups and downs along the way. By mixing a variety of asset classes in your portfolio, you can further minimize the probability of making one large error.

Withdrawing your savings gracefully. So you've reached your goal and are ready to reap the rewards. You'll begin cashing in your investments instead of cashing a paycheck. But you still need a strategy. For example, if you tap your taxable accounts first, you know that you'll get the most bang for your invested buck if you can leave money to grow in your tax-deferred accounts. But if you leave your IRAs intact as long as possible and draw down your outside funds, you're also setting yourself up to maximize your estate. (For more on estate planning, turn to Chapter 7.) Here's why. When you leave your heirs tax-deferred accounts, they'll be able to take withdrawals based on their own life expectancies and possibly stretch out the deferral for another generation. There's one caveat, however. The rules governing inherited IRAs are devilishly complex. So be sure to consult a tax adviser.

Grabbing breaks on your company's stock. Here's a nifty way to cut your tax bill if you have a hefty chunk of your 401(k) plan invested in your company stock. If you keep the stock in your account, you'll pay regular income taxes on it as you withdraw money over time. But before you take your first distribution, you can elect to withdraw some or all of your stock separately. You'll be taxed not on the full value of the stock but only on the cost basis, which is what the shares were worth when they went into your account. Your employer can tell you the exact amount. When you sell the stock, you'll owe capital gains taxes totaling no more than 20% on your profits. Say you're in the 31% federal tax bracket, you have $90,000 in company stock in your 401(k) and your cost basis is $10,000. If you leave the stock in the plan and withdraw it over time, you'll pay 31% in taxes, or $27,900. But if you take the stock separately, you'll pay 31% on the $10,000 cost basis, or $3,100. If you then sell the stock, you'll owe 20% capital gains tax on the remaining $80,000, for a total bill of $19,100. Of course, once you take the stock you do not need to sell it right away. You can hold it as long as you like, paying capital gains taxes on your profit when you sell.

Sorting out Roth IRA options. When you leave a traditional IRA to your heirs, it will be included in their gross income and they'll owe tax on whatever amount is distributed to them. But if you want to leave them untaxed money, consider a Roth IRA. If you convert your regular IRA to a Roth, you'll have to pay income tax on the money you convert (it can be some or all of your IRA). But you never have to take mandatory withdrawals from a Roth. And when you or your heirs do pull the money out, it will be tax-free as long as the Roth has been open for five years. Meanwhile, you'll have access to that money. If you pass it on, your heirs will have the choice of emptying it out within five years of your death or maximizing the tax-free growth by withdrawing minimum payments based on their life expectancy. You will have already paid the tax on it for them. Now you can provide for your family after you're gone. For additional advice, see "When a Roth IRA Is Right for You" later in this chapter.

✒ It's Never Too Late to Save More

Many baby boomers will not glide into their retirement years unless they step up their savings pace. For one thing, they probably will receive a less generous stipend from Social Security than their parents' generation. When most baby boomers retire, there will be two workers paying into Social Security for every retiree, compared with a ratio of 3.2 to 1 in recent years. Unless Washington beefs up Social Security financing or reduces its benefits, the system will start running in the red around 2020. Dwindling Social Security payments are not the only financial hurdle confronting baby boomers. Increasing healthcare costs also seem certain because, sooner or later, Congress must hack away at the ballooning Medicare/Medicaid budget. Reduced corporate retirement benefits are likely too as businesses continue to slash costs to remain competitive.

Living well in retirement will be more difficult for women because they tend to live longer than do men. As a result, a woman needs a larger nest egg than a man to maintain the same level of investment income through retirement. At the same time, she may have a harder time accumulating what she needs. Women earn 30% less than men, on average, and they are also less likely to hold jobs that offer a company retirement plan.

Single and divorced women are most at risk because they are less likely to share a spouse's benefits and full Social Security income. One study found that the typical single woman in her thirties who lacks a pension will retire with only 20% of the income she needs.

Why there's no need to panic. Assume that a married couple in their early thirties earn around $65,000 annually, have a company pension and 401(k) plan and get steady wage hikes of 1.5 percentage points above inflation each year. If inflation averages 3% for the next 30 years, they would be earning the equivalent of $155,000 in today's dollars when they reach retirement at 67. Since their total outlays, including taxes, should be 20% to 30% lower in retirement, they could probably maintain their pre-retirement standard of living on an annual income equal to roughly $109,000 today. But look what happens if they save like most Americans in their income bracket, putting away only 5% of their pretax salary each year. They should figure on generating no more than $62,000 a year in income, including pension and Social Security. That would leave them some $47,000 a year shy of what they need.

What would it take to prevent such a shortfall? If the couple promptly triple their savings to a conscientious 15% of income and allocate roughly 85% of their investments to stocks, their annual retirement income would nearly double to $120,000. And by stashing more of their savings in tax-deferred accounts, such as 401(k)s and IRAs, the couple could get a full 100% increase in retirement income. The easiest way for most investors to try to accumulate such retirement riches is through mutual funds, which conveniently allow you to put away regular amounts of money.

Why you probably aren't saving enough. The exact amount that you decide to sock away depends on several factors, including your age, the generosity of your company's retirement benefits, the amount that you have already saved and your income goals. For a rough idea of your savings target, take time to complete the worksheets beginning on page 164 and page 166. On average, a man in his thirties should be setting aside a little over 10% of his salary. One who waits until his forties ought to aim for 15% or more. And women, who are blessed with longer life expectancies, may need to be even thriftier.

You can put away a lot more than you think. Start by scrutinizing your budget. Do you really need to eat out three nights a week? Or even twice? Can you forgo that luxury coupe for the less costly sedan? And what about basic, money-saving moves such as shopping at warehouse clubs or improving your home's energy efficiency? Many families can save 10% or more just by cutting back on unnecessary expenditures. Before you start locking away that newfound money, make certain that you have built up an emergency cash reserve that's equivalent to three to six months' worth of expenses. You should keep that money in a safe account such as a short-term certificate of deposit or money-market fund. Once you get your savings plan under way, keep it in the groove by signing up for an automatic investing plan. Such plans authorize your mutual fund company to transfer a fixed amount every month from your bank account to funds of your choice. Most fund groups offer these programs. And many of them will waive or reduce their initial investment minimum if you agree to make automatic contributions of as little as $50 a month.

❧ Learn From Today's Golden Agers

In a recent poll, we asked retirees key questions about their finances and what they wished they had done differently to prepare for the day they stopped working. We then distilled our findings into steps you can take now to profit from your elders' experience. For example, to support their lifestyles, the retirees require roughly 70% of their pre-retirement income. That was much more than many of them expected while they were employed. In fact, nearly two in five retirees said they're spending more than they thought they would.

Sure, you can expect to get the price break that most insurers offer to retirees on homeowners and auto policies. You can save on clothing costs because you will no longer have to buy business attire. But your entertainment outlays will typically double in retirement because you will have more time to travel and attend cultural events. You'll pay more for utilities and to maintain your residence because you'll be there more often. You also can expect your healthcare costs to increase as you get older.

Our poll hammers home the fact that you may have to budget for more people than just you and your spouse. More than a third of retirees with children and grandchildren told us that they are helping to support them financially. And of the 36% of retirees whose parents are living, 23% are giving them monetary assistance. Such generosity is laudable. But if you can't afford it, your first priority has to be taking care of yourself in retirement.

Start building your nest egg sooner. One of the biggest regrets of retirees we polled is that they didn't begin saving at a younger age. They typically waited until they turned 32 to sock away that first retirement dollar. Consider this example, however. Say you want to have $1 million by the time you're 65. Let's also say your investment money is going to grow by an average 9% a year. If you start at age 22, you'll have to put away $186,190 ($4,330 a year for 43 years) to make that million. If you wait until you're 32 to start, you'll have to shell out $291,850 ($8,844 for 33 years). The reason is compound interest. The 10-year head start means you'll already have $63,100 compounding for you by age 32, rather than having to start from scratch. Wait until you're 40 and your annual investment skyrockets to reach your $1 million goal.

Shield your savings from the taxman. The only acceptable excuse for not plowing the max into tax-deferred plans is if you need cash to build your emergency fund for daily living. And there's never a reason for not investing as much in your retirement account as your company will match, typically half of the first 6% or so of your salary that you contribute. Let's say you put $100 into a 401(k) and your company matches half of it dollar for dollar. Already you're up to $150. If that investment annually earns 10%, you'll turn your initial $100 investment into $165 in one year. Add in tax savings of, say, $35, and you've nearly doubled your money that year.

What if you don't have a pension or company retirement plan? Self-employed people can use SEPs (simplified employee pensions) that allow you to defer taxes on 13% of your net business income, up to $22,500. A business owner can set up a Keogh plan. The three types are defined-benefit, profit-sharing and money-purchase. You are allowed to contribute anywhere from 13% of net business income to as much as $120,000, depending on the type of Keogh you establish. Then there are IRAs. If you are covered by a pension at work, the income limits for deducting your contribution to a standard IRA will gradually rise over the next several years to $80,000 for couples by 2007 and $50,000 for singles by 2005.

If you earn more than that, consider the new Roth IRA. You can open a Roth IRA regardless of whether you have a pension plan. But your adjusted gross income can't top $95,000 if you're single or $150,000 if you're married. Note that you won't get a tax deduction for your contribution. Instead, you can make tax-free withdrawals provided you're at least 59.5 and your money has been in the account at least five years.

Bet on stocks over the long haul. Forty percent of retirees wish that they had invested more heavily in stocks. If you're like the people we surveyed, you risk feeling the same remorse when you retire. If you won't tap your portfolio for 10 years or more, you ought to keep 60% or more of your holdings in stocks. Since 1926 stocks have returned an average of nearly 11% annually, compared with 5.6% for long-term corporate bonds. True, stocks are likely to deliver a bumpy ride along with those higher average returns. Thus the percentage of your retirement portfolio that you devote to stocks should depend on your ability to tolerate the roller-coaster movements of the market. Are you at least 20 years from retirement? Then consider putting 60% to 100% of your assets in stocks because you will have many years to recover from any market swoons. Even if you have recently retired, you should keep about 40% in stocks. That's because you will need inflation-whipping growth to make your money last for the next 20 or more years.

Make your health a top priority. Your goal is to avoid having your retirement blighted physically and financially by illness. You should take preventive measures such as getting plenty of exercise, quitting smoking and following dietary guidelines for a healthy heart. Make sure your health insurance will protect you until you qualify for Medicare at 65 and will then pay for the bulk of any medical needs that the government program won't cover. If your company's insurance coverage will end when you retire, sign up for a so-called COBRA before you leave your job. COBRA, named after the federal law known as the Consolidated Omnibus Budget Reconciliation Act, requires your company to continue your health benefits for 18 months. Ask your employee benefits office for details.

In addition, half of women and a third of men will spend at least some time in nursing homes that typically charge $41,000 a year. The average stay lasts more than two years. So you might consider insurance coverage for long-term care if your family's medical history indicates that you run a high risk of a long, debilitating illness. Note that premiums can be prohibitively expensive, especially as you get older. A policy that provides a $100 daily nursing home benefit and a $50 daily home healthcare benefit could cost a 55-year-old around $1,500 a year. Buy the policy at 68, and your annual premium will jump to more than $3,600.

Scrutinize your pension options. Nearly 25% of retirees said they wished they had spent more time analyzing their pension plans before leaving work. A fumbling decision about your pension distribution can be a particularly costly error. For example, many newly retired people opt to take their pensions as annuities even though employers seldom pay more than 6% a year on money left in their care. That's why financial pros usually advise clients to take their pensions as lump sums. You can roll over your payout into an IRA, invest it in stocks and bonds and figure on your money growing tax deferred much faster than 6% annually.

Prepare a contingency plan. It's a good idea to give yourself a few years of lead time before you quit working. You may find it difficult to drop your current spending and working habits abruptly. So try to live on your expected retirement income at least three years before you leave your job. Also use these years to test your retirement plans. If you think you want to do volunteer work three times a week in retirement, try doing it once a week now to see if you really like it. If you want to work part time, begin setting up contacts as soon as possible. If you start now you can reach retirement with all the money you need. Let's say you are 40 with a household income of around $84,000. Let's also say that you want to retire on an ambitious, inflation-adjusted 80% of your current income. You put 10% of your salary every year into a 401(k) with a typical 50% in matching funds from your employer and earn 10% on your money (a little below the stock market's average over time). You will hit 65 with $1.7 million in your account even if you are starting from zero today. All right, by the time today's 40-year-olds retire, inflation will have made a million dollars a less awesome figure than it is now. Even so, it will never be chump change.

You will inevitably face obstacles on the way to accumulating such a sum. If you are just starting out, you may find that your beginner's salary leaves you barely enough to cope with student loans, let alone max out on your 401(k) contribution. If you're married with kids, you will have to find some way to finesse college expenses that loom just one step ahead of your own retirement bills. But the fact is, at every stage of your life, you can control your retirement prospects in terms of how much you save and when you save it; how aggressively you invest; and when you plan to retire.

✍ Run the Numbers on Your Retirement

You know you must save regularly and invest wisely to have enough money for a worry-free retirement, particularly an early one. But how much is enough? Well, let's assume that you will have a pension and Social Security. But those checks most likely will replace less than half of your pre-retirement income. For investments to make up the difference of, say, another $20,000 a year that increases annually with inflation, you would need to retire with a $310,000 portfolio earning 8% pretax. Instead of panicking about falling short or having to catch up, think instead about how your life will change when you leave work and then estimate the cost of that lifestyle.

The traditional rule of thumb that retirees need 70% to 80% of their pre-retirement income may not hold true for you. You might consider it a hardship to have to make do with less just when you have time to enjoy the fruits of years of work and savings. Some frugal people may find that they need no more than 50% of their pre-retirement income. Healthcare aside, Americans over 65 spend 25% to 40% less than younger people do on food, clothing, housing, transportation and other everyday expenses. Whether you aim for 50% or 120% of your pre-retirement income depends on when you plan to stop working and how well you hope to live. Do you envision an early retirement of two homes and country clubs? Or quieter years making do with one car and fewer dinners out? Moreover, with retirement possibly lasting as long as 30 years, don't forget that your living costs will diminish as you age. Expenses tend to be highest for early retirees who travel extensively. Older ones typically spend less on such discretionary items as well as necessities.

To calculate your tab for retirement, start with the worksheet "Estimate Your Future Costs Now" on page 164. Then let the worksheet titled "How Much You Must Sock Away" on page 166 guide you to an annual savings goal based on your anticipated retirement lifestyle, your current savings and your expected pension and Social Security benefit. For example, housing (line 1 in the worksheet "Estimate Your Future Costs Now") will continue to be your biggest expense even if you don't have a mortgage to pay now. Figure that your property taxes, homeowners insurance, utilities and upkeep will cost you no less than they do now unless you move to a smaller house or to a lower-cost area.

Your food costs (line 3) may decline 25% or so in retirement if you eat out less (obviously you won't buy lunch at work anymore). Transportation costs (line 4) will drop because you will no longer incur commuting expenses. And you may find that you don't need to replace a car so often or even keep two, especially later on. Unless your job never required pricey suits or dresses, you can expect to shave 20% to 35% off clothing costs (line 2). How much travel and entertainment costs (line 12) may change depends on your tastes. If early retirement means that you'll be going on more long trips, be sure to budget for them, since travel is often such retirees' single biggest new expense.

Chances are (you hope) you will have finished paying for your children's education by the time you retire. But think about

Estimate Your Future Costs Now

Line 1: If you pay off your mortgage and take care of all necessary maintenance problems before you retire, housing costs should drop by as much as 25% to 30%. Count on even more shrinkage if you sell your house and buy a smaller one. Condominium owners and renters should factor in the expense of periodic maintenance and rent increases. And anyone who plans to spend more time at home should anticipate paying higher utilities charges.

Line 2: Financial planners estimate that if you are moving from business suits to jeans, you can expect to reduce clothing expenses by 20% to 35%.

Line 4: Scratch commuting costs. Other transportation expenses will increase if you intend to be very active. Planners recommend that two-car couples keep both autos during retirement, especially if both are fairly active.

Line 6: Most people keep giving the same amounts to charitable, political and educational institutions, as well as to family members outside the immediate household. But the overall figure drops, usually by the amount you used to give at the office.

Line 7: If your kids will be grown by the time you retire, you can eliminate education expenses, unless you plan to help pay your grandchildren's college bills. And if you intend to return to school yourself, check into reduced tuition costs for senior citizens.

Line 8: There will be little change in your payout for property, personal liability and automobile insurance. But retirees can generally reduce their life insurance coverage by at least 50% or, if their spouses are fully provided for under their pension plan, eliminate the policy altogether.

Line 9: If you are currently covered by a company health plan, expect medical and dental costs to spurt by about 50% because of increased illnesses combined with reduced insurance coverage. Medicare pays part of doctors' fees and hospital bills. Check your company's coverage for retirees.

Line 10: Most retirement experts say you should plan to be debt-free by the time you retire, thereby eliminating loan repayment expenses.

Line 12: How much you continue to spend for entertainment depends on how active you are. Expect such expenditures to rise an average of about 20% during your retirement.

Line 13: You probably should be prepared to budget for higher veterinary bills if you will have an aging dog, cat or other pet.

Line 14: While your contributions to pension plans cease at retirement, many financial planners encourage clients to continue setting aside about 10% of their income as a hedge against inflation.

Line 15: If you don't work, it's farewell to Social Security (FICA) taxes. Also check laws in your state because some don't tax income from retirement plans. The conventional wisdom that you will be in a lower tax bracket after retirement is no longer true for high earners. You will be taxed on up to 50% of your Social Security benefits if the total of your adjusted gross income, nontaxable interest, and half your Social Security benefits exceeds $25,000 ($32,000 if you are married). If that total is over $34,000 ($44,000 for married couples), you'll owe tax on up to 85% of Social Security benefits.

Line 16: With more adult kids expecting some form of financial help from Mom and Dad and Americans' increasing longevity, you could be contributing to the down payment on a child's first house while paying for a parent's nursing home.

The figure for total current expenditures should equal approximately 100% of your current before-tax income. By dividing your total expenditures at retirement by your current gross income, you will arrive at the percentage of your current income that you will need to live comfortably in retirement.

EXPENDITURES	AT RETIREMENT	CURRENT YEAR
1. Housing. Rent or mortgage payments, property taxes, utilities (gas, oil, electricity and water), telephone, home furnishings, household services, maintenance, improvements		
2. Clothing. Purchases and cleaning		
3. Food. (including tobacco and alcohol)		
4. Transportation. Car repair and maintenance, installment payments, gas, commuting costs, other		
5. Gifts.		
6. Contributions.		
7. Education.		
8. Insurance. Life, medical, auto, property, liability		
9. Medical and dental care. Premiums, deductible and out-of-pocket costs		
10. Loan repayment costs.		
11. Personal care. Grooming, health club, other		
12. Entertainment. Vacations, dining out, movies, plays, concerts, sports events, cable TV, videocassettes, entertaining, sports, hobbies, other		
13. Pet expenses.		
14. Investments and retirement savings. Contribution to company plans, IRAs, Keoghs, SEPs and other investments		
15. Taxes. Federal, FICA, state, local		
16. Support of relatives.		
Total Expenditures. (add lines 1 through 16)		
Total Current Expenditures Divided by Current Gross Income.		
Total Expenditures at Retirement Divided by Current Gross Income.		

How Much You Must Sock Away

The worksheet at right will tell you how much you need to start saving now to hold on to your standard of living in retirement. The multipliers that are used in lines 7, 9 and 11 allow for inflation by assuming that your investments will grow at three percentage points over the inflation rate, before and after retirement. This keeps all of the figures in today's dollars.

  Line 3: You and your spouse can easily keep tabs on what you have coming to you from Social Security. Just call Social Security (800-772-1213) and ask for a copy of its Personal Earnings and Benefit Estimate Statement (PEBES) request form. Four to six weeks after submitting it to the agency, you should receive a statement that notes your annual earnings to date and estimates your monthly Social Security benefit at retirement. You can start receiving Social Security at 62. If you do, however, your benefit will be permanently reduced. The reduction's size depends on how close you are to your full retirement when you start collecting checks. The longer you postpone filing for benefits after age 65, the bigger your check will be.

  Line 4: Your company benefits department may be able to estimate your pension. Make sure the estimate assumes that you continue working until your retirement age at your current salary. That will understate your likely eventual payout but will keep the figure in today's dollars.

  Line 7: The multipliers in column A incorporate the cautious assumption that men will live to 90 and women to 94—longer than 85% of them do now. Single men should use the multiplier under "men." Women and married couples should use the one under "women," since wives usually outlive their husbands.

  Line 8: Personal retirement portfolio includes any investments earmarked for retirement, aside from an IRA or Keogh. For your employer-sponsored savings plans, check the most recent statement from your 401(k), profit-sharing, thrift or stock ownership plan and total your vested balance in each account.

  Line 12: You should consult the annual statement from these plans to find and total the amount that your company contributed on your behalf to each of the plans last year. Then enter the total.

AGE AT WHICH YOU EXPECT TO RETIRE	MULTIPLIER A	
	MEN	WOMEN
55	22.1	23.5
56	21.8	23.2
57	21.4	22.8
58	21.0	22.5
59	20.6	22.1
60	20.2	21.8
61	19.8	21.4
62	19.3	21.0
63	18.9	20.6
64	18.4	20.2
65	17.9	19.8
66	17.4	19.3
67	16.9	18.9

TIME UNTIL YOU EXPECT TO RETIRE	MULTIPLIER B	MULTIPLIER C
1 year	1.03	1.000
3 years	1.09	.324
5 years	1.16	.188
7 years	1.23	.131
9 years	1.30	.098
11 years	1.38	.078
13 years	1.47	.064
15 years	1.56	.054
20 years	1.81	.037

1. Current gross income _____

2. Annual income needed in retirement, in today's dollars
(70% of line 1) _____

3. Annual Social Security retirement benefits _____

4. Annual pension benefits _____

5. Guaranteed annual retirement income
(line 3 plus line 4) _____

6. Additional retirement income needed
(line 2 minus line 5) _____

7. Capital required to provide additional retirement income
(line 6 times multiplier from column A at left) _____

8. Amount you have saved already

_____ + _____ + _____ = _____
    personal   IRA/Keogh   employer-   total savings
    retirement   sponsored
    portfolio   savings plans

9. What your current investments will have grown to by
the time you retire
(total from line 8 times multiplier from column B at left) _____

10. Additional retirement capital required
(line 7 minus line 9) _____

11. Total annual savings still needed
(line 10 times multiplier, column C at left) _____

12. Annual employer contributions to your company savings plans _____

13. Amount you need to set aside each year
(line 11 minus line 12) _____

whether you want to take courses yourself (line 7). You may also want to help your grown children buy a home or pay for their children's schooling. Members of the so-called sandwich generation may have to budget for care of aging parents (line 16). As for loan payments (line 10), you should strive to reduce credit-card balances and other debt while you are still working.

Life insurance costs (line 8) usually go down or, in the case of disability insurance, disappear in retirement, since you will no longer have earnings from work to protect. Your income from investments, including those in retirement plans, doesn't need to be safeguarded by life insurance. Nor does your pension plan because federal law requires that a surviving spouse be paid a reduced benefit—unless he or she has formally waived it. On the other hand, you may decide that you need life insurance to provide liquidity in your estate or supplement a small pension for a surviving spouse.

Your biggest savings on taxes (line 15), assuming that you don't opt to work in retirement, will be the Social Security and Medicare tax on wages. In addition, some states exempt some income from Social Security benefits and pensions from taxes. Trying to predict medical expenses (line 9) is tough because you don't know what health problems you may face. For purposes of the worksheet, assume that healthcare costs could be higher. In addition, early retirees may face higher medical costs until they qualify for Medicare at 65 if they have to buy their own insurance. You also should figure on your health costs staying high after 65 because of higher out-of-pocket medical expenses and insurance premiums.

Now go to the worksheet "How Much You Must Sock Away" to help you determine the amount you should save every year until you finally stop working. As the line-by-line instructions specify, you'll need estimates of your future Social Security benefit and your company pension. If you're getting close to retirement, your firm's benefits department may be willing to project a pension benefit that has been based on your planned retirement age. Such a projection typically will be more accurate than one that's based on your current years of service with the firm.

Project your future Social Security check by reviewing your Personal Earnings and Benefit Estimate Statement. You can get an application form at your local Social Security office, by calling 800-772-1213 or visiting the agency's website (ssa.gov). About five weeks after submitting the form, you'll receive a statement showing the earnings that Social Security has on file for each year you worked and a projection of your benefit. Alas, you'll likely find that your pension and Social Security won't equal your expected retirement living costs.

✒ *Make the Most of Social Security*

If you've been following the debate in Washington over how to keep Social Security from eventually going broke, you may be worried that your benefits will be a pittance or that you won't get anything at all. Relax. The politicians can't afford to let America's most popular entitlement program wither or die. After all, 30 million people receive Social Security retirement benefits today, and most of them vote. While the pols argue over ways to prevent the program from slipping into the red, it's wise to do whatever you can to get the most out of Social Security.

If you're employed, you pay half of the 12.4% Social Security payroll tax on earnings up to $72,600. Your employer pays the other half. Self-employed people pay the whole amount. What can you expect at retirement? To qualify for a check, you must earn income in at least 10 years and make a minimum amount that is set by law each year. The biggest possible payout now is $1,373 a month for someone who starts collecting benefits this year at age 65. To get it, you must work at least part time for 35 years and earn the maximum amount that is taxed for Social Security purposes in each of those years. If you work for more than 35 years, the Social Security Administration will replace your lowest earning years with higher earning years in the bene-fits calculation. With those basics in mind, consider the following moves to increase your retirement benefit.

Increase your future benefit by moonlighting. If your day job doesn't pay you at least as much as the maximum amount that's taxed for Social Security, developing a profitable sideline could dramatically increase your future benefit. The further you are from earning the max, the greater the effect any additional earnings will have on your ultimate payout.

Plan career hiatuses carefully. When you're deciding how much time to take off to care for a newborn child or an ailing parent, your Social Security benefit is probably not uppermost in your mind. But it's worth considering. That's because years in which you earn nothing can count against you when your benefit is calculated. If you must leave your full-time job, try to work part time to earn money that will count toward your retirement benefit.

Protect your rights in divorce. You're entitled to Social Security checks based on your ex-spouse's earnings if you meet the following tests. One half of your ex-spouse's benefit (at age 65) is larger than the benefit you would receive based on your own work history; you were married for at least 10 years; you've been divorced for at least two years; and you are not married to someone else at the time you start to get the benefit. You can begin receiving checks as soon as both you and your ex are 62 even if neither of you is retired. Your ex is not involved in the filing process. If you remarry after you start to collect, you lose the ex-spousal benefit. For more on the fallout of divorce, see "How Divorce Can Derail Your Plan" later in this chapter.

Consider starting one spouse early. If you earn less than your spouse, begin collecting your Social Security at 62. In general, if you and your spouse have both been employed, the lower earning spouse is entitled to either a benefit based on his or her own work history or one half of his or her spouse's benefit at full retirement age, whichever is larger. The catch is that the lower earner, usually the wife, cannot collect the spousal benefit until the higher earner starts taking his. Note that she can apply for her own benefit as early as 62. Then, when the husband files for his benefit, presumably at 65, the wife's check will automatically be bumped up. In the meantime, however, she will have pocketed her own benefit based on her work record.

Collect benefits for children. When you start receiving Social Security, you qualify for an additional amount if you have a child under 18, or under 19 and still in high school full time. The youngster usually must be your biological or adopted child, and you must be able to claim him or her as a dependent on your tax return. The child may also be a grandchild who lives with you. The additional amount can be 50% of your benefit if you have one qualifying child and as much as 88% for two or more.

Delay can pay until age 70. The longer that you postpone filing for benefits after age 65, the bigger your check will be. That's because for each year you delay, your benefit will increase 5% to 8%, depending on your year of birth. At age 70, the increases stop. You can start receiving Social Security at 62. If you do, however, your benefit will be permanently reduced. The reduction's size depends on how close you are to your full retirement when you start collecting checks. One important consideration is that, unlike private pensions, Social Security is regularly adjusted for inflation. As you age and the purchasing power of your other retirement income shrinks, you may be glad you waited for the full benefit.

Be alert to bureaucratic bungles. You should strive to track down errors in your Social Security records by thoroughly reviewing your Personal Earnings and Benefit Estimate Statement. You can get an application form by calling 800-772-1213 (or going online at ssa.gov.) You will receive a statement showing the earnings that Social Security has on file for each year you worked and a projection of your benefit. If you find a mistake, such as an error in your earnings record, report it to the agency. It will require proof of the correct information, such as a tax return. If you don't have documentation, give Social Security your employer's name, and the agency will try to correct the error using data from its own records. Note that variations on a name can cause havoc in Social Security records. Did you ever use Bill instead of William on payroll forms? Did you change your name when you married, but neglect to inform Social Security? Make sure that the name that appears on your employment records, such as W-2 forms, is identical to that on your Social Security card.

Don't be too coy about your true age. Okay, so you've lied about your age. People do it all the time. But your little secret can cost you some big bucks when you're ready to retire. So it's generally best to sacrifice personal vanity and tell the truth about your age to Social Security and to your employer. If your boss thinks you're a springier chicken than you really are, you can still tell your benefits counselor the truth. He or she is professionally bound to keep your age confidential. And you could retire with a larger nest egg.

✑ Take the Pulse of Your Pension

Each year hundreds of companies get into financial trouble and default on their pension plans, effectively stranding both their retirees and workers who are anticipating regular pension checks at retirement. The victims typically turn to the federal PBGC (Pension Benefit Guaranty Corporation). This government insurance agency gets its money from the terminated plans' assets and from premiums paid by most companies that provide employees with traditional defined-benefit pensions. For many white-collar retirees, however, the PBGC replaces only part of the pension that was once promised by their employers. With payouts that are capped by law, the agency lately paid a maximum benefit of around $3,050 a month.

Even if your company's program isn't one of the weaklings, it may not be flush enough to keep paying benefits throughout your retirement. Whether you're retired or still working, it's crucial to determine the odds of your pension lasting the rest of your life. If your pension looks shaky, you can at least get an early start on boosting your savings to ensure that your retirement is comfortable. Here's how to take the pulse of your pension's health.

Within 90 days of becoming eligible for a pension, you automatically should receive a booklet summarizing how it operates. For specific information, however, you must ask your employee benefits office for a copy of Form 5500, which the company files each year with the U.S. Department of Labor. If you prefer, you can request the document from the department. Just send your employer's identification number (on last year's W-2) and the plan number (in the summary booklet) to the Public Disclosure Facility, Pension and Welfare Benefits Adm., U.S. Department of

Labor, 200 Constitution Avenue N.W., Washington, D.C. 20210 (phone 202-219-8771). When you receive the Form 5500, you should pay attention to the actuary's report in the back. If the actuary expresses reservations about the plan's financial health, you have good reason to worry. Even if your plan is sound today, you can't be sure that it will be healthy in the future. So obtain Form 5500 every few years to check the actuary's report.

Most companies fund their pension obligations appropriately, of course. If they don't and the companies fail to correct shortfalls after repeated warnings, they risk legal action by the Department of Labor and tax penalties from the IRS that could equal as much as the amount of underfunding. Congress has tightened the pressure on underfunded pensions in part by raising insurance premiums for underfunded plans and requiring any plan less than 90% funded to alert all its beneficiaries. What can you do if your pension is underfunded? Start by dealing with the problem the same way you would any financial setback. Try to economize so that you can get by if you're already retired or save more if you're still working. If you're employed, you should invest as much money as you can in tax-deferred retirement plans. In short, if Washington can't reform your employer, you probably can't either. So you'll have to take charge of your own retirement.

✌ How Divorce Can Derail Your Plan

Couples can be torn apart when children move out, careers plateau, aged parents die or future options seem to dwindle. If you get divorced, your shattered emotions may eventually heal. But your retirement plans might not after you and your ex split your assets. Just how a divorcing couple's assets are divided up can depend on the state they live in. While all courts must follow federal law in dealing with company-sponsored retirement plans, states have their own laws on splitting assets in IRAs and Keoghs. Courts in the community property states (Arizona, California, Idaho, Louisiana, Nevada, New Mexico, Texas, Washington and Wisconsin) usually require divorcing spouses to share assets in those plans equally. Other states give judges more discretion, often to the detriment of lower-paid spouses. Judges in these states generally award as much as two-thirds of the marital property to the higher wage earner. Whatever your share, it probably won't be enough to finance the retirement you've been planning. Here's how a retirement stockpile dwindles in divorce.

Dividing defined-contribution plans. These may be 401(k)s, 403(b)s or SEPs (Simplified Employee Pensions) if you're salaried, or Keoghs and SEPs if you're self-employed. You may also have an IRA. If your plans and your spouse's are roughly equal in value, the court will likely let you both keep your plans intact. Otherwise, the judge may divide the total between you, instructing your employers in a court order which share belongs to each of you. Such plans are relatively easy to split up because they consist of company stock or money invested in securities. If the court divides your 401(k) in half, most companies will set up a separate account for your spouse's share. Henceforth, your contributions will go entirely into your account. Some companies will let ex-spouses withdraw everything in their accounts as lump sums that they can roll over into IRAs or take as cash. Other companies allow withdrawals over time, as with any retirement account. Either way, the law imposes no 10% penalty on withdrawals by ex-spouses who are younger than 59.5.

Sorting out defined-benefit pensions. To make things simple, many divorcing couples agree to let one spouse keep the traditional pension, while the other takes all or a portion of the 401(k)s and other defined-contribution accounts. If you must split a pension with your ex, most companies prefer that you use the so-called fixed date method. Here's how it generally works. Based on your salary and years of service, your benefits office will calculate what your pension would be if you were to retire on the day you expect your divorce to be final. Say you would qualify for a $10,000 pension on that date. A court might order your company to give your spouse $5,000 a year of your pension no matter how big your benefit actually turns out to be when you really retire. Your spouse would start to collect the $5,000 when he or she reaches retirement age (usually at age 65, though some companies permit earlier retirement) even if you're still working and not receiving your share of the pension.

Calculating the fractional method. Here's how it works for employees of companies that permit this maneuver. Divide the number of months you were married and employed at your company by the total number of months you've worked for your company, married or not. Next, multiply the result by your estimated pension benefit on the date you plan to retire. Finally, multiply that amount by the percentage of your pension the court has awarded to your spouse. Let's say you've been married 10 years, have worked at your company for 15 years and expect a $20,000 pension when you retire at age 65. Divide 120 by 180 and multiply the result (0.666) by $20,000, resulting in $13,320. If the court gives your spouse half your benefit, he or she would get $6,660 a year. You both take a gamble with this method, however. That's because you might opt to work beyond 65, thereby boosting your pension and your ex's share of it. If you take early retirement, your pension and your ex's share would be smaller. Whichever method you use, your ex can file for a cut of your pension at the earliest retirement age your company allows. But doing so freezes the amount your ex receives even if you continue to work and your benefits keep growing.

❧ *When a Roth IRA Is Right for You*

The Roth IRA continues to confuse individuals as well as some of the experts whom they turn to for answers. The upshot is a lot of bad advice. Maybe that's understandable. The Roth is a very tricky vehicle that has required a seemingly endless stream of clarifications. If you're struggling to decide whether to convert, bad advice can hurt you. "It's frustrating for people when they get three different opinions from three different professionals," says C.P.A. Ed Slott, who specializes in tax planning. Slott received hundreds of questions from people who don't feel confident of answers they've received elsewhere. So he set up a tax website (irahelp.com) with an IRA question-and-answer bulletin board. We checked around to see which questions are yielding incorrect or incomplete responses so we could set the record straight.

Let's start with the fact that there are three types of IRAs. The traditional deductible IRA gives you a tax benefit right away. If you're eligible for one, you deduct contributions from your taxable income in the tax year that you make them. The earnings grow tax-deferred until you take out the money and pay taxes on the withdrawal. A nondeductible IRA is funded with after-tax dollars. It gives you tax-deferred earnings, but you pay taxes when you make withdrawals. The third type, the Roth IRA, is also funded with after-tax dollars and grows tax-free. Rather than simply deferring taxes on your investment earnings, it eliminates them forever. The longer you have until retirement, the greater your earnings and the more you will save by avoiding taxes on those gains.

You can contribute up to $2,000 a year ($4,000 for couples) to a Roth if your AGI (adjusted gross income) is $95,000 or less for singles, $150,000 or less for married couples filing jointly. Singles with an AGI up to $110,000 and couples with an AGI up to $160,000 qualify for a smaller partial contribution. Unlike other IRAs, Roths do not require that you start withdrawals from your account at age 70.5. You can keep contributing as long as you have earned income.

Which type of IRA should you choose? A Roth always beats a nondeductible IRA because, as we just noted, a Roth allows you to escape taxes entirely on the earnings of your after-tax contributions. If you're not eligible for a deductible IRA, the Roth is your best deal. A Roth beats a deductible IRA if your tax bracket will stay the same or rise after you retire. Because the decision between a Roth and a deductible IRA boils down to taxes now vs. taxes later, one big factor in choosing between the two is how your tax bracket will change over time. Most people find their tax bracket declines in retirement because their pension, Social Security benefit and portfolio income fall short of their former paychecks. If you expect your tax bracket will fall, a deductible IRA will most likely put you ahead. But if you think you have a good chance of maintaining or even boosting your income in retirement, then the Roth wins.

Take the case of a 30-year-old couple who pay a combined federal and state tax rate of 32% and put $4,000 into an IRA every year until age 65. Say that they earn an 8% annual return and withdraw their money over 20 years in retirement. If they choose a Roth, they would wind up with about $1,404,000 to spend over the course of their golden years. Now assume they put the same amount of money in a traditional tax-deductible IRA and faithfully invest their tax savings on annual contributions in a taxable account that also grows at 8%. Their 20-year retirement spending would come to about $233,300 less. One reason is that they would have to pay nearly $479,500 in income tax as they withdrew retirement money over those two decades.

The longer you can wait to tap your IRA after you retire, the more attractive a Roth becomes. Since you needn't begin taking distributions from a Roth IRA at age 70.5, you can get a huge financial lift by keeping your retirement stash tucked away in a Roth into your 70s and beyond. If you're age 70 and earn a modest 7% a year in a Roth IRA, you can literally double your money by age 80 by leaving it there instead of withdrawing it and spending it.

What if you're over 70.5 and want to keep saving?

A Roth IRA is your only option. With a deductible or nondeductible IRA, once you hit 70.5, you have to start taking money out of your account and stop contributing. But just as you can keep your money in a Roth for as long as you like, you can keep adding to it each year too, so long as you have earned income. Those attributes make the Roth a powerful estate-planning tool for people who will continue to work part time in retirement. When you die, the Roth will go to your beneficiary and no one will have to pay income tax on the money. But your estate might owe taxes on the IRA just as it might on any other asset you own.

Can you convert an existing IRA to a Roth? If you

do that, you'll owe income taxes on your earnings and (if the IRA was deductible) the original contribution. Much of the IRA confusion has centered on conversions from old IRAs to Roths. For starters, your AGI must fall below $100,000 (single or married) to qualify for a conversion from a deductible IRA. If you make a conversion during the year and your AGI jumps above the limit for the year, you're subject to severe tax penalties. But you're given the option of changing. If, say, a generous bonus puts you over the $100,000 limit, the IRS will let you annul the Roth and switch the funds back to your old IRA penalty-free.

Because you can change your mind for any reason, this rule can save you from more than goofs. Say you roll over $60,000 from a deductible IRA into a Roth. You'll owe $18,600 in income taxes if you're in the 32% bracket. But if a subsequent market drop cuts the value of your Roth to $40,000 before you file your tax return, you can avoid paying taxes on money you've already lost. Just reverse the conversion and then roll the money into a new Roth. You'll owe taxes on $40,000, for a $6,200 saving. Congress also has clarified when you can take money out of a converted Roth. You can't tap converted funds without tax penalties in the first five years unless you're over 59.5 or you're using the money for medical or college expenses or a first home. But you can tap nonrollover Roth contributions penalty-free at any time and for any reason.

If you're eligible to convert to a Roth, should you?

Converting to one lets you make tax-free withdrawals later but gives you a big tax bill today. Remember, you'll owe income taxes on all deductible contributions you made to your IRA and on all its investment earnings. For some rules of thumb, you should strive to answer the following questions.

Do you expect to fall into a lower tax bracket when you reach retirement age? (When estimating your potential retirement income, remember to include your annual pension, projected investment income and taxable Social Security benefits.) Will you need the money within five years of opening a Roth account? Would you have to tap the IRA to pay for the taxes you would owe by converting? To pay the conversion taxes, would you be forced to sell investments and incur substantial capital gains taxes? Will the extra income tax liability that you incur by converting your IRA end up pushing you into a substantially higher tax bracket or cause you to forfeit any significant tax deductions, credits or exemptions?

If you answered yes to any of the questions, we don't think it's a good idea for you to convert to a Roth. If you answered no to all of the questions, it makes sense to convert to a Roth.

Chapter 7

Keeping Wealth in The Family

*T*he World War II generation of Americans created history's first mass middle class. After enduring the Depression, they enjoyed the postwar boom, benefited from exploding real estate values in the 1960s and 1970s and rode the bull market of the past 17 years. Now their assets are tumbling toward their 76 million children. These baby boomers, born between 1946 and 1964, stand to inherit more than $10 trillion. It would be nice to report that you're about to hit the big time. But it's not that simple. This intergenerational transfer of family wealth will proceed more like a series of rummage sales than a national lottery.

Consider Ann Perry of Encinitas, Calif, a freelance journalist and former staff writer for the *San Diego Union-Tribune.* "We inherited an estate worth $500,000," she says. "But it's not like someone hands you a check for half a million dollars." When Perry's mother died in 1993, Ann, 45, and her husband Anthony, 52, had to sort through the contents of a house in Texas and a summer place in Michigan. They had to decide what to do with her antiques and her TV sets. They had to get an old oil painting appraised and find a home for her cat. And then there were her Bell South and Exxon stock, her savings account and her IRA. "My mother had been critically ill for a year and a half, and it was just awful from beginning to end," remembers Perry. "I had helped care for her, and I started thinking, 'Gee, now I'm going to have to take care of her things.' I didn't think of it as an inheritance. I thought of it as all of my mother's belongings."

Family money is as complicated as the lives that create it. An estate serves as a vessel for feelings and memories, as well as property of all kinds. And when the bric-a-brac of a lifetime passes from one generation to another, it's not just estate taxes and probate laws that a family confronts. Survivors also suffer the collateral damage of death, including exhaustion, fear and guilt. Still, there is money involved. No amount of planning can fully prepare you for the loss of your mother or father. But if you're a baby boomer, taking a look at the impending transfer of wealth can open your eyes. The wave of estates moving toward our nation's largest generation will transform this country's culture, society and economy. Maybe it's time to get ready.

🌿 Your Stake in a $41 Trillion Bequest

Trying to get a handle on the size of the inheritance wave is tough because different experts produce different numbers, all of which have to be put into proper context. The best-known estimate of the estate bonanza is about $10 trillion, a figure derived in 1993 by Cornell economists Robert Avery and Michael Rendall, who studied how much wealth would be passed by people age 50 and over to their children. The latest research indicates the windfall could be much larger. John Havens and Paul Schervish, economists from Boston College, recently projected wealth transfers by all Americans to all sources over roughly the next 50 years and estimated the total will be at least $41 trillion.

Now, $41 trillion is a lot of money even if you're Bill Gates. But its impact on most individual families will be smaller than you might think. For starters, the heap will be split among a huge number of people. After all, boomers are called boomers because there are so many of them. Furthermore, much of the wealth that's changing hands is concentrated in a small number of portfolios. According to Avery and Rendall at Cornell, a third of the transfer will go to the richest 1% of boomers. Another third will pass to the next wealthiest 10%, and the remaining third will be scattered among the bottom 90% of the baby boomer pyramid. Havens and Schervish at Boston College teach a similar lesson in inequality. Their research shows that the wealthiest 57,800 estates in America will bequeath more than $582 billion to heirs over the next 17 years. That's an average inheritance of more than $10 million. The poorest 1.3 million estates will have zero or negative worth and will leave zilch to the next generation.

Boomers' parents also have financial obligations apart from those to their children. Uncle Sam currently takes a cut from estates worth more than $675,000 (see "A Quick Course in Estate Taxes" on page 186). Charitable organizations will also rake in part of the transfer. Havens and Schervish project that of the $41 trillion that estates will distribute by mid-century, taxes will devour $8.5 trillion, and $6 trillion will flow to charities. For all these reasons, many inheritances are likely to be quite modest. Avery and Rendall estimated that the average estate passed to boomers will be worth about $90,000. Other studies have put the amount as low as $23,000.

Get a grip on your expectations. Whatever your personal prospects, you can make sure a bequest makes a difference in your life by calibrating your expectations. An inheritance can help you meet a specific financial goal or make meaningful changes to your lifestyle. Perhaps you'll be able to afford a new car, take better vacations or start a business at home. But you almost certainly will not be able to replace your stream of income. "I'm amazed by how often a client will say something like, 'I'm going to use my inheritance to buy a $100,000 boat,'" says Dee Lee, a financial planner based in Harvard, Mass. "And I have to say, 'Okay, great, have fun. But you've just burned through a chunk of your principal, so don't count on retiring at 55.'"

That's a lesson taught by Jeff and Joan Bendix of Cleveland. When Jeff's mother died in 1993, the Bendixes inherited about $333,000 in a trust for their children, Peter, 14, and Lia, 11, plus some $166,000 in cash. They used part of the cash for a down payment on a new house, and they draw $3,000 a month from the income generated by the inheritance. Meanwhile, Jeff has reallocated the trust so that two thirds is invested in stocks, with the remainder in bonds. Though the fund is held in trust for Peter and Lia, Jeff says that "its purpose is to enhance the lives of our children. So it can pretty much fund anything, even building on to our house."

So while Jeff, 45, and Joan, 44, earn a combined $55,000 a year, they're living in a $300,000 home. "It's mostly the small things that have changed for us," says Jeff. "We eat out more, and we donate more to our favorite charities." The Bendixes also used part of their cash inheritance to start investing for college costs. Their savings funds now total $140,000 for Peter and $90,000 for Lia.

These are the kinds of changes echoed by other boomers who have successfully handled bequests, whatever the amount. Susan Hughes, 49, of Seattle, received about $26,000 when a trust set up by her father liquidated in 1985. She spent $6,000 on a piano and decided to devote the rest of her inheritance to a trust for her sons. "At the time my husband, who was a broker, thought that was superfluous because we could pay for their education out of his salary," Hughes recalls. After splitting with her ex in 1988, Hughes assumed control of the trust, then worth $19,000, and took an investing class with a local planner. Eventually, she shifted the bulk of the trust into small-cap stock funds that grew to the point where the trust could fund $40,000 in college costs for her sons Steve, 26, and Joseph, 24.

Prepare to be an heir one day. Of course, there is one catch to carefully managing your inheritance. You and your parents must be in accord about how and when they are going to divvy up all their property. And you can't be fainthearted about helping them get their estate in order. "If you thought talking to them about sex was tough," says financial planner Lee, "just wait until you try talking to them about estate planning." For tips, see the box "Talking to Your Parents About Money" on page 188.

Parents of any age can grow wary when children approach them about money. But boomers' parents, many of whom have lived through tremendous adversity, can become especially irritated with their children, who are easily caricatured as spendthrift and undisciplined. Nevertheless, the sooner you bring up the topic of estate planning with your parents, and the more fully you explore it, the better. Once your parents are gone, you will have to do right by their wishes and take care of your family's needs. That's never an easy task. But it may be nearly impossible without some instruction.

For example, after surveying her mother's belongings, Ann Perry deliberated for months before deciding what to do with each asset. "We sold her home in El Paso but kept the summer house in Michigan," she says. "We held on to her Bell South holdings and sold some of her Exxon. We adopted her cat, and I've got that painting hanging in our living room. All of these choices had to do with what we knew she would have wanted but also what we could manage."

Perry is an only child. In families with many siblings, or where there are divorces, remarriages and stepchildren, it's even more important to establish your parents' intentions. "If you treat your wealth as a hidden kingdom, a box that no one can open until you're gone, you're setting your family up for disaster," says Norman Ross of Hirschfeld Stern Moyer & Ross, a New York City estate planning firm. "You must talk about it when you are alive to eliminate problems when you're dead."

How to broach the subject tactfully. So how do you ease into the most difficult discussion you may ever have? First, lead by example. Get your own estate in order, and it will be much easier to discuss planning without seeming like your goal is getting your hands on your parents' money. You can talk to your parents about providing for the care of a spouse, setting up a living trust and seeking tax advantages as you work through these topics yourself. This shouldn't be any kind of ruse. If you are in your forties or fifties, you should be thinking about your own estate anyway. "When I'm talking to people in their seventies and eighties, I tell them that everything I say applies to their children as well," says Stuart Kessler of Goldstein Golub & Kessler, an accounting firm based in New York City. "And when I give advice to boomers, I tell them their parents also need it."

Put it all down on paper. If your parents are a bit bewildered by the task of assembling an estate plan, try this tactic recommended by Ross. Suggest that they write down where they come from, where they have worked and what they have saved, and list their most significant purchases and investments. Encourage them to take stock of how they have come to accumulate their most important possessions. It's a simple way to connect the work they have done with the things in their lives that mean the most to them. That way, when they look at their inventory to divide up their estate, they will be working from a sense of pride in their accomplishments, not anxiety about death. What's more, you may be fascinated by the details that emerge about their lives.

Making Charity Part of Your Plan

Talk to your parents about what charities they have supported. Try to make that conversation an overture to a discussion about what causes or groups they would like their estate to aid on an ongoing basis. In doing this, you can take a page from Ralph Edwards, 61. He says that facing his own mortality led him to bring his family into managing his estate through charitable giving.

The appeal of community foundations. Edwards meets with his daughters Colie, 27, and Tyler, 24, at least once a year to discuss his donations to the Community Foundation in Atlanta. This regional trust invests individual donations, pools the gains and allocates grants, usually to nonprofits in the area. Edwards made an initial donation of $500,000 three years ago and plans to keep making donations in the form of appreciated securities. That way, he enjoys a tax deduction for the market value of the securities and avoids taxes on his capital gains. His goal is to contribute enough annually so that his total grows to $1 million even though the fund gives away 20% of assets every year. Over the next 10 years, he will gradually give complete control of the donations to his daughters.

Edwards directed the Community Foundation to aid causes such as the Trust for Public Land and the Atlanta Opera. He enjoys the fact that those targets may change as his children make decisions about their family giving. "As a parent," he says, "I face the question of what my legacy is. How do I teach them to be good stewards? I think one way is to teach them to give it away, and this is a way to have them involved so when they inherit what I have they will know what they are doing."

The lesson here is that communication and clarity lead to control. Only by talking with your parents about exactly what they want to achieve with their life savings can you help them tailor an estate plan that fits their objectives and your needs. "I

A Quick Course in Estate Taxes

When you hear presidential hopeful George Bush and House Majority Whip Tom DeLay denouncing the "death penalty," you might think that these Texas politicians no longer were supporters of capital punishment. Wrong. Their rhetoric actually reflects the animosity that growing numbers of Americans feel toward estate taxes.

Where did today's death taxes originate? During the 18th and 19th centuries, the estate tax was used on rare occasions to raise money during national emergencies. By the 1880s, the idea had gained favor as a way to encourage people to distribute their wealth charitably before death and to close the gap between rich and poor. Steel magnate Andrew Carnegie, for example, wrote approvingly that "by taxing estates heavily at death, the state marks its condemnation of the selfish millionaire's unworthy life." A few decades later, Woodrow Wilson signed legislation that taxed estates worth more than $5 million (in 1916 dollars) at a 10% rate. The law provided a significant source of revenue during an age when wealth was more concentrated and there were fewer taxes and taxpayers. During the Depression and the early 1940s, in fact, the estate tax brought in as much as 7% of the government's total tax take.

How big are the loopholes? Ever since the tax's inception, benefactors have tried to figure out ways to dodge it. Among them were giving huge untaxed gifts to their spouses, children and friends, a tactic Congress soon discouraged by passing a gift tax. Since then, the feds have closed other loopholes while creating many new ones. The cumulative result? These days you can avoid the estate tax altogether unless you're extremely wealthy or unaware of your planning options. The tax is now paid by fewer than 1% of households and contributes less than 1% of federal tax dollars. And its basic function is to curb very large inheritances. At last count, estates valued under $1 million had average net estate taxes of just $47,000, while estates valued at $20 million or more paid average estate taxes of $11.2 million.

What's the taxman's bite now? The estate tax ranges from 37% to 55%. Estates worth less than $675,000 per benefactor (or $1.35 million for married couples) are exempt. Those figures will rise to $1 million ($2 million for couples) by 2006. And while it's true that Americans are accumulating wealth so quickly that the IRS expects the number of people filing estate taxes to grow 5.5% a year through 2004, only a very slender fraction of Americans will ever pay them.

What's my family's liability? Still wondering if you're subject to death taxes? Reviewing will and trust options with your children or parents and a lawyer will take any guesswork out of the matter. Until then, don't worry about unloading heirlooms or the family home to qualify for the exemption. Odds are you won't have to.

never said, 'Gee, Mom, how much do you own?'" says Jeff Bendix. "I wasn't comfortable having that conversation before my mother got ill. Then afterward, I was thinking of her health and, besides, it seemed ghoulish. But if you want to be prepared, you should have that conversation."

Coping with an abundance of charity. The U.S. is now a far tonier place than when baby boomers' parents were in their prime earning years. One basic measure of the difference is that real disposable income (what people earn after adjusting for inflation and deducting taxes) is up 452% since 1960, according to data from the Federal Reserve. Because of this, many observers have anticipated that part of the wealth transfer will surge toward charities. Parents might leave less to boomers who already own so much, and some boomers might actually keep less for themselves. Sensing the inheritance wave, individual charities have stepped up their solicitation campaigns. And newly convenient ways to make donations are popping up at a rapid rate.

Community foundations, like the one Ralph Edwards uses in Atlanta, make up the fastest growing sector of U.S. philanthropy. And financial services companies, eager to manage the expected wave of giving, are also getting in on the action. Fidelity and Vanguard, among others, now have charitable gift funds that allow you to take an immediate tax deduction for an initial investment, then let it grow tax-free and direct portions to specific nonprofits whenever you like.

Although the share of personal income donated to charities has held fairly steady at 2% for years, recent IRS data show that the percentage of estate wealth dedicated to charities is rising. For example, from 1992 to 1995, the amount left to heirs rose 14%. But the amount bequeathed to charities jumped 28%.

Passing It on to Your Offspring

So far we've given you the big picture divined from national demographic data and the projections of economists. But there's something else to consider about the great estate coming your way. Simply put, what would you like your own world to look

Talking to Your Parents About Money

Aging parents are often reluctant to discuss their financial situation with their children, who are often reluctant to ask. This uncomfortable minuet, involving so many delicate issues of trust and power, sometimes means that important financial decisions are made under the worst of circumstances, such as when a parent suddenly falls ill and needs long-term care. To open lines of communication that will benefit both generations, experts recommend these strategies.

Don't wait for a crisis. The ideal time to start talking is when your parents are in their sixties and still able to handle their own lives. People 85 and over are the fastest-growing segment of the elderly population. So the odds are good that eventually you'll have to take some responsibility for their financial affairs. No matter how difficult talking about money may seem, it's far safer to begin now than to put it off until there's an emergency.

Examine your own motives. If you want only what's best for Mom and Dad, that's fine. If you're concerned about the size of your inheritance, that's okay too. What's not okay is trying to impose your financial philosophy. You should be making plans with your parents, not for them. Ultimately this is a discussion about death. So you are bound to feel guilty, and your parents are likely to be fearful. Recognizing your emotions, and theirs, gives you a better chance of separating feelings from the matters at hand.

Strive to include the whole family. If you have brothers or sisters, consider whether one of you should talk alone with your parents, or whether there should be a family powwow. If you're chosen to do the talking, be sure to keep everyone informed. A sibling left out of decisions now may be the cause of an angry scene later.

Pick your moment, then go slowly. You'll want a setting where no one is likely to feel threatened. That might be a family dinner, a walk with the dog, a round of golf. Elder care experts suggest that you keep the initial talks general. You don't need to know exactly how much money your parents have the first time out. If you can be direct, by all means do so. You may find that your parents are relieved. If you need to ease into the subject, think about bringing up an article you read on Medicare, then asking your parents about their health plan. Saying "I'm sure you've already talked to someone about..." will help you give the impression that you think they're in control.

Consider calling in an intermediary. Bring in a trusted friend or a professional planner if years of family dynamics make this topic too hot to handle. Sometimes only an outsider can hear what is really being said. If your parents still resist, accept that they're not ready. Then start educating yourself so you'll be prepared for a crisis.

like once your parents' slice of wealth passes into your hands? And remember that a bequest doesn't mean only that you can acquire more. It can also allow you to subsidize a change in your lifestyle. In fact, that may be the greatest kindness from your forebears.

Recall Ann Perry. The inheritance of her mother's estate allowed her to keep working only part time, spend more time with her kids and ultimately pursue a dream of her own. It was a gift beyond appraisal. "I was able to serve on the PTA board and run the school talent show," she says with pride. "The inheritance made it possible for me to work at home as a writer." What's more, boomers such as Perry, Susan Hughes and the Bendixes all used part of their inheritances to fund their children's education. In that sense, the passing of wealth has given them an opportunity to honor the values of earlier generations and provide for those to come. Keep that in mind when your turn comes.

✒ The Sandwich Generation's Pickle

Margie White, her husband and their two teenage sons had just moved back to Plano, Texas, near their families, in 1993. There were boxes everywhere. Tradesmen were handing her estimates for repairs. And then her parents called. "We're at the bank," her mother said tearfully. "There's nothing left."

"I'll be right there," White said, flying out the door and into a financial disaster. Piecing together some 25 bounced checks, White realized that her mother had been an easy mark for every sweepstakes, every telemarketer, every traveling salesperson. She bought scores of Michigan bulbs to improve her chances of winning a sweepstakes. She purchased $800 worth of cosmetics over the phone. "She'd write a check, and my father would sign it," White recalls. "And neither of them balanced the checkbook." But the hit to their assets was just a symptom. The problem, she quickly understood, was that her parents were no longer able to take care of themselves. Both, in fact, eventually were diagnosed with Alzheimer's.

The fate of some 9 million Americans. Within weeks, White, 49, had become a full-fledged member of the sandwich generation, that growing group of adult children who are caring for aging parents while raising their own kids. According to a study from the National Alliance for Caregiving and the American Association of Retired Persons, there are more than 9 million Americans in this situation, 40% of them between 35 and 49. For White, a stay-at-home mother, her parents became a second full-time job. Every morning she'd rush out of her house to beat her father to his mailbox. If he got there first, some bill would go missing. Whenever he wandered off, she'd get a call to go find him. "No matter what we did, it wasn't enough to keep him safe," she says. "We changed the locks and covered the burners on the stove. But he'd put a metal pot in the microwave and ruin that."

Then there were the financial headaches. They were compounded by the fact that she didn't have power of attorney, which would have let her make decisions for her parents. One supplemental Medicare policy had lapsed. The keys to their safe-deposit box were missing. They hadn't paid taxes for years. When her father went into a nursing home and her mother needed a full-time companion, Social Security and Medicare covered only a third. To pay the rest, White began liquidating her parents' six-figure portfolio.

The fact that they had significant investments meant that White, unlike nearly half of all family caregivers, suffered no financial hardship. She didn't have to dip into her own assets or choose between saving for her own old age and paying their bills. But that doesn't mean she wasn't paying a price. Her absence from her own family strained relations with her husband and sons. "It cost me my marriage," she says sadly. Today, she and her husband are separated.

They're not suffering alone. The stress of belonging to the sandwich generation is taking a toll countrywide. All of a sudden you're struggling with this huge balancing act. How do you fulfill all your roles? How do you balance your marriage, your children and your work with elder care? Everyone's answer is different. And no one's is easy.

Doing double duty to support a family. They call it parenting your parent. But that term is off the mark. If your third-grade daughter belongs in advanced math, you go to see the principal. If your teenage son needs special surgery, you spend hours interviewing doctors until you find the right one. You do this for your kids because they can't do it for themselves. They may not appreciate every gesture, but they certainly expect it. Caring for your parents is another matter entirely. Handling their physical needs, at least at the start, feels inappropriate. So does battling their doctors, insurers and creditors, particularly if they don't want your help. "It's much, much worse than caring for a child," says Joan Gruber, a Dallas financial planner who specializes in helping adult children with aging parents. "You can't tell your parents what to do."

John Strohl has gotten that message loud and clear. Strohl, 47, a program manager at Dell Computer in Texas, has what you'd call a houseful. He and his wife Joyce have five children vying for their attention and support. Surprisingly, none are more in need of it than their eldest daughter, 21-year-old Katie. Almost three years ago, she went off to college. It was her first time away from the nest, her first step toward financial and emotional independence. And it was a total failure. Eighteen months later, Katie had earned zero credits, was two months pregnant and had spent the night in the county jail. She'd been arrested for shoplifting.

The next morning, her parents picked her up and took her out for breakfast. "Over eggs and strong coffee, we told her she had to have a decent job before she hit her seventh or eighth month, or she'd never find one," Strohl recalls. "We got her lined up with Medicaid for the pregnancy. And I was her birthing coach." It was torture to see his daughter struggling, he admits. There were days when he wanted to say, "Stay home. Put your feet up. Rest." But he held his tongue. And she found a job helping to manage a local apartment complex. She's been promoted twice. Yet her salary isn't enough to make ends meet, so her mother watches Katie's daughter. Not for free, mind you; she pays about half of the cost of outside care. Strohl believes that the only way to make his daughter learn to take responsibility for herself and her child is to insist that she pay something.

Meanwhile, he feels increasingly responsible for his parents, who live 1,200 miles away, in San Diego, on a modest pension and Social Security. They haven't been able to go to the theater or to concerts as they've done all their lives, and the only restaurant they can afford is a cafeteria. To make things worse, Strohl's 76-year-old father is suffering a relapse of prostate cancer. Despite Strohl's pleas, his parents wouldn't accept help even when he presented it as payback for their support in the early '90s when the defense industry, where he'd been working, turned sour.

Then his daughter Alenna, a high school junior, decided that she'd like to go to a California college. The Strohls realized that sending Alenna to live with his folks would solve two problems. She could establish residency, thus qualify for in-state tuition. And he could send his parents $500 a month for her room and board. Not that it was an easy choice. "It was hard for us to let her go," Strohl says. "But it was the best thing for her." Alenna, now a student at Mesa College, moved out of her grandparents' house in January. But Strohl still sends his parents the checks.

Improvising in a one-woman show. It's not sexist to say it: most family care duties fall to the daughters. According to the National Alliance for Caregiving, 73% of family caregivers are women. And it's not because they have more time. Three in five female caretakers from 35 to 49 hold down full-time or part-time jobs. About half have to change their work schedules. It's also a fact that caregiving is typically a solo enterprise. Even when there are several siblings, the job of taking care of Mom and Dad generally falls to just one.

That's what happened to Roz Schaffer, 46. Three years ago, when she was a commercial lender with a bank in Philadelphia and the mother of a teenage son, she decided she was ready to kick her career into high gear. Her 20th high school reunion had convinced her that she needed an advanced degree. So she'd started the course work for her M.B.A. Classes were just beginning when her mother, Tina Horn, fell and broke her back. She lay on the floor of her Seattle apartment for 12 hours before she was found.

While Horn recuperated in the hospital, Schaffer and her siblings convened. "My sisters, one in Detroit, the other in New York, gave me two choices," recalls Schaffer. "Move her to Philly or move her to Philly." All of a sudden, doing her course work wasn't her highest priority. Schaffer began scouring the city for an assisted living facility. Her husband Charles was supportive.

But as a commercial pilot, he was often away. Finally she found a place she liked. It was clean and bright, and the staff seemed energetic. But after only a few weeks, Schaffer says, "I would show up in the dining room and see a full plate of food in front of my mother. They'd say, 'Tina's not hungry.' But as soon as I'd cut it up so she could handle it, she would eat." So Schaffer started spending more and more time with her mother.

Then last summer Horn developed Crohn's disease, became incontinent and lost her ability to swallow. "Terminal," the doctor said. Simultaneously, Schaffer's son was diagnosed with learning problems. It seemed that if she wasn't sitting at her mother's bedside with one doctor, she was shuttling her son to another. She used up all five weeks of her vacation time, not to mention any chance of scaling the corporate ladder. "When clients would call with referrals, I'd have to turn them over to other loan officers," she says. Her bank transferred her to a suburb, where she was closer to her mother but invisible to her bosses.

Something had to give. She hired a private nurse to come in eight hours each day and monitor her mom's care. The bill came to $3,500 a month. In response, Horn rebounded. Now she's back in assisted living with the private nurse by her side. And Schaffer has a new challenge on her hands. She recently was offered a promising new job—and a chance to use that M.B.A.—working in organizational development at a marketing startup. With her mother and son stable, she said yes. Then she put out the call to her brothers and sisters that she was going to need more help. No dice. So she's forging ahead, taking it one day at a time. "After all," she says, "my mother could live another 20 years."

Who takes care of the caregivers? Diane and Darin Aldrich have three children (the two oldest are Diane's from a previous marriage). A year ago they were living in Washington, D.C., where Darin, 34, was a Navy officer and Diane, 44, was a special education kindergarten teacher. Her mother, in the early stages of Alzheimer's, was in an assisted living facility nearby. And nothing was working, in part because her mother hated where she was living. She wouldn't let the attendants bathe her; she didn't trust the staff to wash her clothes; and she didn't like the food. So Diane ran over to bathe her three times a week.

She did her mother's laundry. And every other night, she would bring her mother home for dinner. The facility certainly wasn't worth the $3,600 a month her mother was spending.

The price Diane's family was paying was even higher, however. "I never saw her," Darin recalls. "She was always watching her mother or the kids." Finally, he'd had enough. "If you brought your mother here to live with us," he told Diane, "then maybe we'd get to see you sometimes." But their D.C. place wasn't large enough for six. After mulling things over for a few months, they moved to Maine, where Diane had bought her family's six-bedroom house 20 years before, and where Darin's mother also lived. "We did what needed to be done," says Darin. "If it were my Mom, Diane would feel the same way."

It's been a strain financially. The original plan was for Darin to go back to school on Uncle Sam's dime (courtesy of the Montgomery bill) and for Diane to find a job. But as her mom's condition worsened, she decided to stay home. She expects that this may be the last year there are still flashes of her mother left. The family's only source of income is her mother's savings. Diane, who has power of attorney, learned from a lawyer that she could pay herself a monthly stipend for caring for her mother. It amounts to about 65% of what she could earn in the work force. Diane and Darin fill in gaps from their shrinking savings. To make sure they'd have funds for an emergency, they refinanced the Maine house, cashing out $15,000.

"I don't want to put my own family in financial jeopardy because of this," Diane says. Nor does she want her family to feel the sacrifice so heavily that they come to resent her and her mother. "My kids don't have to have their own cars. They don't have to go to Europe. But I don't want to say, geez, we can't go to Florida this year because we have to pay for Grandma." For the kids, at least, the situation is livable. For Diane and Darin, it's harder. "I'm jealous of my 17-year-old son out at the lake at nights with his friends," Diane says. "I want to be out there with my husband. And I feel terrible about that."

Preparing for the sandwich years. As we continue to have children later in life and our parents continue to live longer, more and more of us will find ourselves in situations similar to those detailed earlier. This prospect is responsible for the growth of lifetime care facilities, where people can move in as independent adults and segue into nursing home care if needed. It's also fueling a boom in insurance covering long-term care. If parents aren't buying their own policies, many of today's wary, workaholic kids are offering to ante up. For advice on buying such coverage, see "Choosing Long-Term Care Insurance" on page 196.

Jodi Van Kirk has her own strategy—save as much as she can. Van Kirk, 31, her husband and three kids, ages 8, 7, and 2 live in Juneau, Alaska, near her mother, 49, and her maternal grandmother, 81, neither of whom has any significant savings or investments. Van Kirk knows the financial responsibility will fall on her. Already the groceries and sundries she buys for her grandmother add up to about $200 a month.

"I just took out a large life insurance policy on myself," says Van Kirk, a stay-at-home mom who also cares for other children to supplement her husband's income as a salesman for Coca-Cola. "So if something happens to me, my husband and my kids will be covered." Her husband puts 15% of each paycheck into his 401(k); his employer matches 35¢ on the dollar. They've maxed out his Roth IRA contribution for the year and stashed $700 in hers. She may take in two more kids, which would let her put away another $500 a month. "We'll do what we can," she says.

Kathy Hampton, 36, a legal librarian in Washington, D.C. with two kids, is taking a different tack. She's pushing her mother Faye Snoddy, 60, to help herself. Today Mom is self-sufficient and lives comfortably, outside Atlanta, on disability since a stroke forced her to stop working as a teacher seven years ago. She owns her home outright. But Hampton and her sister have long suspected that she had little in the way of retirement savings.

"When she turned 60, we decided to ask her some questions about money," Hampton recalls. As it turned out, they were right. Snoddy's disability would take her to age 65, when she'd start to receive Social Security and a small pension. She had no IRAs, no investments, no other savings to speak of. "She said she'll sell the house; she doesn't realize that won't be enough," Hampton says. "My sister and I will have the burden of carrying her financially, and we can't do that right now." So they got their mother started with an automatic investment plan and sent her back to school.

Medicare and private health insurance do not cover lengthy nursing home stays or extended homecare. With nursing home fees averaging $41,000 a year, many baby boomers are realizing that they may ultimately bear the cost of their parents' long-term care. And some are attempting to guard against those losses by purchasing long-term care insurance for their parents. The coverage is expensive. Annual premiums average $2,100 at age 65, and $4,500 at age 75. Buying long-term care coverage may be a good move if you have a family history of debilitating illness. But it could also be a waste of money. Here's what you need to know on the subject.

Understand your options. The main types of long-term care covered by insurance are nursing facilities, assisted living and homecare. Policies vary in the services offered under each category. Choose the broadest range of care options you can afford. A policy limited to homecare, for example, is usually a bad idea. Anyone frail enough to use those benefits may well need a nursing home someday.

Keep premiums under control. Most companies let you choose a daily nursing home benefit, typically between $50 and $250. Homecare is covered at 50% to 100% of the nursing home rate. Before you decide how much insurance to buy, call nursing facilities and homecare agencies to get an idea of rates. Then peg your daily benefit to those costs. You can select coverage for a period ranging from one to six years or for an unlimited time. A policy covering four or five years is a safe bet. The average stay for seniors who enter a nursing home is a bit less than 2.5 years.

Factor in an inflation rider. You need inflation protection when buying long-term care coverage because benefits may not kick in for several years. Go for the standard rider if the insured is age 68 or younger. It increases the policy's daily benefit by 5% compounded annually. And it will add 25% to 35% to the premium. You can probably get a somewhat cheaper inflation rider by not compounding the annual increase. Opt for this if the insured is 69 to 75.

Look into innovative state programs. Insurers in California, Connecticut, Indiana and New York have teamed up with state Medicaid agencies to develop so-called partnership policies. These allow residents with long-term care insurance to go on Medicaid when the policy benefits are exhausted without first having to deplete their own assets. For information, call 800-434-0222 in California, 860-424-4943 in Connecticut, 317-233-1470 in Indiana and 518-478-1030 in New York.

Consider the alternatives. Your parent might pay for long-term care by borrowing from the cash value of a whole life insurance policy. In addition, many policies allow for accelerated death benefits paid while the insured is still alive.

She's enrolled in computer classes to learn word processing and spreadsheets. "We think she's going to be healthy enough to sit at a computer and take in work at home," Hampton says. "And she's loving it. It's opened up a whole new world for her."

Taking back your personal life. Being in the sandwich generation does not have to be all negative. "Every night," says Diane Aldrich, "my mother kisses me and says, 'I don't know what I'd do without you.' And that's enough." In fact, most of the caregivers we spoke to hope that their efforts for the older generation provide a lesson for the younger one. If Aldrich ever falls ill, she says, she'd like to think one of her kids would care for her.

Not Margie White. Now that her father has passed away and her mother is in a nursing home, she's taken back her life. She's traveling, going to church and exercising regularly, shedding an impressive 50 pounds. Her mother's money is in the hands of a financial planner. And White has gotten her own finances in order. One prized asset is a sizable long-term care policy. "There was a definite lack of foresight and planning on my parents' part," she says. "I can understand. They never expected to live that long. But it took five or six years out of my life. I don't want my sons to have to do this for me."

How to Hire a Financial Planner

People usually look for professional advice when they get serious about saving for retirement and setting up an estate plan. Do you need a pro to overhaul your whole financial life or just to make sure your investments are on track? Here's what you should know about the world of brokers, bankers, accountants and financial planners who are all competing for your business.

A thorough estate plan provides an accurate snapshot of your current financial status, maps out strategies to help you achieve long-term goals and sets up a safety net of insurance to protect your financial stability. To develop such a plan, an adviser will meet with you to review how you spend and invest your money. He or she will want to see your pay stubs, a description of your benefit plans, your investment statements and your tax returns. These will provide the numbers to crunch. A good planner will ask about your specific wants and needs as well as tolerance for risk. The report you receive may be only a few pages or a booklet filled with tables and charts. What's valuable is that it spells out the most important things you need to do. The tough part is finding an adviser who's competent and has relevant experience (for tips, see the box "A Planner You're Proud to Call Your Own" at right). Here are the major players.

Traditional planners. These consultants take a holistic approach to financial planning rather than focusing simply on your investments. Most prefer working from extensive plans that they develop. They typically use lawyers and accountants (yours or theirs) to handle technical concerns such as estate plans or taxes. The three major types of planners are certified financial planner (C.F.P.), chartered financial consultant (Ch.F.C.) and chartered financial analyst (C.F.A.). A candidate for these certifications must undergo a rigorous training program and pass an exam that covers all the elements of a full-scale plan.

Brokerages, mutual funds, insurers. A growing number of financial services firms are also positioning their brokers or service representatives as "financial advisers" or "financial consultants." If what you're really looking for is investing advice, a broker or a mutual fund rep may be fine. But their expertise on broader planning issues depends on their training.

Certified public accountants. These pros are also migrating to financial planning as the prevalence and popularity of tax software packages continue to erode their income. A C.P.A. with expertise in investing and insurance can be especially helpful to business owners or individuals with complicated taxes or uneven cash flow.

Wealth managers. More traditional planners and financial firms are now positioning themselves as "wealth managers" who do more than recommend investments. They either run clients' money directly or match them with private money managers in exchange for a percentage of the client's assets or net worth.

A Planner You're Proud to Call Your Own

Even when a financial planner comes with glowing recommendations from a friend, the fit has got to be right for you. Before hiring an adviser to prepare a retirement plan, review the following pointers.

Consider only licensed or accredited advisers. While no form of accreditation guarantees competence or honesty, certified financial planners are monitored by the C.F.P. Licensing Board of Standards, which disciplines members who violate ethics codes. Although brokers may not be certified as planners, they must have a Series 7 license to sell securities.

Examine regulatory and disclosure records. Anyone who is compensated for dispensing financial advice must register with the Securities and Exchange Commission if he or she oversees assets of $25 million or more. An adviser must register with state securities regulators if assets are less than $25 million. Being registered doesn't guarantee competency. It means the adviser filled out an ADV (short for advisers) form and paid a fee. Advisers are legally required to give you a copy of ADV Part II, which discloses the terms of their compensation, including all commissions and payments received from sponsors of financial products that the adviser recommends. Review this carefully for any potential conflicts of interest. Also ask for Part I, which details any run-ins with regulators or other disciplinary history. If a planner refuses to give you this information, find the information yourself by calling the SEC (800-732-0330) or your state securities regulators (call the North American Securities Administrators Association at 888-846-2722 for a local contact). You can also call The National Association of Securities Dealers (800-289-9999) to review records of brokers' regulatory violations.

Interview several prospective planners. Most will agree to a free half-hour session to learn what you need and present their qualifications. The International Association for Financial Planning (888-806-7526) and the Institute of Certified Financial Planners (800-282-7526) can provide lists of advisers in your area by specialties or fee arrangements. In your preliminary meetings, pose questions about some challenge you face to see how different planners would approach these problems. Be concerned if the planner offers answers without asking follow-up questions or quickly changes answers if you express reluctance. Here are some questions to ask. What is your typical client like? What are your areas of expertise? How do you prepare a plan? What's your investment philosophy? Then ask for a list of clients who have worked with the adviser. Call the clients and ask specific questions. Example: Did recommended investments perform as expected?

Specialized planners. It is increasingly common for advisers to develop specialties. Some focus on advising corporate executives on stock options, retirement accounts and estate plans, for instance. Others concentrate on divorced or widowed women.

Putting a price on planners. If you think finding the right type of adviser is tough, try figuring out the best way to pay him or her. The important factor is the amount you pay, not the method used to calculate it. Planners normally charge set fees (per hour, per project or as a percentage of your assets) or commissions on financial products they sell you. Fees can range from $75 to $350 per hour, or from $1,500 to $5,000 for a typical plan, depending on the complexity of your situation and the amount of your assets. A commission-based planner usually won't charge you for drawing up a plan. But you may wind up paying more than you would a fee-only planner once you factor in costs related to the investments recommended in the plan. A hybrid category of "fee-based" advisers is emerging who will reduce their fees if you buy commission-generating investments from them.

Consumer advocates often contend that fee-only advisers are superior because their recommendations are not influenced by potential income from products. Others argue that conflicts of interest exist for fee-only planners too. For example, if a client asks a planner whether a sizable lump sum distribution is preferable to a monthly pension payout, there is a potential conflict of interest if that planner's fee is based on a percentage of assets under management. The key consideration is an adviser's integrity, regardless of how he or she is compensated.

✒ Get the Lowdown on Life Insurance

Most people, regardless of the size of their estate, need some kind of life insurance. The longer you wait to tackle the subject, the more you will pay and be at greater risk of leaving your loved ones in financial danger. We examine why it's so hard to understand the costs of various forms of life insurance and what you can do to clear away the cobwebs. Consider this intimidating tidbit. There's no such thing as sticker shock in the life insurance business. That's because there are no stickers on policies. Life insurance policies carry no unit pricing, no breakdown of what you are paying per quantity of what you are buying. With term insurance, that's no big deal because you pay a defined price (your premium) over a fixed period of time (the term). You know exactly what your heirs will receive if you are hit by a bus (the amount for which you are insured).

So-called permanent insurance is more complicated. This type of policy builds up savings under such product headings as whole, universal and variable insurance. Your insurer invests part of your premiums and credits you with dividends; your policy accumulates a cash value that grows tax-free. But it's often unclear exactly how much gets invested, where it goes and how much you get back. The illustrations used to sell policies rely on assumptions made by your insurer that may or may not turn out to be accurate. Illustrations almost never itemize all the costs. As a result, most customers don't have a clue what they are buying.

Simplify those complex policy pitches. Your only protection against bad life insurance deals is to equip yourself with the information that you need to evaluate cash-value policies. It's easiest to begin by viewing all life insurance as variants of the same product. Agents often hype the cash-value, dividend and tax advantages of whole life. Some even say that you're only "renting" insurance if you buy term. But the truth is that you can think of whole, universal or variable life as term insurance plus an investment account that accumulates as you contribute to it. Your insurer has to make the money in that account available not just if you die but also if you want to borrow against it or cash out your policy. That's why premiums are much higher for permanent life than for term.

The first type customarily carry staggering charges in their early years. Let's say that the first year's premium for a $200,000 whole life policy would be $3,036. Suppose you put that money in another low-risk, tax-free investment such as a municipal bond fund that returns 6% a year. At the end of a year, your investment would be worth $3,218. Your policy, however, has a cash value of zero at the end of the year. So the cost of your first year of insurance is $3,218. Where does the $3,218 go?

Typically, an insurance company needs only 10% to 20% of your premium to cover the cost of insuring you against death. The rest is split among everyone involved in selling your policy and managing its cash value. Your agent will take at least 50% of your first year's premium as a commission. This explains why so many are eager to sell you permanent insurance.

There also are sales and administrative charges, investment management fees and "mortality expenses," basically your share of claims paid to the estates of policyholders who have died. What's left is added to your cash value. Agent commissions and surrender charges plunge after the first two or three years. So the cost of permanent life generally drops steeply for a decade or more before rising again in the latter years of a policy, when your age drives up the cost of insuring you against death. Thus it's usually a terrible deal to surrender a permanent life policy in the first few years before you see the investment returns that come later. Yet some 25% of policyholders do just that, giving up or cashing out in the first three years.

Beware of coverage shell games. A recent study by the Consumer Federation of America found that early policy terminations cost policyholders more than $6 billion a year. Lose sight of how the rewards of permanent life grow over time, and you could find yourself "churned." Churning, a practice that was rampant in the industry in the 1980s and early 1990s, takes the cash value of one policy and uses it to pay the premiums of another. If you are still with us, you know that switching simply wastes the investment returns of the first policy on the up-front costs of the second. Don't do it.

Sounds like permanent life insurance can't possibly be worth the trouble. But if you have a high income and are contributing the maximum allowable to your tax-deferred savings accounts, the investment component of a permanent life policy may well suit your needs. Just keep in mind that comparison shopping takes some effort. To assess your options, ask your insurer what investment assumptions underlie the policy illustration. Ask for an illustration of a worst-case scenario. What would your cash value look like if your insurer pays its rock-bottom guaranteed rate, usually about 4%? And ask for a complete breakdown of costs, including

Paying Policies Over Time Is Costly

If you're like most Americans, you buy insurance on some schedule other than a single annual payment—say, $90 every month for 12 months rather than $1,000 once a year. But it's easy to lose sight of just how costly so-called fractional premiums can be.

Suppose your yearly life insurance premium is $1,200 and your provider lets you make two semiannual payments of $620. That comes to $1,240. It would be natural to conclude that the extra $40 you're paying for convenience constitutes a 3.3% surcharge ($1,240 divided by $1,200). Natural but wrong. Think about it this way. After you make your first payment, you're essentially taking out a $580 loan ($1,200 minus $620) from your insurer to get coverage for the rest of the year. So you're paying $40 to borrow $580 for six months, and that translates into an annual interest rate of 14.3%, not 3.3%. Unfortunately, federal truth-in-lending laws don't require insurance companies to disclose the interest rates associated with fractional premiums, and almost none do. "Using conservative assumptions, fractional premium charges cost consumers an estimated $5 billion a year," says Joseph Belth of the *Insurance Forum*, an Ellettsville, Ind. trade journal.

To find out what your insurance company is charging if you pay your premiums on a monthly, quarterly or semiannual basis, consult the table below. It shows the interest rates associated with varying fractional premium factors. To calculate your policy's factor, divide a single payment by your total annual premium. For example, if your annual life insurance premium is $1,500 and your monthly payment is $135, your factor would be 135 divided by 1,500, or 0.09. Then your rate would be 18.6%. That's ample incentive to pay your next premium in one pop.

Your Real Interest Rate: Use this table to estimate what rate you're being charged if you pay your insurance premium in installments. Start in the section of the table that corresponds to how often you are billed—monthly, quarterly or semiannually. Then calculate your policy's fractional premium "factor" by dividing a single payment by your annual premium. Once you find the factor closest to yours, look in the third column for your rate.

BILLING FREQUENCY	FACTOR (PAYMENT ÷ PREMIUM)	INTEREST RATE
Semiannually	0.5100	8.3%
	0.5150	12.8
	0.5200	17.4
	0.5300	27.2
Quarterly	0.2600	11.2
	0.2625	14.1
	0.2650	17.1
	0.2700	23.3
Monthly	0.0850	4.4
	0.0875	11.3
	0.0900	18.6
	0.0950	34.1

Source: *Insurance Forum.*

commissions, loads and fees. Then calculate your costs for a few years on alternative policies. Or consult the Consumer Federation of America (202-387-0087), which for $45 will evaluate the rate of return your life insurance policy is providing.

Guard against loss of a breadwinner's income. This continues to be the key reason people buy life insurance. But changes both in Americans' lifestyle and in the financial services industry have complicated the issue. As families have become increasingly dependent on both spouses' earnings, more policies are being sold to women. Trends toward later marriage and childbearing mean many of today's parents can expect to need some coverage for dependents well into their fifties and sixties. And advances in medicine mean that people are living longer, which lowers costs. On the other hand, no potential mortality risk is likely to go undetected by insurers. A vegetarian long-distance runner who doesn't smoke can look forward to great rates. But most of us don't fit into that category.

At the same time, the long bull run on Wall Street has increased competition for the dollars that once went into low-yielding whole life policies. Trying to recapture those dollars, insurance companies have introduced an array of products, several of which have an investment component. All of this means that generic insurance advice is irrelevant. You really need to know what is right for you and your family.

The first step is to figure how much money your dependents would need, and for how long. To come up with a meaningful estimate, you'll have to think seriously about lifestyle choices, goals and expectations. Will your spouse continue to work? How will the kids be cared for? Will the kids go to private colleges or public ones? At what age can they fend for themselves? After college? After graduate school? Total the assets and income that would be available for the years the family would need support after your death. Then subtract the estimate of expenses and the money the family would need for those years, which is probably 75% to 85% of current expenses. The shortfall between assets and expenses is the coverage you need. You should be sure to recalculate and update your coverage if necessary after major life changes, like a birth, divorce or remarriage.

Why term insurance usually is tops. Term life provides a death benefit only during the period covered by the contract, from one year to 30 years. An ART (annual renewable term) policy generally guarantees you the right to renew, although your premium will go up. Most guaranteed level-term policies guarantee the premium for the entire term. To renew at a favorable rate, however, you usually have to take another health exam. Premiums, expenses and commissions are lower for term than for whole life. No cash value builds up. But a convertible term contract allows you to convert to a cash-value policy later.

Intense competition between savings banks and big insurance companies has driven down term life premiums. This trend may be ending, however, as states adopt regulations requiring insurers to keep larger cash reserves for 15- to 30-year guaranteed level-premium policies. Rates for some policies could rise 40%, industry sources say, or premium guarantees could be shortened. Term is unquestionably the best choice for most young families. After age 50, premiums can run into thousands of dollars a year even if you're in good health. By 60, premiums are often prohibitive.

That's why middle-aged and older people often turn to permanent or cash-value coverage. Many consumer advocates are quick to criticize the cost of such insurance. Yet these policies can make sense if you married or had kids late, have a much younger spouse, have maxed out on your tax-deferred savings, expect to incur federal estate taxes or are concerned about continuing a business. Permanent policies provide a death benefit for as long as the premiums are paid. There's also a savings or investment component that policyholders can borrow from or draw down as retirement income. Commissions and expenses slow the accumulation of cash value in the early years of the policy. So you should buy permanent life only if you'll keep the policy for at least 20 years. And except for traditional whole life policies, permanent life needs to be actively managed.

The limited appeal of whole life. This is the kind of fixed-premium policy your father or grandfather might have had. Premiums in the early years are higher than the cost of providing the protection. In later years they're usually less. The insurance company invests the premiums in low-risk instruments, mostly bonds and mortgages, as required by law. The policyholder has no say in how these funds are managed. In participating policies, a share of the surplus mortality charges is returned to policyholders in the form of dividends, which may be used to help reduce premiums. Nonparticipating policies have no dividends. The most attractive feature of any permanent life insurance is that earnings aren't taxed until they're withdrawn, and then only to the extent that they exceed the amount paid as premiums. But tax-deferred 401(k)s and IRAs and the phenomenal growth of mutual funds have made traditional whole life less popular as a means of retirement saving.

Who should buy universal life. This lets you adjust the death benefit and the amount and timing of premiums as long as you keep enough cash value to cover administrative expenses and mortality charges. The part of the premium not going toward the mortality charge is invested in a separate account of intermediate-term bonds. The flexibility of universal life appeals to consumers who want to adjust their payments to an uneven cash flow. Take waterproofing contractor Karl Kardel, 58, of Piedmont, Calif. Kardel's $2 million-a-year business is cyclical. Most of his other assets are tied up in real estate. If he died suddenly without insurance, his family would have no income until they could liquidate the business. To further complicate the situation, Kardel started a second family when he was over 40. His youngest child is only 11. To combine the lower cost of term life with the flexible premiums and permanence of universal, Kardel bought a $350,000 10-year level-premium term policy and a $350,000 universal policy. His annual premium is a hefty $12,900 because of his age and a heart problem. He acknowledges that the 4% return he expects on his universal policy doesn't compare favorably with what he'd earn from a mutual fund. But he doesn't have a long time horizon and needs protection now.

Sorting out variable and variable universal life.
These allow policyholders to invest their premiums in a stock portfolio. If you invest wisely and the market is up when you die, your beneficiaries may realize a considerable windfall. If the

market is down, they may wind up with a smaller death benefit than expected, though most policies do guarantee a minimum. Variable policies have a fixed premium. The hottest commodity in today's life insurance market is variable universal. It combines the investing feature and the fluctuating cash value and death benefit of variable with the adjustable premiums of universal.

When it's time to comparison shop. If term insurance is what you need, group insurance offered by your employer is often a good buy especially if you can take your policy with you once you change jobs. Otherwise, the internet is a good place to begin your search for the policy you want at the lowest price. Check these websites for quotes from a variety of national insurers: insuremarket.com, insweb.com, lifeinsurance.net, quickquote.com and rightquote.com. Note, however, that quotes on the web generally apply only to the healthiest people. Extra pounds, a slightly high cholesterol count or a family history of heart disease will boost your premium. If you decide to buy a policy online, you won't know your exact premium until underwriting is complete and you've been screened by a medical technician.

If you'd rather do business with a person, call an agent who sells policies from several companies and see if he or she can beat the quotes you found online. For permanent coverage, you will probably need a broker. For leads, contact the local chapter of the National Association of Life Underwriters (202-331-6000; nalu.org) or the Society of Financial Service Professionals (888-243-2258; financialpro.org). Look for an agent with at least five years' experience and a C.L.U. or Ch.F.C. designation. If you're buying a variable policy, your agent must be registered to sell securities. If a different agent's name appears on your application, it may mean your agent isn't registered.

Try to resist the temptation to fib on your application. If you smoke, just say so. If you die within the first two years of the policy and it's found that you lied on your application, the insurer can refuse to pay. And don't make your estate your beneficiary unless you're advised to do so by your attorney or financial planner. Doing so will tie up the death benefit in probate and delay your survivors the protection you've gone to all this trouble to provide.

Ways to Leave a Lasting Legacy

In a perfect world you would segue effortlessly from a lifetime of work to a comfortable retirement. When you died, your fortune would amply provide for your spouse and eventually flow to your children, who would in turn use their inheritances as you always hoped they would. The problem with this scenario, however, is how quickly it can be undone by circumstances of real life, including divorce, remarriage, stepchildren, illness, untimely death and the vagaries of human nature itself. That's not to imply that life is so unpredictable you can't secure your wealth. You can. But doing so requires more than having a will that simply divvies up your assets. As the real-life examples in this chapter illustrate, addressing a family's unique circumstances requires setting up trusts that can be tailored more precisely than a will to reflect both your wishes and your family's needs.

If you're like many people, you may assume that trusts are only for the wealthy who need to cut taxes. Not so. Trusts are the most versatile tools in estate planning. They allow you to accomplish such disparate goals as providing for heirs who are minors, disabled or from previous marriages and naming a loved one to manage your assets if you become incapacitated. Indeed, many estate attorneys now recommend using a living trust (discussed later in this chapter) as the foundation of your plan and from there devising more intricate trusts to address special situations. You will need to consult an attorney to set up the ones that best meet your particular goals. The cost? Depending on the complexity of your situation, the size of your estate and your attorney's customary legal fees, you could pay anywhere from $1,500 for a simple trust to $5,000 for a complicated one that is incorporated into a thorough estate plan.

Hammer Out a Bullet-Proof Will

If you go to your grave without a will, you could leave behind chaos. For example, a judge would decide who raises your children. That's right. In your will you name guardians to raise your children and manage their inheritances. Fail to do so, and a probate court judge will select the caretakers for you. Even if the judge makes a good choice, it may not satisfy everyone. Custody fights could result, prolonging the trauma and possibly depriving the children of relationships you might want them to have.

Loved ones could be left in the cold. In most states, if you're single, childless and die without a will, your parents get almost everything you own outright. Your significant other will be left out unless you state your intentions in a will. If you are married with children and die without a will, a portion of your wealth generally goes in equal parts to your kids. That may sound fair until you consider that one child (say, one with special needs) may have greater financial requirements than another. If you're married and childless and die without a will, you could leave a mess behind even if all your property is owned jointly with your spouse. Say the husband dies and the surviving wife becomes the sole owner of their jointly owned assets. When she dies, all of the former joint property goes to her family, unless she has written a will that names his kin as her heirs. Want to provide for your elderly mother or for children from a first marriage? Then say so in a will.

Revisions are needed as circumstances change. If you move to another state, ask a local lawyer to make certain your will complies with your new state's statutes. He or she can also tell whether you've done all you can to diminish state death taxes. You needn't tear up your old will and begin anew to make minor changes. You can add or remove a beneficiary, change the amount of someone's bequest or replace an executor or guardian by asking your attorney to draft an amendment to your will called a codicil. Like wills, codicils must be signed and witnessed. After you've added a couple of codicils, you should draw up a fresh will to avoid possible confusion. Whatever you do, don't alter the original copy of your will yourself. If you do, its validity can come into question.

Leave the original copy of your will with your lawyer for storage. Or you can file your will at your county probate court for a small fee. Don't stash the original in a safe-deposit box. Banks in many states will seal boxes until a court orders them opened. If you include burial instructions in your will, your survivors may not get to read them before your funeral.

When a revocable living trust beats a will. Experts in estate planning increasingly are urging well-off clients to replace their wills with so-called revocable living trusts. The attraction of such trusts is to bypass probate, the process involved in court approval and execution of a will. Living trusts are more complicated and expensive to draw up than wills. For transferring sizable or complicated estates, however, estate attorneys favor living trusts. You can change the trust terms at any time and serve as the trustee. As a result, you don't have to give up control of the assets while you're alive. When you die, the trust assets are distributed to the beneficiaries that you have named, according to instructions you set forth in the trust document. Or you can instruct that the assets flow into a different type of trust, such as a special needs trust for a disabled heir. For the pros and cons of setting up such vehicles, see the box "Why Living Trusts Are on the Rise" at right.

Name the Best Beneficiary for IRAs

When setting up tax-deferred accounts such as IRAs, you might automatically name your spouse and children as beneficiaries. But opening separate accounts for each heir could end up being a far smarter move. Here's some background. You should already know that you must begin taking minimum withdrawals from your tax-sheltered accounts by age 70.5. You can always take heftier bites if you need the dough. But in general your goal should be to take out as little as possible, so your money can keep growing tax deferred. And that's where the question of beneficiaries can make a big difference.

Your IRA's compulsory withdrawal schedule is designed to empty the account in the last year of your expected life span. But you can lengthen the schedule, and trim mandatory withdrawals, by adding a beneficiary's life expectancy to yours. A couple of restrictions apply: If you name multiple beneficiaries, you must use the age of the oldest. And when you name anyone other than

Why Living Trusts Are on the Rise

More and more people are replacing their wills with revocable living trusts, which are much harder to contest. They protect your privacy. And trusts allow you to bypass probate, the often tedious process during which a court approves your will and oversees its execution. Once the trust is established, you transfer ownership of all your assets to it while you are still alive. You can be your own trustee, manage the assets and receive income from the trust until you die. The "revocable" part of the deal comes from the fact that you can change, amend or dissolve the trust during your lifetime. As a result, you never give up control of your belongings. The flip side, however, is that you must still pay taxes just as if the assets had remained in your own name.

The biggest payoff occurs after you die. Because the trust owns your property, there are no assets to go through probate. As a result, bequests can be distributed as soon as your debts and taxes have been paid. And a trust rarely becomes public record. To get the most from yours, follow these steps.

Take inventory of your assets now. If you forget to include any in the trust, they will go through probate, thus defeating the purpose of the trust. Make a list of all of your belongings, then meet with your lawyer and discuss what should and should not be part of the trust. Personal property like jewelry and art can usually be placed in the trust simply by listing the articles in the trust document. But there is usually no point in retitling assets such as life insurance policies. These don't go through probate anyway because they have a named beneficiary that overrides a will.

Write separate assignment letters. Your lawyer should have the form letters you need to send to each brokerage firm, mutual fund and bank where you have accounts. In these letters you announce that you are transferring ownership of the assets to the trustee of your trust. Do not use a so-called global assignment form letter that you fill out once and copy to all the firms. You have to list all your accounts in such a letter, thereby letting everyone know what you've got and where it is. After all, one reason you're setting up the trust is to protect your privacy.

Retitle the deed to your house. You will have to get a new deed and change ownership of your home to the trust. This could cause problems if you later decide to refinance your house. Banks and title companies occasionally balk at lending on a home that's owned by a trust because they don't understand that the place is still owner-occupied. If your bank is unwilling, you may have to shop around for other lenders. You could retitle the deed in your name and then retitle it back when you are finished.

Put a pour-over will in place. This scoops up any assets that are not in the trust at the time of your death and deposits them there. Then you can finally relax.

your spouse, you have to calculate your joint life expectancy as though the beneficiary were no more than 10 years younger than you are. So if you're 70.5, even your grandchild will be considered to be age 60.5. Thus you usually will be able to take smaller withdrawals from accounts where a child, not your spouse, is the beneficiary. Single and joint life expectancies are listed in IRS Publication 590 (800-829-3676 or irs.ustreas.gov).

After you die, your choice of beneficiaries has an even bigger impact. If you have multiple beneficiaries, they must withdraw the money on a schedule determined by the life expectancy of the oldest heir. But single beneficiaries have much more flexibility. A widow who inherits an IRA can, after age 59.5, roll it over into a new one in her own name, designate her own beneficiary and begin a new withdrawal schedule. A nonspouse beneficiary can't roll the assets into a new IRA. But he or she is allowed to recalculate the original withdrawal schedule using his or her true life expectancy. Doing so may enable the beneficiary to stretch out the withdrawals for many years, leaving more money in the account to enjoy the benefits of tax-deferred growth.

A final note. If you have a 401(k), its rules on beneficiaries will probably be more restrictive. Rolling over your money into an IRA after you retire will give you more options for calculating withdrawals.

❧ Build a Tax-Saving Family Trust

This vehicle, also called a bypass or credit-shelter trust, has taken on added luster with the hike in the estate-tax exemption. Here's why. These trusts ensure that a husband and wife can ultimately double the amount of tax-free assets that they leave their kids. The tax-free threshold now is $675,000 per person or $1.35 million for a married couple. But it rises to $1 million ($2 million per couple) in 2006 and beyond. To understand how such a trust works, consider the fairly typical situation of Doug and Maureen Wulf, both 35, of Denver.

For the first several years after they were married, the Wulfs spent much of their income on travel and paying down student loans and credit-card debt. Since then they have picked up two priceless assets, tots Conor and Kathleen. Doug, a real estate broker, earns roughly $200,000 a year. The couple have amassed an estate worth nearly $2 million, including their $500,000 home, a $560,000 investment portfolio and $450,000 in term life insurance policies ($300,000 for Doug and $150,000 for Maureen). With both a family and their wealth to protect, the Wulfs' estate-planning goals are twofold. The first priority is to ensure that the surviving spouse will be financially secure after the other dies. They also seek to preserve as much of the family wealth as possible for their children.

The Wulfs could take care of each other by simply writing wills in which Doug leaves everything to Maureen and vice versa. Such a transfer would automatically be tax-free. A provision in the tax law known as the marital deduction lets you bequeath any amount to your spouse without owing tax (as long as your spouse is a U.S. citizen). But passing everything to the spouse merely postpones the tax hit until he or she dies, undercutting the Wulfs' second objective of shielding the family fortune from tax. To address this problem, Doug and Maureen each wrote a will bequeathing to a trust property valued up to the maximum estate exemption at the time of death. Each stipulated that the trust income go to the surviving spouse and that the principal pass to their kids after the survivor dies.

Assume, for example, that Doug dies first, decades from now. Under the terms of his will, assets worth $1 million will flow into his trust estate tax-free thanks to the $1 million exemption. The remainder of his estate will pass directly to Maureen, escaping estate tax because of the marital deduction. When Maureen dies, the contents of Doug's trust will be distributed to their children. No estate tax will be due on those distributions no matter how much the trust has grown since Doug's death. That's because the original contribution was covered by the $1 million exemption. In addition, Maureen's estate will qualify for its own $1 million exemption, enabling her to bequeath her own assets, up to that amount, free of estate tax.

A family trust can be funded only with separately owned assets. If you and your spouse own most of your assets jointly, you'll need to retitle them to ensure that they can pass into the trust as planned.

❧ Create Hybrids for Blended Clans

As the Wulfs illustrate, a husband or wife typically leaves his or her assets to a spouse with the understanding that the survivor will then arrange to convey the estate to the couple's children. But what if you have children from a previous marriage whom you want to provide for after you're gone, in addition to providing for your spouse? Can you assume your spouse will provide for children who are not his or her biological offspring?

Those questions worried retired Navy officer Jim Jefferson, 73, and his wife Diane, 60, who recently retired from IBM. When the Pacifica, Calif. couple were married 27 years ago, Jim and Diane each had three children from previous marriages. With an estate now worth roughly $800,000, they want to ensure that all six kids share in the stash. "We've seen cases where family members start out with high ethics and good will," says Jim. "But somehow the children of the first to die get cut out, and the surviving spouse's children get the lion's share of the assets. We wanted to avoid that." Accordingly, the Jeffersons' estate plan includes a so-called QTIP trust, which stands for qualified terminable interest property.

Here's how one works. Let's say that a husband puts property intended for his wife in a QTIP. When the husband dies, the wife is entitled to all of the trust income. After her death, however, the trust principal passes to beneficiaries who were named by the husband when the trust was established. Assume that Jim dies first. Upon his death, assets intended for Diane go into the trust. Diane will receive the trust income during her lifetime. But she can withdraw trust principal only if she has no other means to pay for her healthcare, education, maintenance or support. When Diane dies, whatever is left in the trust goes to all six kids. If Diane dies first, the trust will operate the same way, but with the trust income going to Jim before the principal is divided among the kids.

❧ Tailor Minor's Trusts for Grandkids

As your circumstances evolve, so must your estate plan. Take Ron Eastman, 62, and his wife Joanne, 61, of Naples, Fla. Both have wills that include family trusts. After the Eastmans die, the trust assets will go to their two children, Randall, 38, and Julie, 36. In the years since the Eastmans established that basic estate plan, however, both their family and their fortune have grown. The clan now includes a daughter-in-law and three grandchildren. Meanwhile, Ron and Joanne's estate has exploded to $7.2 million, made up mainly of their 51% share of a sporting-goods dealership they own with their children, their $950,000 primary residence, a $300,000 lakeside vacation home in Minnesota and their stock portfolio.

The Eastmans' estate has outgrown their original plan. Since Randall and Julie are already financially secure, the Eastmans have set their sights on sharing their wealth with their grandchildren. To do so in a tax-savvy way, they've earmarked nearly $2 million for a generation-skipping trust. In such a setup, the trust beneficiaries, typically your grandchildren, must be at least two generations your junior. You can, however, stipulate in the trust document that your own children may receive the trust income. They can tap the principal to pay for virtually anything that can be said to benefit the grandchildren, such as housing, healthcare for the entire family and college education.

In the Eastmans' case, the three grandchildren are the beneficiaries of the generation-skipping trust. But their father, Randall, is entitled to the trust income and he has control over the principal. When Randall dies, the assets remaining in the trust will go to his kids without ever being diminished by taxes in his estate. The most you should allocate to this type of trust is $1 million ($2 million if you give jointly with your spouse). Bequests above those amounts are subject to the stiff 55% generation-skipping transfer tax, which is separate from estate tax. Note that this transfer tax doesn't apply if you leave assets to the children of a deceased son or daughter.

Graduating from college is the focus of minor's trusts that were established by 67-year-old retired bank executive Wolfgang Schoellkopf of New York City. Motivated by memories of his struggle as a young man to raise a family, buy a house and pursue a career, Schoellkopf was determined to help his son and daughter-in-law. His solution was to set up college funds for his grandchildren, Julie, 7, and Jason, 1. On the advice of his attorney, Schoellkopf created a $20,000 minor's trust for Julie and a $20,000 minor's trust for Jason. He appointed the children's uncle, who is a stockbroker, as trustee.

The trust documents dictate that the funds must be used to pay for tuition, books, room, board and other living expenses while Julie and Jason are attending a four-year college or university. Each also will receive $10,000 upon graduation. Whatever is left in the trusts goes to them at age 30. If either of them doesn't attend college or goes to a two-year junior college, she or he gets half of the money at 30 and the rest at 35.

There's one caveat, however. While minor's trusts let you hold on to hefty sums for a long time, they're not entirely leakproof. In exchange for tax breaks on your trust contributions, you must generally give the beneficiaries limited access to the trust principal. Schoellkopf's trusts, for example, include typical provisions that require the trustee to notify the children (through their parents) whenever Schoellkopf makes subsequent contributions to the trust. The children then have 45 days from the date of notification to withdraw an amount equal to the contribution. In practice, however, most beneficiaries never demand the money.

Care for Heirs With Special Needs

Providing for a disabled relative requires a more complex type of trust. That's because money that is paid to a disabled person, either directly or from a minor's trust, could disqualify him or her from vital government aid such as Medicaid and Supplemental Security Income. Thus the aim of a special-needs trust is to preserve an heir's eligibility for public assistance while providing support that will allow for a higher standard of living than would be possible on government aid alone. Without such a trust, a disabled heir is likely to quickly deplete an inheritance, leaving him or her with only public assistance to live on.

Jeannette Stevenson, 46, an insurance claims adjuster and single mother in Fair Oaks, Calif. has directly confronted the legal and emotional complexities of special-needs trusts. Her son Scott, 17, suffers from schizo-affective disorder. With medication and psychotherapy, the 12th-grader is at times well adjusted. But he also experiences delusions and depression and can become violent. "Scott could get better, or he could get worse," says Stevenson. "I have to plan for both."

So far, Stevenson has amassed assets worth $380,000. Upon her death, her estate plan directs that the assets are to be placed in a trust with Scott as the beneficiary. Under the trust terms, however, Scott can never demand money from the trust. Rather, trust distributions are at the discretion of the trustee, Stevenson's sister Betty. In the event Betty is unable to serve as trustee, the trust instructs her to appoint a professional trustee or to name a trustee who is recommended by the Planned Lifetime Assistance Network, or PLAN, a nonprofit program that helps adults with lifelong disabilities. Since Scott doesn't control the money, the government isn't likely to include the trust payouts in the formulas it uses to determine his eligibility for government aid.

To further ensure that trust payouts won't disqualify Scott from public assistance, Stevenson has included a provision that forbids the trustee to pay for anything that would otherwise be covered by government aid. These include housing, food, clothing and necessary medical care. Instead, Stevenson expects the trustee to use some of the money to support Scott's passion for car racing. "He eats, sleeps and dreams race cars," she says.

As a last resort to preserve both his government benefits and his inheritance, Stevenson's trust also has a provision that calls for the trust to terminate if the state tries to seize its content as payment for the public aid. At that point, the trust assets would be paid out to Betty. Although Stevenson has faith that Betty would continue to support Scott financially, Betty would not be legally obligated to do so. "A situation where a trust terminates is far from ideal," says Trudy Nearn, an attorney who drew up the trust for the Stevensons. "But without these carefully worded trusts, parents wouldn't have a prayer of preserving a child's government benefits."

✒ Use Partnerships for Family Firms

Like many Americans, a family business is the largest asset in the estate of Sonny Rianda, 65, and his wife Lillian, 66. The Riandas own a $6 million vegetable farm in Gonzalez, Calif. Sonny's child Michael wants to continue running the farm after his parents die. But the Riandas also want to give their other three children an ownership stake in the farm. The couple's biggest estate-planning challenge was to ensure that the children won't have to sell so much of the land to pay estate tax that there won't be any farm left to run.

The solution was a family limited partnership. In effect, the Riandas are giving away the farm while they're alive rather than bequeathing it in their wills or transferring it through a trust. The partnership arrangement lets the couple control the farm as general partners while gradually bestowing interests in the business on their children as limited partners. Since the kids don't control the business, however, the value of their interests is heavily discounted from the fair market value of the farm itself.

In the Riandas' case, the discount came to 30%. So far, Sonny and Lillian have given their children interests with a fair market value of nearly $3 million—or just under 50% of the farm. But the couple haven't incurred any tax. The first transfer, which they made in 1991, had a fair market value of $1.7 million but a discounted value of just $1.2 million. That discounted amount was, at that time, equal to the maximum estate tax exemption for the two of them. Each subsequent transfer has had a discounted value of no more than $20,000 per child each year. You can make tax-free gifts of up to $10,000 a year to as many people as you wish. The amount is $20,000 if you make the gift jointly with your spouse.

As the Riandas demonstrate, leaving a financial legacy is not the only aim of estate planning. Through judicious use of trusts or partnerships, you can also leave a legacy of family harmony.

Index